An OPUS book

An Introduction to
Political Philosophy

Jonathan Wolff is Reader in Philosophy in the Philosophy
Department at University College London.

An Introduction to
Political
Philosophy

Jonathan Wolff

Oxford   New York
OXFORD UNIVERSITY PRESS

Oxford University Press, Walton Street, Oxford OX2 6DP

Oxford New York
Athens Auckland Bangkok Bombay
Calcutta Cape Town Dar es Salaam Delhi
Florence Hong Kong Istanbul Karachi
Kuala Lumpur Madras Madrid Melbourne
Mexico City Nairobi Paris Singapore
Taipei Tokyo Toronto
and associated companies in
Berlin Ibadan

Oxford is a trade mark of Oxford University Press

British Library Cataloguing in Publication Data
Data available

Library of Congress Cataloging in Publication Data
Wolff, Jonathan.
An introduction to political philosophy / Jonathan Wolff.
Includes bibliographical references and index.
1. Political science—Philosophy.   I. Title.
JA71.W67   1996   320'.01—dc20   95-38873
ISBN 0-19-289251-7

3 5 7 9 10 8 6 4 2

Typeset by Best-set Typesetter Ltd., Hong Kong
Printed in Great Britain by
Biddles Ltd
Guildford & King's Lynn

For Elaine and Max

Contents

Preface

My purpose in this book is to give the reader a sense of the central problems of political philosophy, and the most interesting attempts, throughout its history, to solve them. In doing so I have explored the subject through a series of linked questions, raiding the treasure houses of political philosophy in search of answers and approaches. Rather than trying to provide a systematic account of contemporary debates, or a thorough and scholarly history, I have often jumped centuries (sometimes millennia) to explore the most thought-provoking writings on the most important topics—or so I think.

Some will disagree with my choice of the central problems, with my view of the relations between these problems, and with my choice of thinkers to take seriously. This is no bad thing. The last thing I want to do is to present the illusion of a finished or completed subject, or even one that is straightforward to chart. Too many introductory books give the impression that the area of study was created by decree, and that understanding is a matter of mastering the manual or rule book. I have tried to avoid this type of over-simplification.

The book is written so that each chapter develops a theme arising from the previous one, but I also hope that any of the chapters can be read as a self-standing unit, as an introduction to a particular issue. Readers often feel that they have virtually a moral obligation to start at the beginning of any book and read it page by page (my grandmother used to say that Hitler would always read the last page of a book first). In the case of this book the reader is hereby invited to follow his or her own interests.

Much of the material has been presented as lectures to students at University College London and Birkbeck College, and to students on the London Inter-Collegiate Lecture Programme. In return I have received many helpful criticisms. Indeed, I have managed to amass an almost indecent amount of help and advice for such a short book. Those who have discussed parts of the book with me, or have commented on all or part of drafts (in some cases, on many versions) include Paul Ashwin, Richard Bellamy, Alan Carter, Elaine Collins, Issi Cotton, Virginia Cox, Tim Crane, Brad Hooker, Alya Khan, Dudley Knowles, Annabelle Lever, Veronique Muñoz Dardé, Mike Martin, Lucy O'Brien, Sarah Richmond, Mike Rosen, Mike Saward, Mario Scannella, Raj Sehgal, John Skorupski, Philip Smelt, Bob Stern, and Nigel Warburton. I am very grateful to them all.

Introduction

> We do not say that a man who shows no interest in politics
> is a man who minds his own business; we say that he has no
> business here at all.
>
> (Pericles' funeral oration, in Thucydides,
> *The Peloponnesian War*, 147)

It has been said that there are only two questions in political
philosophy: 'who gets what?', and 'says who?' Not quite true,
but close enough to be a useful starting-point. The first of these
questions is about the distribution of material goods, and of
rights and liberties. On what basis should people possess property? What rights and liberties should they enjoy? The second
question concerns the distribution of another good: political
power. Locke defined political power as 'the right of making
laws with penalties of death, and consequently all less penalties'.
This probably goes further than we need, but we can see the
point. Political power includes the right to command others, and
to subject them to punishment if they disobey. Who should hold
this power?

As soon as we reflect on these questions puzzles emerge. Is
there any good reason why one person should have more property than another? Are there any justified limits to my liberty?
And what should the relation be between political power and
economic success? In some countries few obtain political power
unless they are already wealthy. In others, those who gain political power soon find themselves rich. But should there be any
connection at all between possession of wealth and enjoyment of
political power?

Indeed, political power is puzzling enough on its own. If someone has legitimate political power over me then they have the
right to force me to do certain things. But how could another
person justify the claim to have such rights over me? It often
seems outrageous that someone else should tell me what to do,

worse still that they think they are entitled to punish me if I disobey. Yet there is, of course, another side to this. Perhaps I should also consider how others might behave—how unpleasant they could make my life—if they were left unrestrained by the law and the threat of punishment. Reflecting on this, perhaps there is something to be said, after all, for the existence of political power. So we can identify with both the anarchist's plea for the autonomy of the individual, and the authoritarian's claims for the power of the state.

One task for the political philosopher, then, is to determine the correct balance between autonomy and authority, or, in other words, to determine the proper distribution of political power. This example also illustrates what is distinctive about political philosophy. Political philosophy is a *normative* discipline, meaning that it tries to establish norms (rules or ideal standards). We can contrast the normative with the *descriptive*. Descriptive studies attempt to find out how things are. Normative studies try to discover how things should be: what is right, just, or morally correct. Politics can be studied from both a descriptive and a normative standpoint.

Characteristically, descriptive political studies are undertaken by the political scientist, the sociologist, and the historian. So, for example, some political scientists ask questions about the *actual* distribution of goods within a given society. Who in the United States of America holds wealth? Who in Germany holds power? The political philosopher, like all of us, has good reason to be interested in the answers to these questions, but his or her primary concern is elsewhere: *what rule or principle should govern the distribution of goods?* ('Goods' here includes not only property, but power, rights, and liberty too.) The political philosopher will ask, not 'how is property distributed?', but 'what would be a just or fair distribution of property?' Not 'what rights and liberties do people have?', but 'what rights and liberties *should* people have?' What ideal standards, or norms, should govern the distribution of goods within society?

The partition between normative and descriptive studies, though, is not quite as clear-cut as it might seem. Consider again the question 'who holds wealth?' Why are we interested in this descriptive question? Primarily because the distribution of wealth is relevant to normative questions about *justice*. (Compare the question: 'who holds string?'—inequalities in the possession of string are of no political interest.)

Furthermore, questions about human behaviour often seem to straddle the descriptive/normative divide. A sociologist seeking to explain why people generally obey the law, for example, is likely to appeal at some point to the fact that many people believe that they *ought* to obey. And, of course, factual questions about human behaviour are just as relevant to normative issues. For example, there is no point in putting forward a theory of the just society without having some knowledge of human behaviour and motivation. Some theories of justice, for example, might make unrealistic assumptions about people's capacity (or lack of capacity) for altruism. In short, studying how things are helps to explain how things can be, and studying how they can be is indispensable for assessing how they ought to be.

But how can we answer the question of how things ought to be? We know, broadly, how to go about answering purely descriptive questions: we go and look. This is not to say that political science or history is easy, for very subtle and detailed work is often involved. But in principle we do think we know how to do it, even if often we cannot find the information we seek. But what can we do to find out how things ought to be? Where can we look?

The uncomfortable fact is that there is no easy answer. But, despite this, very many philosophers have attempted to solve these normative political problems, and they have not been short of things to say. We will examine some of the most important contributions throughout this book, and we will see that, by and large, philosophers reason about politics in just the way they do about other philosophical issues. They draw distinctions, they examine whether propositions are self-contradictory, or whether two or more propositions are logically consistent. They try to show that surprising theses can be deduced from more obvious ones. In short, they present arguments.

And philosophers argue about politics for good reason. In political philosophy, unlike many other areas of philosophy, there is no hiding-place. In philosophy, agnosticism ('the English translate their ignorance into Greek and call it agnosticism', said Engels) is often a respectable position. Perhaps I cannot find a satisfactory position on the question of whether or not we have free will, so I profess no view. In a wider context this hardly matters. But in political philosophy agnosticism is self-defeating. It may not matter if a society has no official policy on the solution to the problem of free will, but in every society someone (or no one) holds political power, and property is distributed in some way or other. Of course, any one individual's influence on society's decisions is likely to be minute. But potentially we all have some say, if not by voting then by making our views known through debate and discussion, whether on the public stage, or by 'underground' means. Those who prefer not to participate will find their political decisions made for them, whether they like it or not. To say or do nothing is, in practice, to endorse the present situation, however repellent.

In the course of this book we shall raise and discuss the main questions of political philosophy, examining some of the most influential answers, from the ancient Greeks to the present day. Each chapter takes on a particular question or controversy. The natural starting-point is political power, the right to command. Why should some have the right to pass laws to regulate the behaviour of others? Well, suppose no one had such a right. What would life be like? This is the question pursued in the first chapter: what would happen in a 'state of nature' without government? Would life be unbearable? Or an improvement on how things are now?

Suppose we come to accept that life under government is preferable to life in the state of nature. Does it follow from this that we have the moral duty to do as the state decrees? Or is there another argument that will deliver this conclusion? This is the problem of political obligation, which we shall discuss in Chapter 2.

If we have a state, how should it be organized? Should it be democratic? What does it even mean to say that the state is democratic? Is there any rationale for preferring rule by the people to rule by an expert: a benevolent dictator? These are the questions pursued in Chapter 3.

How much power should the state have? Or, viewed from the other side, how much liberty should the citizen enjoy? Chapter 4 considers the theory that, to avoid the 'tyranny of the majority', we should be given the liberty to act just as we wish, provided that we do no harm to others.

If we give citizens such liberty, should this include the liberty to acquire and dispose of property however they see fit? Or are there justified restrictions on economic activity in the name of liberty or justice? This is the topic of Chapter 5: distributive justice.

The five main chapters of this book take us through topics of enduring concern: the state of nature, the state, democracy, liberty, and property. The final chapter looks briefly at some of the assumptions underlying my choice of topics, and examines those assumptions in the context of recent work in feminist political theory. By this point, with two and a half thousand years of hindsight, we may have some sort of answer to a question raised, yet not satisfactorily answered, in this Introduction—how do we do political philosophy? On this topic, as on all those discussed here, my aim is not to force an opinion on you; I hope instead to present some materials that will help you form your own view. Of course it will be possible to read this book and end up as uncertain as before. But we must not underestimate the progress made by advancing from muddled ignorance to informed bemusement.

1

The State of Nature

Introduction

'I should have thought that a pack of British boys—you're
all British aren't you?—would have been able to put up a
better show than that—I mean—'
'It was like that at first,' said Ralph, 'before things—'
He stopped.
'We were together then—'
The officer nodded helpfully.
'I know. Jolly good show. Like the Coral Island.'

(William Golding, *Lord of the Flies*, 192)

R. M. Ballantyne's *Coral Island* is a story in which three English
boys are marooned on a desert island. Through courage, intelligence, and co-operation they repel pirates and native savages to
enjoy an idyllic life in the South Seas. William Golding's charac-
ters also find themselves on a bountiful coral island, but soon fall
first into dispute, and then into desperate tribal warfare. In
telling their stories as they do, Ballantyne and Golding suggest
opposing pictures in answer to our first question: what would life
be like in a 'natural' state, a world without government?

Why ask this question? What is its relevance for political
philosophy? We take for granted that we live in a world of
political institutions: central government, local government, the
police, the law courts. These institutions distribute and administer political power. They place people in offices of responsibility,
and these people then claim to have the right to command us to
act in various ways. And, if we disobey and are caught, we will be
punished. The life of each one of us is structured and controlled,
in part, by the decisions of others. This level of interference in
our lives can seem intolerable. But what is the alternative?

A natural starting-point for thinking about the state is to ask: what would things be like without it? To understand why we have something, it is often a good tactic to consider its absence. Of course, we could hardly abolish the state just to find out what life would be like without it, so the best we can do in practice is carry out this process as a thought-experiment. We imagine a 'state of nature'; a situation where no state exists and no one possesses political power. Then we try to decide what it would be like to live under those conditions. This way we can come to a view about how things would be without the state, and this, we hope, will help us to see just why we have a state. Perhaps we will come to understand how the state is justified, if it is, and also what form it should take.

Was there ever a state of nature? Many philosophers seem reluctant to commit themselves on this topic. Jean-Jacques Rousseau (1712–78), for example, thought that so much time would have been required to pass from a state of nature to 'civil society' (a society governed by a formal state) that it would be blasphemous to assume that modern societies had arisen in this way. He argued that the amount of time needed for the transition was longer than the age of the world, as recorded in the scriptures. Yet, on the other hand, Rousseau also believed that there were contemporary examples of peoples living in a state of nature, while John Locke (1632–1704) thought this was true of many groups living in seventeenth-century America.

But even if there never has been a true state of nature we can still consider the question of what life would be like if, hypothetically, we found ourselves without a state. Thomas Hobbes (1588–1679), deeply worried by the English Civil War, thought he saw his country falling into a state of nature. In *Leviathan* he drew a picture of how unpleasant this would be, hoping to persuade his readers of the advantages of government. Accordingly, for the purposes of this chapter we need not spend much time discussing the question of whether, as a matter of fact, human beings have ever lived in a state of nature. All we need to argue is that it is possible.

Is it possible? Sometimes it is claimed that not only have

human beings always lived under a state, but that it is the only way they possibly could live. On this view, the state *exists naturally* in the sense of being *natural to human beings*. Maybe we would not be human beings if we lived in a society without a state. Perhaps we would be a lower form of animal. If human beings exist, then so does the state. If this is true then speculation about the state of nature is redundant.

In response some theorists claim that we have plenty of evidence that human beings have been able to live without the state, and such claims have been vital to the case made by anarchist writers (we will return to these later in the chapter). But even if human beings have never actually lived for any length of time without a state, it is very hard to see how it could be established that it is absolutely impossible. And so, as a way of trying to work out why we have the state, we will assume that human beings could find themselves in a world without it. What would that world be like?

Hobbes

> In [the state of nature] there is no place for Industry; because the fruit thereof is uncertain: and consequently no Culture of the Earth; no Navigation, nor use of the commodities that may be imported by Sea; no commodious Building; no Instruments of moving, and removing of things as require much force; no Knowledge of the face of the Earth; no account of Time; no Arts; no Letters; no Society; and which is worst of all, continuall feare, and danger of violent death; And the life of man, solitary, poore, nasty, brutish, and short.
>
> (Thomas Hobbes, *Leviathan*, 186)

Hobbes's greatest work, *Leviathan* (published in 1651), pursues a theme that had obsessed him for more than twenty years: the evils of civil war and the anarchy by which it would be accompanied. Nothing could be worse than life without the protection of the state, Hobbes argued, and therefore strong government is essential to ensure that we do not lapse into the war of all against all.

But why did Hobbes believe that the state of nature would be so desperate, a state of war, a state of constant fear and danger of a violent death? The essence of Hobbes's view is that, in the absence of government, human nature will inevitably bring us into severe conflict. For Hobbes, then, political philosophy begins with the study of human nature.

Hobbes suggests that there are two keys to the understanding of human nature. One is self-knowledge. Honest introspection tells us a great deal about what human beings are like: the nature of their thoughts, hopes, and fears. The other is knowledge of the general principles of physics. Just as to understand the citizen (the individual in political society) you have to understand human nature; Hobbes believed, as a materialist, that to understand human nature you must first understand 'body' or matter, of which, he urged, we are entirely composed.

For our purposes, the most important aspect of Hobbes's account of matter is his adoption of Galileo's principle of the conservation of motion. Prior to Galileo, philosophers and scientists had been puzzled by the question of what kept objects in motion. By what mechanism, for example, does a cannon-ball remain in flight once it has been fired? Galileo's revolutionary answer was to say that this was the wrong question. We should assume that objects will continue to travel at a constant motion and direction until acted on by another force. What needs to be explained is not why things keep going, but why they change direction and why they stop. In Hobbes's lifetime this view was still a novelty, and, he pointed out, defied the common-sense thought that, just as we tire and seek rest after moving, objects will naturally do this too. But the truth, he claims, is that 'when a thing is in motion, it will eternally be in motion, unless somewhat els stay it' (*Leviathan*, 87). This, he thought, was true for us too. Becoming tired and desiring rest is simply to have a different motion act upon us.

So the principle of the conservation of motion was used by Hobbes in developing a materialist, mechanist view of human beings. The broad outlines of this account are laid out in the introduction to *Leviathan*: 'What is the *Heart*, but a *Spring*; and the *Nerves* but so many *Strings*; and the *Joynts*, but so many *Wheeles*, giving motion to the whole Body . . . ?' (p. 81). Thus human beings are animated through motion. Sensation, for example, is a 'pressing' on an organ. Imagination is a 'decaying relic' of sensation. A desire is an 'internal motion towards an object'. All of this is meant quite literally.

The importance of the theory of the conservation of motion is that with it Hobbes paints a picture of human beings as always searching for something, never at rest. 'There is no such thing as perpetuall Tranquillity of mind while we live here; because Life it selfe is but Motion, and can never be without Desire' (*Leviathan*, 129–30). Human beings, Hobbes argues, seek what he calls 'felicity', continual success in achieving the objects of desire. It is the search to secure felicity that will bring us to war in the state of nature. Ultimately, Hobbes thought, our fear of death would bring human beings to create a state. But without a state, in the state of nature, Hobbes thought that the search for felicity would lead to a war of all against all. Why did Hobbes think this?

One clue can be found in Hobbes's definition of power: one's 'present means to obtain some future apparent Good' (*Leviathan*, 150). So to be assured of achieving felicity one must become powerful. Sources of power, Hobbes claims, include riches, reputations, and friends, and human beings have 'a restlesse desire of Power after power, that ceaseth onely in Death' (*Leviathan*, 161). This is not only because humans can never reach a state of complete satisfaction, but also because a person 'cannot assure the power and means to live well, which he hath present, without the acquisition of more' (*Leviathan*, 161). For others will also seek to increase their power, and so the search for power, is by its nature, competitive.

Everyone's natural, continual, attempt to increase power—to have riches and people under one's command—will lead to competition. But competition is not war. So why should competition in the state of nature lead to war? An important further step is Hobbes's assumption that human beings are by nature 'equal'.

An assumption of natural equality is often used in political and moral philosophy as a basis for the argument that we should respect other people, treating one another with care and concern. But for Hobbes the assumption is put to a quite different use, as we might suspect when we see how he states the point: we are equal in that all humans possess roughly the same level of strength and skill, and so any human being has the capacity to kill any other. 'The weakest has strength enough to kill the strongest, either by secret machination or by confederacy with others' (*Leviathan*, 183).

To this Hobbes adds the reasonable assumption that in the state of nature there is a scarcity of goods, so that two people who desire the same *kind* of thing will often desire to possess the same thing. Finally, Hobbes points out that no one in the state of nature can make himself invulnerable against the possibility of attack. Whatever I possess, others may desire, and so I must constantly be on my guard. Yet even if I possess nothing I cannot be free from fear. Others may take me to be a threat to them and so I could easily end up the victim of a pre-emptive strike. From these assumptions of equality, scarcity, and uncertainty, it follows, thinks Hobbes, that the state of nature will be a state of war:

From this equality of ability, ariseth equality of hope in the attaining of our Ends. And therefore if any two men desire the same thing, which neverthelesse they cannot both enjoy, they become enemies; and in the way to their End, (which is principally their owne conservation, and sometimes their delectation only) endeavour to destroy, or subdue one another. And from hence it comes to pass, that where an Invader hath no more to feare than an other mans single power; if one plant, sow, build, or possesse a convenient Seat, others may probably be expected to come prepared with forces united, to dispossesse, and deprive him, not only of the fruit of his labour, but also of his life or liberty. And the Invader again is in the like danger of another. (*Leviathan*, 184)

Worse still, Hobbes argues, people seek not only the means of immediate satisfaction, but also power in order to satisfy whatever future desires they will have. Now, as reputation of power *is* power, some people will attack others, even those who pose no threat, purely to gain a reputation of strength as a means of future protection. As in the school playground, those with a reputation for winning fights are least likely to be attacked for their goods, and may even have goods surrendered to them by others who feel unable to defend themselves. (Of course, those with a reputation for strength cannot relax either: they are the most likely victims of those seeking to enhance their own reputations.)

In sum, Hobbes sees three principal reasons for attack in the state of nature: for gain, for safety (to pre-empt invaders), and for glory or reputation. At bottom, Hobbes relies on the idea that human beings, in the search for felicity, constantly try to increase their power (their present means to obtain future goods). When we add that human beings are roughly equal in strength and ability; that desired goods are scarce; and that no one can be sure that they will not be invaded by others, it seems reasonable to conclude that rational human action will make the state of nature a battlefield. No one is strong enough to ward off all possible attackers, nor so weak that attacking others, with accomplices if need be, is never a possibility. The motive to attack falls into place when we also recognize that attacking others in the state of nature is often the surest way of getting (or keeping) what you want.

Should it be objected that this depiction of our likely plight in the state of nature relies on an assumption that human beings are unrealistically cruel, or unrealistically selfish? But Hobbes would reply that both objections miss the point. Human beings, Hobbes argues, are not cruel, 'that any man should take pleasure in other mens great harms, without other end of his own, I do not conceive it possible' (*Leviathan*, 126). As for selfishness, he would agree that human beings do generally, if not always, seek to satisfy their self-centred desires. But of equal or greater importance as a source of war is fear: the fear that others around you may try to take from you what you have. This can lead you to attack, not for gain, but for safety or perhaps even reputation. Thus we come close to the idea of a war in which everyone is fighting everyone else in self-defence.

Still, it might be said, it is unreasonable to suppose that everyone will be so suspicious of each other that they will always be at each others' throats. But Hobbes accepts that there will be moments without actual conflict. He defines the state of war not as constant fighting, but as a constant readiness to fight, so that no one can relax and let down their guard. Is he right that we should be so suspicious? Why not assume that people in the state of nature will adopt the motto 'live and let live'? But consider, says Hobbes, how we live even under the authority of the state. What opinion of your neighbours do you express when you lock your doors against them? And of other members of your household when you lock your chests and drawers? If we are so suspicious when we live with the protection of law, just think how afraid we would be in the state of nature.

At this point it might be argued that, while Hobbes has told us an amusing story, he has overlooked one thing: morality. Although creatures with no moral sense might behave as Hobbes outlines, we are different. The great majority of us accept that we should not attack other people or take their property. Of course in a state of nature a minority would steal and kill, as they do now, but there would be enough people with a moral sense to stop the rot spreading and prevent the immoral minority from bringing us to a general war.

This objection raises two central questions. First, does Hobbes believe that we can make sense of the ideas of morality in a state of nature? Second, if we can, would he allow that the recognition of moral duty, in the absence of the state, is sufficient motivation to override the temptation to invade others for their goods? Let us consider Hobbes's position on the first of these questions.

Hobbes seems to deny that there can be a morality in the state of nature: 'To this warre of every man against every man . . . nothing can be Unjust. The notions of Right and Wrong, Justice and Injustice, have no place' (*Leviathan*, 188). The argument Hobbes uses at this point is that injustice consists of the breach of some law, but for a law to exist there must be a lawgiver, a common power, able to enforce that law. In the state of nature there is no common power, so no law, so no breach of law, and so no injustice. Each person has 'the Liberty . . . to use his own power . . . for the preservation of his own Nature; that is to say of his own Life; and consequently, of doing any thing, which in his Judgement, and Reason, he shall conceive to be the aptest means thereunto' (*Leviathan*, 189). One of the consequences of this, claims Hobbes, is that 'in such a condition every man has a Right to every thing; even to one anothers body' (*Leviathan*, 190). Hobbes calls the liberty to act as you think fit to preserve yourself the 'right of nature': its consequence seems to be that, in the state of nature, you are permitted to do anything, even take another's life, if you believe that this will help you survive.

Why does Hobbes take such an extreme position, granting everyone liberty to do anything they think fit in the state of nature? But perhaps his position is not so extreme. We would find it hard to disagree that people in the state of nature have the right to defend themselves. That said, it also seems evident that individuals must decide for themselves what reasonably counts as a threat to them, and further, what is the most appropriate action to take in the face of such a threat. No one, it would seem, could reasonably be criticized for any action they take to defend themselves. As pre-emption is a form of defence, invading others can often be seen as the most rational form of self-protection.

This, then, is the simple initial account of Hobbes's view. In the state of nature there is no justice or injustice, no right or wrong. Moral notions have no application. This is what Hobbes calls the 'Natural Right of Liberty'. But as we shall see, Hobbes's view does have further complications.

In addition to the Natural Right of Liberty, Hobbes also argues that what he calls the 'Laws of Nature' also exist in the state of nature. The first 'fundamental law' is this: 'Every man ought to endeavour Peace, as farre as he has hope of obtaining it; and when he cannot obtain it, that he may seek, and use, all helps, and advantages of Warre' (*Leviathan*, 190). A second law instructs us to give up our right to all things, provided others are willing as well, and each should 'be contented with as much liberty against other men, as he would allow other men against himselfe' (*Leviathan*, 190). The third, which is particularly important for Hobbes's later social contract argument for the state, is to perform whatever covenants you make. In fact, Hobbes spells out a total of nineteen Laws of Nature, concerning justice, property, gratitude, arrogance, and other matters of moral conduct. All these laws, Hobbes supposes, can be deduced from the fundamental law, although he realizes that few people would be able to carry out the deduction, for most people 'are too busie getting food, and the rest too negligent to understand' (*Leviathan*, 214). But the Laws of Nature can be 'contracted into one easy sum . . . Do not that to another, which thou wouldest not have done to thy selfe', a negative formulation of the biblical 'golden rule' (do unto others as you would have them do unto you).

The Laws of Nature, then, could easily be called a moral code. But if Hobbes intends these as a set of moral rules which govern the state of nature, then this seems to contradict his earlier statement that there is no right or wrong in such a condition. Furthermore, if people are motivated to obey the moral law perhaps this will make the state of nature rather more peaceful than Hobbes allows. However, Hobbes does not describe the Laws of Nature as moral laws, but rather as theorems or conclusions of reason. That is, Hobbes believes that following these laws gives each person the best chance of preserving his or her own life.

This, however, seems to lead into a different problem. The fundamental Law of Nature tells us it is rational to seek peace. But Hobbes has already argued that the state of nature will be a state of war, because it is rational, in the state of nature, to invade others. How can Hobbes say that rationality requires both war and peace?

The answer, I think, is that we have to distinguish between *individual* and *collective* rationality. Collective rationality is what is best for each individual, on the assumption that everyone else will act the same way. The Laws of Nature express what is collectively rational. We can illustrate this distinction with an example from Jean-Paul Sartre. Consider a group of peasants, who each farm their own plot on a steep hillside. One by one they realize that they could increase the usable part of their plot by cutting down their trees and growing more crops. So they all cut down their trees. But in the next heavy storm the rain washes the soil off the hill, ruining the land. Here we can say that the individually rational thing for each peasant is to cut down his or her trees, to increase the amount of land available for farming. (Cutting down the trees on just one plot will not make any significant difference to soil erosion.) But collectively this is a disaster, for if they all cut down their trees everyone's farm will be ruined. So the collectively rational thing to do is leave most, if not all, of the trees standing.

The interesting feature of cases of this nature (known in the literature as the 'prisoners' dilemma') is that, where individual and collective rationality diverge, it is very hard to achieve co-operation on the collectively rational outcome. Every individual has an incentive to 'defect' in favour of the individually rational behaviour. Suppose the peasants understand the structure of their situation, and so agree to refrain from cutting down trees. Then any given peasant can reason that he or she will personally increase yield by felling trees (remember that clearing just one plot will not lead to significant soil erosion). But what is true for one is true for all, and so they may each begin to clear their plots, to gain an individual advantage. Even if they make an agreement, everyone has good reason to break that agreement. Hence the collectively rational position is unstable, and individuals will tend to defect, even if they know the consequences of everyone acting that way.

With this in mind, one way of thinking about Hobbes's argument is that, in the state of nature, the *individually* rational behaviour is to attack others (for reasons we have already seen) and this will lead to the state of war. However, the Laws of Nature tell us that the state of war is not the inevitable situation for human beings because another level of behaviour—*collective* rationality—may also be available. If only we could somehow ascend to the level of collective rationality and obey the Laws of Nature we can live in peace, without fear.

The question now is whether Hobbes believed that each person in the state of nature has a duty to obey the Laws of Nature, and if so whether the recognition of such a duty should be sufficient to motivate people to obey the Laws. Hobbes's answer here is subtle. He says that the Laws bind '*in foro interno*' (in the internal forum), but not always '*in foro externo*' (in the external forum). What he means is that we should all desire that the Laws take effect, and take them into account in our deliberations, but this does not mean that we should always obey them under all circumstances. If other people around me are disobeying the Laws, or, as will often be the case in the state of nature, I have reasonable suspicion that they will break the Laws, then it is simply stupid and self-defeating for me to obey. If someone does obey in these circumstances then he will 'make himselfe a prey to others, and procure his certain ruine' (*Leviathan*, 215). (In the technical language of contemporary game theory, anyone acting this way is a 'sucker'!)

In sum, then, Hobbes's position is that we have a duty to obey the Laws of Nature when others around us are known (or can reasonably be expected) to be obeying them too, and so our compliance will not be exploited. But if we are in a position of insecurity, the attempt to seek peace and act with moral virtue will lead to an individual's certain ruin and so we are permitted to 'use all the advantages of war'. The real point, then, seems to be, not exactly that moral notions have no application in the state of nature, but that the level of mutual suspicion and fear in the state of nature is so high that we can generally be excused for not obeying the law. We should only act morally when we can be assured that those around us are doing so too, but this is so rare in the state of nature that the Laws of Nature will, in effect, almost never come into play.

Hobbes sees the way out of this predicament as being the creation of a sovereign who will severely punish those who disobey the Laws. If the sovereign is effective in keeping people to the Laws, then, and only then, can no one have reasonable suspicion that others will attack. In that case there is no longer an excuse to start an invasion. The great advantage of the state, argues Hobbes, is that it creates conditions under which people can securely follow the Laws of Nature.

We should conclude this section by recalling Hobbes's account of the state of nature. It is a state where everyone is rightly suspicious of everyone else, and this suspicion, not mere egoism or sadism, leads to a war, where people will attack for gain, safety, and reputation. The war is self-fuelling and self-perpetuating, as reasonable suspicion of violent behaviour leads to an ever-increasing spiral of violence. In such a situation life is truly miserable, not only racked by fear, but lacking material comforts and sources of well-being. As no one can be sure of retaining any possessions, few will plant or cultivate, or engage in any long-term enterprise or plan. People will spend all their time grubbing for subsistence and fighting battles. Under such circumstances there is absolutely no chance that the arts or sciences could flourish. Our short lives would be lived without anything to make them worthwhile.

Locke

> The State of Nature, and the State of War, which however some Men have confounded, are as far distant as a State of Peace, Good Will, Mutual Assistance, and Preservation, and a State of Enmity, Malice, Violence, and Mutual Destruction are from one another.
>
> (John Locke, *Second Treatise of Civil Government*, s. 19, p. 280)

It is a matter of scholarly debate whether Locke had Hobbes explicitly in mind when he wrote this passage (published in 1689). His official target was the view of Sir Robert Filmer (1588–1653), a defender of the doctrine of the Divine Right of Kings—that the king ruled with authority granted by God. Nevertheless it is hard to deny that, at a number of points, Locke seems to be arguing with Hobbes, whose work must have been well known to him. As we shall see, comparing the two accounts of the state of nature casts light on them both.

While, as we saw, Hobbes identified the state of nature with a state of war, Locke is keen to emphasize that this is a mistake. Locke supposed that it would generally be possible to live an acceptable life even in the absence of government. Our question must be how Locke managed to draw this conclusion. Or, in other words, how, according to Locke, does Hobbes fall into error?

Let us start at the beginning. The state of nature, says Locke, is first, a state of perfect freedom; second, a state of equality; and third, bound by a Law of Nature. Verbally, of course, this sounds just like Hobbes's view, but each of these three elements is given quite a different interpretation by Locke. Hobbes's principle of equality was a claim about the mental and physical capabilities of all people. For Locke it is a moral claim about rights: no person has a natural right to subordinate any other. This assertion was explicitly aimed against those, including Filmer, who accepted the feudal view of a natural hierarchy, headed by a sovereign, ruling by divine appointment. Filmer argued that God had appointed Adam first sovereign, and contemporary sovereigns can trace their title back to God's initial grant. For Locke it is self-evident that no one *naturally* has a right to rule, in the sense that no one has been appointed by God for this purpose. Although Hobbes did not mean this by his assumption of equality, he would accept Locke's position here. Hobbes thought that whoever did, in fact, exercise power over the community was, for that reason, to be recognized as its sovereign.

There is, however, greater disagreement between the two on the nature and content of the Law of Nature. For Hobbes the fundamental Law of Nature was to seek peace, if others are doing so, but otherwise to use the advantages of war. This, and Hobbes's other eighteen Laws, were said to be 'theorems of reason'. Locke, too, believes the Law of Nature to be discoverable by reason, but Locke's Law has a theological aspect absent in Hobbes's Laws. The Law, says Locke, is that no one ought to harm another in his life, health, liberty, or possessions. The reason for this, according to Locke, is that while we have no natural superiors on earth, we do have one in heaven. In other words, we are all creatures of God, his property, put on earth as his servants, 'made to last during his, not one anothers Pleasure'. Therefore 'Every one . . . is *bound to preserve himself*, and not to quit his station wilfully; so by the like reason when his own Preservation comes not in competition, ought he, as much as he can, *to preserve the rest of Mankind*' (*Second Treatise*, s. 6, p. 271). The Law of Nature, for Locke, is simply the idea that mankind is to be preserved as much as possible. So, Locke argues, we have a clear duty not to harm others in the state of nature (except for limited purposes of self-defence), and we even have a duty to help them if we can do so without damage to ourselves.

Clearly, then, Hobbes and Locke have significantly different views of the nature and content of the Laws of Nature. A still greater difference lies in their use of the term 'natural liberty'. For Hobbes, we saw, to say that we have natural liberty is to say that it can often be entirely rational, and beyond moral criticism, to do whatever is appropriate to help secure our own survival, even if this means attacking the innocent. Locke's understanding is very different, claiming that although the state of nature 'be a *state of Liberty*, yet it is *not a state of Licence* . . . The *state of Nature* has a Law of Nature to govern it, which obliges every one' (*Second Treatise*, s. 6, pp. 270–1).

Thus natural liberty, on Locke's view, is no more than the liberty to do what the Law of Nature allows. That is, we are given the liberty to do only what is morally permitted. So, for example, although Locke's Law of Nature prevents me from invading the property of others, this is in no sense a limitation of my liberty. Locke would certainly disagree with Hobbes's claim that in the state of nature everyone has a right to everything, even each others' bodies (although he does accept that we have considerable rights of self-defence).

Do these disagreements between Hobbes and Locke add up to enough to establish Locke's conclusion that the state of nature need not be a state of war? Clearly it is important for Locke that even in the state of nature we have a moral duty to restrict our behaviour. Yet this, on its own, does not seem enough to show that in the state of nature fear and suspicion would not exist. And, as Hobbes argues, fear and suspicion may be enough for the state of nature to tumble into war. To avoid this Locke requires not only that the state of nature be subject to moral assessment, but that somehow or other people will be motivated to act as the Law of Nature instructs.

This suggests a strategy for resisting Hobbes's pessimistic conclusion. Hobbes argued that human beings would be driven by the search for felicity (the continued satisfaction of their desires), and this, at least initially, leads them into conflict. If Hobbes has misdescribed human motivation—if human beings, say, really are strongly altruistic—then peace might easily be achieved. This would be one route to Locke's conclusion. Is it the route Locke takes? Locke does not explicitly put forward a theory of human motivation in the *Two Treatises*, but it seems clear that he did not think that human beings would automatically be motivated to follow the moral law. Indeed he comes very close to sounding like Hobbes: 'For the *Law of Nature* would, as all other Laws that concern Men in this World, be in vain, if there were no body that in the State of Nature, had a *Power to Execute* the Law and thereby preserve the innocent and restrain offenders' (*Second Treatise*, s. 7, p. 271). In other words, the Law of Nature, like all laws, needs a law-enforcer. Without such an enforcer it would be empty.

Hobbes is perfectly prepared to accept that in the state of nature his Laws of Nature are ineffective. Unlike Hobbes, however, Locke cannot accept that the Law of Nature could be in vain: it is, after all, in Locke's view the law of God, who presumably does nothing in vain. Therefore there must be a way of enforcing the law: somebody who has the power to enforce it. But we are all equal in the state of nature, so if anyone has such power then everyone must have it. Therefore, Locke concludes, there must be a natural right, held by each person, to punish those who offend against the Law of Nature. Each of us has the right to punish those who harm another's life, liberty, or property.

The right to punish is not the same thing as the right of self-defence. It is the right not simply to try to prevent or ward off a particular episode of harm or damage, but to make anyone who has overstepped the Law of Nature pay for their transgression. This 'strange doctrine' as Locke calls it, plays a very important role in the derivation of his view of the state of nature. If the Law of Nature can be enforced, then we have good reason to hope that life could be relatively peaceful. Offenders can be punished to make reparation, and to restrain and deter them, and others, from similar acts in the future: 'Each Transgression may be *punished* to that *degree*, and with so much *Severity* as will suffice to make it an ill bargain to the Offender, give him cause to repent, and terrifie others from doing the like' (*Second Treatise*, s. 12, p. 275). It is important that this natural right to punish is not restricted solely to the individual who suffers the wrong. If that were so, then obviously those who commit murders would go unpunished. But, more importantly, the victim may not have sufficient strength or power to subdue, and exact retribution from, the offender. Locke therefore argues that those who break the law are a threat to us all, as they will tend to undermine our peace and safety, and so every person in the state of nature is given what Locke calls the 'Executive Power of the Law of Nature'. Locke has in mind the idea that law-abiding citizens, outraged by the offence, will band together with the victim to bring the villain to justice, and together they will have the necessary power to do this.

Locke realizes that the claim that we all have a natural right to punish offenders may seem surprising. However, in support of his view he claims that, without it, it is hard to see how the sovereign of any state can have the right to punish an alien who has not consented to the laws. If the foreigner has not consented to the sovereign's laws, then he has not accepted that he is liable to punishment for breaching them. Therefore such a person cannot justly be punished, unless there is some sort of natural right to punish. In effect, the sovereign is in the state of nature with the alien, and so the sovereign's behaviour is sanctioned not by the laws of the land, but by the Executive Power of the Law of Nature. (In fact we will see in the next chapter that Locke has a more obvious strategy to explain the sovereign's right: that the alien *tacitly consents* to the law.)

If the Law of Nature is enforceable, then a number of other rights can be secured, even in the state of nature. For Locke, the most important of these is the right to private property. We can already see what the basic form of the argument must be. God put us on earth, and it would be absurd to think that he put us here to starve. But we will starve unless we can rightfully consume objects such as apples and acorns; furthermore, we will do better still if individuals can securely possess plots of land and rightfully exclude others. For then we can cultivate the land, and be secure in our enjoyment of its products. (We will look at this argument in more detail in Chapter 5.)

To the modern reader, Locke's continual invocation of God and God's purposes may seem an embarrassment. Surely it should be possible to consider questions of political philosophy outside a theological framework? However, Locke also appeals to 'natural reason' in establishing the premisses of his arguments, even if he gives it a lesser role. So, for example, he thinks it absurd, and against natural reason, to suppose that human beings may not make use of the earth without the permission of all others, for if this were the case we should starve. This alternative argument certainly seems plausible, and so some followers of Locke have been prepared to drop the theological underpinnings of his view in favour of this 'natural reason' approach.

To return to the main argument, so far the central difference between Hobbes and Locke seems to be that Locke thinks that, even in the state of nature, there is an enforceable and effective moral law, backed by the natural right of punishment, while Hobbes would be highly sceptical of this claim. We can imagine how Hobbes would reply to Locke. According to Hobbes, the only way of subduing any power is through the exercise of a greater power. So we might all gang up on a villain to exact reparation and deter future such acts. But then the villain—who

may well be an unreasonable person with like-minded friends—
might return, armed, with forces united, to gain revenge. Such
thoughts could act as a powerful disincentive to those thinking
of exercising their executive power of the law of nature. If you
want to avoid unpleasantness in the future, don't get involved
now. So Hobbes would probably argue that even if people did
have a natural right to punish offenders, this would rarely be
used with any effect unless a single, stable, authority existed: for
example, within a tribe or group an acknowledged leader to
adjudicate disputes and enforce judgements. But that would
already be a fledgling state. So in the state of nature, even if
there were a right to punish, this would be ineffective as a means
to peace.

However, there is still one seemingly vital difference between
Hobbes and Locke that I have not yet mentioned. Remember
that for Hobbes, one of the key factors that brought people into
conflict was a natural scarcity of goods. Two people will often
desire the same thing, and this will make them enemies. Locke,
on the other hand, appears to make a very different assumption:
nature has given things richly. There is a natural abundance of
land, and plenty of room for everyone, particularly 'in the first
Ages of the World, when Men were more in danger to be lost, by
wandering from their Company, in the then vast Wilderness of
the Earth, than to be straitned for want of room to plant in'
(*Second Treatise*, s. 36, p. 293). Hence, Locke implies, under
these conditions there is very little reason for conflict and dispute. Most people, presumably, would rather cultivate their own
plot than invade their neighbour's, and so we can expect a relatively peaceful climate and few sources of quarrel. If this is right,
then peace in the state of nature is secured not only by the
natural right to punish, but, equally importantly, by the fact that
it would rarely have to be used.

How plausible is this? Hobbes no doubt would point out that
abundance of land does not rule out scarcity of finished and
consumable goods. It will often be far less trouble to take
another's product by stealth, than to go to the effort of plough-
ing, sowing, and harvesting. Furthermore, if others have similar

thoughts then I am wasting my energy by cultivating my own land, for, as Hobbes argued, whatever I will produce will end up in the hands of others. For Locke to refute this he must either show that the natural right to punish can be used effectively, or that human beings have some fairly strong motivation to obey the moral law. Otherwise a few highly anti-social individuals could ruin things for everyone.

Locke, indeed, comes close to admitting that the state of nature may not be as peaceful as he first supposed. After all, he has to be careful not to paint it in too idyllic tones, for then it would be very difficult to explain why we ever left it and created the state. The primary fault, Locke sees, is with the administration of justice. It is not so much that we will squabble over goods, but that we will squabble over what justice requires. We will, in other words, disagree about the interpretation of the Law of Nature. People will disagree about whether an offence has taken place. They will disagree about its proper punishment and compensation. And they might not have the power to exact what they believe to be its proper punishment. So the attempt to administer justice, even between the would-be law-abiding, is itself a powerful source of dispute. This Locke sees as the primary 'inconvenience' of the state of nature. The only thing that prevents serious trouble is the thought that, given initial abundance of land, disputes would be few.

But Locke sees the initial abundance of land eventually turning to scarcity: not through massive population growth, but through greed and the 'invention' of money. Prior to the existence of money no one would have any reason to take more land than is necessary for their own family's survival. If you grew more than you could use, it would simply go to waste, unless you could exchange it for something more permanent. But once money exists then such exchanges become easy, and it is possible to hoard up enormous amounts of money without the risk that it will spoil. This gives people a reason to cultivate more land to produce goods for sale. In turn this leads to pressure on land which then, and for this reason only, thinks Locke, becomes scarce. Now Locke does not say that such scarcity introduces the

Hobbesian state of war, but he recognizes that once land is in short supply and under dispute the inconveniences of the state of nature multiply and multiply. It becomes imperative to establish civil government. So although it is initially peaceful, eventually, even for Locke, the state of nature becomes almost unbearable.

Rousseau

> The philosophers, who have inquired into the foundations of society, have all felt the necessity of going back to a state of nature; but not one of them has got there.... Every one of them, in short, constantly dwelling on wants, avidity, oppression, desires, and pride, has transferred to the state of nature ideas which were acquired in society; so that, in speaking of the savage, they described the social man.

(Rousseau, *Discourse on the Origin of Inequality*, 50)

One way to avoid Hobbes's pessimistic conclusions about the state of nature is to start from different premises. In particular, life without the state might seem a much more attractive possibility if we adopted a different theory of human nature and motivation. Hobbes argues that people continually seek felicity: the power to satisfy whatever future desires they may have. This, together with fear and suspicion of fellow human beings, in a condition of scarcity, drives the argument for the state of war. But suppose Hobbes was quite wrong. Suppose people naturally and spontaneously desire to help each other whenever they can. Perhaps, instead of competing in a struggle for existence, humans offer mutual aid, and act for the sake of each others' comfort. If so, then the state of nature will look very different.

Although Rousseau does not make these optimistic assumptions about the natural goodness of human beings, his view takes a substantial step in this direction. Like Hobbes and Locke he assumes that human beings are primarily motivated by the desire for self-preservation. Yet he also believes that this is not the end of the story. Hobbes and Locke overlooked a central aspect

of human motivation—pity or compassion—and so overestim-
ated the likelihood of conflict in the state of nature. Rousseau
believes that we have 'an innate repugnance at seeing a fellow-
creature suffer' (*Discourse on the Origin of Inequality*, 73). This,
he adds, is 'so natural, that the very brutes themselves sometimes give evident proofs of it'.

Compassion, argues Rousseau, acts as a powerful restraint on
the drives that might lead to attack and war.

It is this compassion that hurries us without reflection to the relief of
those who are in distress: it is this which in a state of nature supplies the
place of laws, morals, and virtues, with the advantage that none are
tempted to disobey its gentle voice: it is this which will always prevent
a sturdy savage from robbing a weak child or a feeble old man of the
sustenance they may have with pain and difficulty acquired, if he sees a
possibility of providing for himself by other means. (*Discourse on the
Origin of Inequality*, 76)

Rousseau does not doubt that if modern citizens, moulded and
corrupted by society, were placed in a state of nature, they
would act just as Hobbes depicted them. But both Hobbes and
Locke have projected the qualities of man-in-society (or even
man-in-bourgeois-society) on to savage man. That is, they have
depicted socialized traits as if they were natural.

Rousseau follows this with a second claim. When we understand how 'savage man' behaves—motivated by both self-
preservation and pity—the state of nature would be far from the
Hobbesian state of war, and even in some respects preferable to
a more civilized condition. This does not mean that Rousseau is
advocating a *return* to the state of nature, for that would be
impossible for us, tainted and softened by society. Still, for
Rousseau, it is something of a matter of regret that we
have grown civilized. For Rousseau took an extreme, and extremely dismal, view of human progress. His treatise on education, *Émile*, begins: 'God makes all things good; man meddles
with them and they become evil.' And his early essay, the *Discourse on the Arts and Sciences*, argues that the development of
the arts and sciences has done more to corrupt than to purify
morality.

However, it is important to make clear that Rousseau's claim that human beings are naturally motivated by pity or compassion is very different from the point we attributed to Locke in the previous section: that human beings in the state of nature will often respect each other's *rights*. Like Hobbes, Rousseau argues that notions of law, right, and morality have no place in the state of nature, and so, clearly, he cannot mean that we have a natural impulse to follow a moral law. But unlike Hobbes and Locke he claims that we generally try to avoid harming others, not because we recognize that harm is immoral, but because we have an aversion to harm, even when it is not our own. We are naturally sympathetic to others, and are upset by their suffering. So we take steps to avoid this if we can.

It is surely very plausible that by nature human beings often have sympathy for one another. But is this enough to prevent war in the absence of government? The trouble is that Rousseau has given natural man two drives—self-preservation and compassion—and it seems more than possible that the two could come into conflict. If another has what I believe to be essential for my preservation, but I can take it only by causing harm, what would I—or rather the savage—do? It would surely be rare for any creature to put a stranger's well-being before their own survival, and consequently if goods are scarce the influence of pity must fade. Rousseau more or less admits this. Pity stops the savage robbing the weak or sick, provided there is hope of gaining sustenance elsewhere. But what if there is little or small hope of this? Perhaps, then, in a condition of scarcity we would suffer doubly. Not only would we be in a state of war, but we would feel terrible about all the harm we were doing to our fellow human beings. But the main point is that in a condition of scarcity, natural compassion does not seem enough to hold off the threat of war.

Rousseau tries to avoid this type of problem by supposing that savage man has few desires, and, relative to those desires, goods are more likely to be obtained by hunting and gathering than by taking them from others. This is not because of nature's munificence, but because the savage, claims Rousseau, is a solitary being, rarely coming into contact with others. Indeed there would not even be families. Rousseau speculates that children would leave their mothers as soon as they could survive on their own, and that among savages there would be no permanent union of man and woman. Compassion is not a strong enough sentiment to create a family bond.

Part of Rousseau's explanation of the solitary life of the savage is that nature has equipped the savage to survive alone. Strong and fleet of foot, not only a match for wild beasts but generally free from disease (which Rousseau claims to be a consequence of indulgence and unhealthy habits), the savage desires only food, sexual satisfaction, and sleep, and fears only hunger and pain.

Natural solitude rules out any desire for 'glory' or reputation, for the savage takes no interest in others' opinions. Indeed, as Rousseau argues that at this stage the savage has not yet developed language, the opportunities for forming and expressing opinions seem greatly restricted. Equally, the savage has no desire for power. Hobbes, we saw, defined power as 'the present means to satisfy future desires'. But, Rousseau argues, the savage has little foresight, and barely even anticipates future desires, let alone seeking the means to satisfy them. Rousseau likens the savage to the contemporary Caribbean, who, he says, 'will improvidently sell you his cotton bed in the morning, and come crying in the evening to buy it again, not having foreseen he would want it again the next night' (*Discourse on the Origin of Inequality*, 62). Consequently all of Hobbes's drives to war—desires for gain, safety and reputation—are either defused or absent in Rousseau's state of nature.

Still, despite its relatively peaceful character, Rousseau's state of nature hardly seems a welcoming prospect. Rousseau's savage may well be king of the beasts, but nevertheless, as portrayed, seems barely distinguishable from the other wild animals. The savage, says Rousseau, is 'an animal weaker than some, and less agile than others; but, taking him all round, the most advantageously organised of any' (*Discourse on the Origin of Inequality*, 52). Given that this is all we would have to boast of in the state of nature, why should Rousseau regret that we have now passed to a more civilized era? Furthermore, it is hard to see how such a transition would even be possible. What dynamic is there for change in Rousseau's picture? It is far from clear how, even hypothetically, we could have got here, from there.

Rousseau himself admits that what he says is no more than 'probable conjecture', for the transition could have happened in many ways. And it has to be admitted that it is not always easy to fit together everything Rousseau says on this topic. However, the key is the thought that human beings, unlike brutes, have two special attributes: free will, and the capacity for self-improvement. As we shall see, this latter capacity, Rousseau supposes, is the source of all human progress and all human misfortune.

The state of nature as set out so far lies deep in human prehistory: the condition of 'infant man', who spends time 'wandering up and down the forests, without industry, without speech, and without home, an equal stranger to war and to all ties, neither standing in need of his fellow-creatures nor having any desire to hurt them, and perhaps even not distinguishing them one from another' (*Discourse on the Origin of Inequality*, 79). We begin the path to civilization through the first exercise of the capacity of self-improvement: the development of tools in the struggle for subsistence, a struggle brought about, Rousseau speculates, by an increase in population. It is interesting that Rousseau sees innovation, and not Hobbesian competition, as the primary response to scarcity. Here Rousseau is probably relying on the idea that, as the savage has a natural aversion to harming others, most will prefer to get what they need by working for it, rather than taking things from others. And it is innovation to make work easier—tool-making—that first awakens man's pride and intelligence.

Another innovation is the idea of co-operation: mutuality of interest spurs collective pursuits, as for example, in the formation of hunting parties. Thus the advantages of living in groups, and making common huts and shelters, become apparent, and the habit of living in these new conditions 'gave rise to the finest feelings known to humanity, conjugal love and paternal affection' (*Discourse on the Origin of Inequality*, 88).

In this condition another novelty arises: leisure time. Co-operation and tool-making conquer scarcity sufficiently well to give the opportunity to create goods which go beyond bare survival needs. Thus the savage now starts to create convenience or luxury goods, unknown to former generations. However, 'This was the first yoke he inadvertently imposed on himself, and the first source of the evils he prepared for his descendants' (*Discourse on the Origin of Inequality*, 88). Why? Because man now develops what we could call 'corrupted needs'. Rousseau tells a familiar and plausible story. We become dependent on what were at first considered luxuries. Having them gives us little or no pleasure, but losing them is devastating—even though we once managed perfectly well without them.

From here a number of other negative elements are introduced: as societies develop, so do languages, and the opportunity for comparison of talents. This gives rise to pride, shame, and envy. For the first time an injury is treated as an affront, a sign of contempt rather than simply as damage, and those so injured begin to seek their revenge. As the state of nature begins to transform itself, causes of dissension and strife break out. But, even so, Rousseau says of this stage that it must have been the happiest and most stable of epochs, 'the real youth of the world' (*Discourse on the Origin of Inequality*, 91): a just mean between the savage's natural indolence and stupidity, and the civilized being's inflamed pride.

Though this is a stable period it cannot last for ever, and the real rot sets in with the long and difficult development of agriculture and metallurgy. From here it is a short step to claims of private property, and rules of justice. But private property leads to mutual dependence, jealousy, inequality, and the slavery of the poor. Eventually:

The destruction of equality was attended by the most terrible disorders. Usurpations by the rich, robbery by the poor, and the unbridled passions of both, suppressed the cries of natural compassion and the still feeble voice of justice, and filled man with avarice, ambition, and

vice. Between the title of the strongest and that of first occupier, there
arose perpetual conflicts, which never ended but in battles and blood-
shed. The new-born state of society thus gave rise to a horrible state of
war. (*Discourse on the Origin of Inequality*, 97)

Thus we arrive at war: not as part of the initial state of innocence
but as a result of the creation of the first rudimentary societies.
And at this point: 'The rich man, thus urged by necessity, con-
ceived at length the profoundest plan that ever entered the mind
of man: this was to employ in his favour the forces of those who
attacked him' (*Discourse on the Origin of Inequality*, 98). This
was a plan, of course, to institute social rules of justice to ensure
peace: rules that bind all equally, but which are greatly advan-
tageous to the rich, for they, after all, are the ones with property
to secure. Thus the first civil societies—societies with laws and
governments—are born. (We will see in Chapter 3 how far from
ideal Rousseau takes these first societies to have been.) And
once more we see the emergence of civil society taken to be a
response to a situation of war or near-war in the state of nature.

Anarchism

> No more laws! No more judges! Liberty, equality and prac-
> tical human sympathy are the only effective barriers we can
> oppose to the anti-social instincts of certain among us.
>
> (Peter Kropotkin, *Law and Authority* (1886),
> repr. in *The Anarchist Reader*, 117)

Even Rousseau, who believed in man's natural innocence,
thought that ultimately life without government would be intolerable. Certain anarchist thinkers, however, have tried to
resist this conclusion. William Godwin (1756–1836), husband of
Mary Wollstonecraft (1759–97) (see Chapter 3), differed from
Rousseau on two counts. First, human beings, when 'perfected'
could become not only non-aggressive but highly co-operative.
Second, this preferred state for human beings was not buried in
the distant past, but an inevitable future in which the state would
no longer be necessary. The Russian anarchist, Peter Kropotkin,

held a somewhat similar view that all animal species, including human beings, profited through natural 'mutual aid'. This he put forward as an alternative to Darwin's theory of evolution through competition. The fittest, suggests Kropotkin, are those species best able to achieve co-operation.

Kropotkin was able to marshal impressive evidence of co-operation within the animal kingdom, and other anarchists have argued—surely correctly—that there are endless examples of uncoerced co-operation among human beings. Many philosophers and social scientists have accepted that even highly selfish agents will tend to evolve patterns of co-operative behaviour, even for purely selfish reasons. In the long run co-operation is better for each one of us. If the state of war is damaging for all, then rational, self-interested creatures will eventually learn to co-operate.

But, as Hobbes would have been quick to point out, however much evidence there is of co-operation, and however rational co-operation can be, there is still plenty of evidence of competition and exploitation, and this will often seem rational too. And, like the rotten apple, a small measure of anti-social behaviour can spread its evil effects through everything it touches. Fear and suspicion will corrode and wear away a great deal of spontaneous or evolved co-operation.

One response open to the anarchist is to insist that there are no rotten apples. Or at least, in so far as there are, that this is a creation of governments: as Rousseau suggests, we have become softened and corrupted. Anarchists argue that we propose government as the remedy to anti-social behaviour, but, in general, governments are its cause. Nevertheless the thought that the state is the source of all forms of strife among human beings seems impossibly hopeful. In fact, the thesis appears to undermine itself. If we are all naturally good, why has such an oppressive and corrupting state come into existence? The most obvious answer is that a few greedy and cunning individuals, through various disreputable means, have managed to seize power. But then, if such people existed before the state came into being, as they must have done on this theory, it cannot be the case that we are *all* naturally good. Therefore to rely on the natural goodness of human beings to such an extent seems utopian in the extreme.

Hence most thoughtful anarchists have made a different response. The absence of governments does not mean that there can be no forms of social control over individual behaviour. Social pressure, public opinion, fear of a poor reputation, even gossip, can all exert their effects on individual behaviour. Those who behave anti-socially will be ostracized.

Furthermore many anarchists have accepted the need for the authority of experts within society. Some people know how best to cultivate food, for instance, and it is sensible to defer to their judgement. And within any sizeable group political structures are necessary to co-ordinate behaviour on the medium and large scale. For example, in times of international conflict even an anarchist society needs generals and military discipline. Deference to the opinions of experts and obedience to social rules may also be essential in peacetime too.

Such rules and structures are said not to amount to states as they allow the individual to opt out: hence they are voluntary in a way no state is. As we shall see in the next chapter, the state claims a monopoly of legitimate political power. No 'voluntarist', anarchist social system would do this. However, the existence of anti-social people who refuse to join in the voluntary society places the anarchist in a dilemma. If the anarchist society refuses to attempt to restrain the behaviour of such people, then it is in danger of falling into severe conflict. But if it enforces social rules against such people, then, in effect, it has become indistinguishable from a state. In sum, as the anarchist picture of society becomes increasingly realistic and less utopian, it also becomes increasingly difficult to tell it apart from a liberal, democratic, state. In the end, perhaps we simply lack an account of what a peaceful, stable, desirable situation would be in the absence of something very like a state (with the exception of anthropological accounts of small agrarian societies).

Yet, as we shall see in the next chapter, anarchism should not be dismissed so quickly. We have seen some of the disadvantages of the state of nature. What about the disadvantages of the state? How rational is it to centralize power in the hands of the few? We are yet to examine the arguments which have been given to justify the state. If it turns out that these attempts to justify the state do not work, then we will have to take a fresh look at anarchism. And in fact, for just this reason, we will need to raise the subject again.

Conclusion

I began this chapter with Hobbes's famous depiction of the state of nature as a miserable state of war of all against all. The basic argument is that individuals, motivated by the drive for 'felicity' will inevitably come into conflict over scarce goods, and, in the absence of a sovereign, this conflict will escalate into full-scale war. A number of counter-arguments were made in response. Locke suggested that the state of nature is governed by a moral law which could be enforced by every individual. He supplements this with the claim that we are initially in a condition of abundance, not scarcity, and with an implicit assumption that people will often be directly motivated to follow the moral law.

While Rousseau agrees with Locke that Hobbes was wrong to suggest that our natural condition is one of extreme scarcity, he denies that ideas of morality and moral motivation have any place in a state of nature. Instead he proposes that natural pity or compassion will prevent war from breaking out, pointedly remarking that we cannot tell how 'natural man' would behave on the basis of our observations of 'civilized man'. But whatever the force of these responses to Hobbes, both Locke and Rousseau admit that the counteracting causes to war they have identified can only serve to delay the onset of severe conflict, and will not avoid it for ever.

The anarchists are more optimistic in their attempts to avoid this conclusion. We considered three main strategies to defend the anarchist position. The first was to argue that co-operation will evolve in the state of nature, even among self-interested creatures. The second was to claim that human beings are naturally good. The third, and most plausible, is the argument that political and social structures and rules, short of the state, can be devised to remedy the defects of the state of nature. Yet, as I suggested, the gap between rational anarchism and the defence of the state becomes vanishingly small. In the end, I think, we must agree with Hobbes, Locke, and Rousseau. Nothing genuinely worthy of being called a state of nature will, at least in the long term, be a condition in which human beings can flourish. But whether this turns out to be a 'refutation' of anarchism remains to be seen.

2

Justifying the State

Introduction

> All that makes existence valuable to any one depends on the enforcement of restraints upon the actions of other people.
>
> (John Stuart Mill, *On Liberty*, 130)

If the arguments of the last chapter are correct, sooner or later, among any fairly sizeable group of people, life in the state of nature will become intolerable. Reason enough, it may be said, to accept that the state is justified without the need of further argument. After all, what real alternative to the state do we have? If we agree with the claim of John Stuart Mill (1806–73), that life without restraints on the behaviour of others would be of little or no worth, and also believe that the idea of 'enforceable restraints' without the state is mere wishful thinking, then any further argument about its justification seems idle.

That we have no real alternative to the state acts as a negative justification: we cannot think of anything better. Still, this does not end the philosophical discussion. The defender of the state should hope to find something more positive to say, in order to show how the state can be justified in terms of some acknowledged moral reasoning. That is, we need an argument to show that we have a moral *duty* to obey the state. Such an argument will also enable us to understand when the state might lose its legitimacy, as was widely believed to have happened, for example, at the time of the fall of the former eastern bloc countries. How we might give a positive justification of the state should become clearer as this chapter progresses. But first we should remind ourselves why it is far from obvious that we do have a moral duty to obey the state.

As we saw, Locke assumed that human beings are naturally free, equal, and independent. This means that they are not naturally under the authority of any other person. Hence legitimate power relations must be, in some sense, artificial, a human creation or construction. Accordingly, Locke concluded that the only way of coming under another person's authority was to give that person your consent (except in the case of justified punishment). This holds, for Locke, whether the person claiming authority is another private individual or the sovereign. Thus the sovereign, who claims authority over you, has no right to that authority unless you have voluntarily put yourself in this position through your own consent. So for Locke the problem of justifying the state is to show how its authority can be reconciled with the natural autonomy of the individual. His answer is to appeal to the idea of individual consent, and the device of the social contract. Essentially, for Locke and the social contract theorists, the state is justified if, but only if, every individual over which it claims authority has consented.

Locke, then, belongs in a tradition of theorists who give great weight to the idea of personal autonomy or natural liberty. Our political institutions, according to these theorists, must be justified in terms of the will, choices, or decisions of those over whom they have authority. This is a very appealing view, as it accords great respect to each individual, giving them the responsibility and opportunity to control their own destinies through their own choices. But there are other important approaches to the defence of the state which downplay the importance that Locke gives to autonomy and put other values in its place. In the utilitarian theory of Jeremy Bentham (1748–1832), for example, the primary value is not autonomy but happiness. The utilitarian theory, in its crudest form, says that we should aim to maximize the sum total of happiness in society. On this account the state is justified if and only if it produces more happiness than any alternative. Whether we consent to the state is irrelevant. What matters is whether it makes the members of society, in total, happier than they would be without it. This chapter will examine consent theory and the utilitarian theory, together with some other approaches to the moral defence of the state.

The state

Before deciding how best to justify the state, we had better be sure what it is. There are, we know from history and contemporary politics, many different types of state. Probably most people reading these words live in modern liberal democracies. Others live under dictatorships, benign or tyrannical, based on military rule, a monarchical family line, or something else again. Some states promote the free market, while others attempt collective forms of production and distribution. When we add to these actual states the theoretical models of the state, especially from communist and utopian writings, it might seem that different real and possible states have so little in common that trying to 'define' the state is a hopeless task.

Nevertheless, it has often been noted that there are some things that all states seem to have in common. We have seen that Locke defined political power as the right to make laws, with the right too to punish those who fail to obey them. States clearly possess, or at least claim to possess, political power. The sociologist Max Weber (1864–1920) made a similar point, if in more startling language: states possess a monopoly of legitimate violence. Within any state, violence or coercion is seen as primarily the state's business, either directly, through its agents—the police and law courts—or indirectly, through the permissions it gives citizens to be violent to each other on occasion: in self-defence, for example. All legitimate violence or coercion is undertaken or supervised by the state.

The other side to this is that the state accepts the responsibility of protecting everyone who resides within its borders from illegitimate violence. Surely it is only for this reason that we are prepared to grant the state its monopoly of violence. We forfeit the right to protect ourselves only on the understanding that we do not need self-protection: the state will do what is necessary for us.

Thus it is often claimed that the state possesses two essential features: it maintains a monopoly of legitimate coercion or violence and it offers to protect everyone within its territory. Is this a 'definition' of 'the state'? One common objection to such a claim is that it is perfectly obvious in practice that no actual state can live up to the ideal. No state can really monopolize violence, nor can it protect everyone within its territory. We need only think of the murder rate in any large city, and the precautions ordinary citizens feel they have to take in order to ensure their personal safety. What we say about such cases is that certain states do not manage to monopolize violence, and, sadly, fail to protect all their citizens: we would not say that such societies do not have states at all. But it would seem that this would be forced upon us if we treated the two 'essential features' of the state as providing a definition.

In answer to this it should be re-emphasized that the proposed definition claims only that the state maintains a monopoly of *legitimate* violence. The existence, then, of illegitimate violence is irrelevant. And the state *offers* protection to all, even if it also often fails to deliver. But both of these replies are problematic. Many people in the USA claim a right to arm themselves in self-defence. But not only do they believe that they should have this right, they also argue that the government has no authority over them in this matter. So, in effect, these people claim, with a great deal of conviction, that the state or government has no business trying to monopolize the means of violence. And the argument that the state offers protection to all hardly seems universally true. Many states simply ignore the plight of unfavoured minorities, particularly those belonging to certain ethnic groups. Worse, in extreme cases, these minorities even suffer illegitimate violence from the state itself, in the form of persecution, purges, or 'ethnic cleansing'. Thus such states fail to possess one of the features all states are said to have, but it would be absurd to deny that they are states.

Both defining qualities of the state, then, are problematic. At this point we have done no more than indicate an ideal type of state, one which does indeed have the two features we indicated.

Let us leave the issue of definition aside and move on to our central question: how can we justify a state such as this?

The goal of justification

At this point it will be helpful to introduce some terminology. The task of justifying the state is often said to be the task of showing that there are *universal political obligations*. To say that someone has political obligations is to say, at least, that they have the duty, in normal circumstances, to obey the law of the land, including paying taxes where these are due. Other duties may also be implied: to fight, if called for, in defence of the state; perhaps to behave patriotically; even to seek out and expose the enemies of the state. But let us concentrate on the duty to obey the law.

Political obligation is the obligation to obey each law because it is the law, and not necessarily because we think it has some independent moral justification. Most of us obey the laws against murder without a second thought. If we were asked why we refrain from killing people most of us would surely answer that the idea of doing so has never entered our heads as a serious option. If called on for a further reason we would probably say that killing is wrong, or immoral. It would cause us great concern, I think, to be told that someone's primary reason for not killing others is that doing so is illegal. Few people, then, need the law to stop them from committing murder. Thus here we have a law which coincides with what morality independently also requires.

But there also exist laws which seem to have little grounding in morality. Take traffic laws, for example. You may believe that you have a moral obligation to stop at a red light at a deserted crossroads, but only because this is what the law tells you to do. Of course, people occasionally think that what the law requires them to do is morally wrong. For example, some of our taxes are used to build nuclear warheads, and many taxpayers think that such a policy is morally reprehensible. But even in this case the 'good citizen' may well feel an obligation to obey the tax laws, and thus reluctantly continue to contribute to this and other projects, simply because this is what the law requires. Any pro-test, such a citizen might suppose, must be carried out by other means. Breaking the law would only be appropriate in the most urgent and serious cases.

'Justifying the state' is normally thought to mean showing that there are universal obligations to obey the law. A 'universal' obligation, in this context, does not mean the duty to obey all laws at all times. Only a certain rather unpleasant kind of fanatic could believe that we are always morally obliged to obey the law whatever it tells us to do; that for example, I ought to stop at a red light even if I am driving a dying man to hospital. Rather, the idea is that political obligations are universal in the sense that they apply to all people who reside within the borders of the state. It may be that the state is prepared to exempt certain people from certain laws (although this is often a sign of corrup-tion) but the point is that the goal of justification of the state is to show that, in principle, everyone within its territories is mor-ally bound to follow its laws and edicts. We should turn now to see whether such justification can be achieved.

The social contract

> I moreover affirm, That all Men are naturally in [the state of nature], and remain so, till by their own Consents they make themselves Members of some Politick Society; And I doubt not in the Sequel of this Discourse, to make it very clear.
>
> (Locke, *Second Treatise*, s. 15, p. 278)

Voluntaristic obligation

Let us use the term 'voluntarism' for the view, mentioned earlier, defended by Locke: political power over me can be created only as a consequence of my voluntary acts. Another person can have political power over me only if I have granted them that power.

This view is sometimes expressed in terms of the so-called 'self-assumption' principle: that no one has any duties whatsoever unless they have 'assumed' those duties, that is, voluntarily undertaken them. Taken literally this is a view of little plausibility and should be dismissed. My duty not to attack the innocent seems not in any way to be conditional on my prior 'assumption' of that duty. We must, it seems, accept that we have some moral duties, whether or not we have agreed to them. But this is not enough to show that anyone has the right to make laws, and compel me to obey them. And that, of course, is what the state does.

On this account it becomes obvious that the problem of political obligation, at least for Locke, is to show how the existence of the state can be explained in voluntaristic terms. It needs to be shown that somehow or other, every last individual—or at least every mentally competent adult—has given the state its authority over them. On this view, in order to justify the state it is not enough simply to point out how much better off we would be under the authority of the state than in the state of nature. We would also have to show that each person has voluntarily consented to the state.

To put this another way, even if it is true that the state is to my advantage, it does not follow, for Locke, that the state is justified. For I have a natural right to freedom, and so political power over me can be brought into existence only through my own consent. Accordingly, a state which purports to exercise political power over me, but which does not have my consent, has no right to govern and hence is illegitimate. This remains so even if life in civil society is far superior to life in the state of nature.

The project of showing that individuals consent to the state lies behind the idea of social contract theory. If, somehow or other, it can be shown that every individual has consented to the state, or formed a contract with the state, or made a contract with each other to create a state, then the problem appears to be solved. We would have shown how the state comes to have universal authority—authority over each one of us—by showing that everyone has consented to that authority. In the abstract, then, social contract theory is an obvious, elegant solution to the problem of political obligation. It satisfies the twin demands of

universalism—every person must be obligated—and voluntarism—political obligations can come into existence only through
consent.

This is all very well in theory, but where can we look for a
social contract in practice? On some accounts the social contract
is thought to be an 'original contract', that is, it was a real
historical event. It was the moment, and mechanism, which took
our ancestors from the state of nature to civil society. This view
is commonly—and probably rightly—met with blank incredu-
lity. Even if we accept that there was a real, historical, state of
nature (and we saw in the last chapter some reasons to question
this) could there have been such a contract? What is the
evidence? Which museum is it in? Such a momentous event
should have left some trace on the historical record. Furthermore, how could such a contract have happened? Aside from
the obvious practical problems of communication and co-
ordination, critics inspired by Rousseau have pointed out that
it is absurd to think that savages in the state of nature could
have the conceptual sophistication to create and respect any sort
of legal agreement.

But much more importantly, even if there had been such a
contract, what would it prove? We could hardly maintain that
it explains the political obligations of existing citizens. After
all, no reasonable legal system allows one generation to make
a contract which binds succeeding generations. Yet this is exactly what the doctrine of the original contract seems to
presume.

If social contract theory depends on a doctrine of the original
contract, then surely it is doomed. Fortunately there are
other ideas which may play a more suitable role. If the goal of
constructing a voluntaristic account of the state is to be
achieved, then it is important that all those presently said to be
bound by the state should have been able to consent to it. This
seems to require some sort of ongoing consent, given by every
individual.

Could it be that every one of us has knowingly, and voluntarily, given our consent to the state? It is hard to see how. I cannot remember ever having been asked whether I agree to be governed, or at least not by anyone with any official status. It is true that Boy Scouts and schoolchildren are often required to pledge their allegiance to the flag or to 'God and the Queen', but they are given no real choice, and, in any case, are not old enough for their pledge to have legal standing. There are few, if any, societies in which literally everyone is required to pledge. As is often observed, the only people in modern societies who explicitly give their consent are those who gain citizenship of a society through naturalization. The vast majority of ordinary citizens are left untouched.

Here it might be replied that consent is given in a less obvious or explicit fashion. One thought is that consent is communicated via the ballot-box. In voting for the government we give it our consent. And it is not wholly implausible that even those who vote against the government nevertheless indicate their consent to the system as a whole through voting. But this leaves us with two problems. Some of those who vote against the government might claim to be expressing their dissent to the system as a whole. Further, what can be said about those who abstain? Refusing to vote can hardly be treated as a way of expressing consent to the government. The situation is not improved by making abstention illegal and forcing everyone to vote. As voting would no longer be voluntary, it could not possibly be represented as an act or sign of consent.

However, a much more interesting development of this line of thought is the claim that political obligations arise only where society is arranged as a 'participatory democracy'. A participatory democracy is one in which all citizens take an active role in government, far more extensive than anything we have encountered in modern democracies. An important consequence of this view is that, as contemporary democracies fail to match the ideal, citizens in such states have no political obligations. The theory of participatory democracy deserves proper attention, and we will return to it in the next chapter. In the mean time we must remember that any conclusions in this chapter about political obligation are conditional on that examination.

Tacit consent

So far we have not been able to see how to develop a plausible theory of explicit or express consent. We have already considered the idea that voting is a way of *tacitly* consenting, but perhaps the idea of tacit consent can be developed in a more promising form. In fact all the major social contract theorists—Hobbes, Locke, and Rousseau—rely in different ways on arguments based on tacit consent. Here the central thought is that by quietly enjoying the protection of the state one is giving it one's tacit consent. And this is enough to bind each individual to the state. Although Locke believed that only express consent could make one a full member of political society, he famously argued that nevertheless political obligations can be created through tacit consent:

Every Man that hath any Possession, or Enjoyment, of any part of the Dominions of any Government, doth thereby give his *tacit Consent*, and is as far forth obliged to obedience to the laws of that Government, during such Enjoyment as any one under it; whether this Possession be of Land to him and his Heirs for ever, or a Lodging only for a Week; or whether it be barely travelling freely on the Highway. (*Second Treatise*, s. 119, p. 348)

Perhaps this seems plausible. I tacitly consent to the state by accepting its protection and other benefits. Now it might be that the mere receipt of benefits is alone enough to bind one to the state, and we shall look at such an argument later in this chapter. But the current proposal is subtly different, for it adds a further step in the argument: receiving benefits is a way of tacitly consenting to the state, and it is the *consent* that binds one. Should we accept this claim?

Perhaps behind the argument is the thought that those who do not like the package of benefits and burdens offered by the state can get up and go. But if the doctrine depends on this, then many would claim that it has been decisively refuted by David Hume (1711–76):

Can we seriously say, that a poor peasant or artizan has a free choice to leave his country, when he knows no foreign language or manners, and lives from day to day by the small wages he acquires? We may as well assert, that a man, by remaining in a vessel, freely consents to the dominion of the master; though he was carried on board while asleep, and must leap into the ocean, and perish, the moment he leaves her. ('Of The Original Contract', 475)

What does this objection show? Hume's idea is that residence alone cannot be construed as consent. Why not? Simply because nothing could count as dissent, except leaving the country. But that is surely too onerous a condition to allow us to conclude that those who stay consent.

This is often taken as a convincing refutation. But on the other hand there might be cases which meet even these demanding conditions. Rousseau, for example, supposes that residence constitutes consent, but only within a 'free' state, 'for elsewhere family, goods, lack of a refuge, necessity, or violence may detain a man in a country against his will; and then his dwelling there no longer by itself implies his consent to the contract' (*Social Contract*, bk. IV, ch. 2, p. 277). It is peculiar, if typical, of Rousseau to think that family or goods render one unfree. But we can see his point, even if we would wish to amend his account. In a free state, Rousseau implies, the act of dissenting—leaving the territories of the state—is simple enough.

The idea that any dissenter can leave might be plausible if we think of a world of walled city-states, which one may leave simply by walking through the gates (as Rousseau, almost by accident, left Geneva in his youth). Hume clearly has in mind something much more like the nation-state, such as Britain, where leaving is no simple matter. Indeed his image of the state as a vessel on the high seas suggests an island like Britain. In the contemporary world, a world of nation-states, the doctrine of tacit consent seems far less appropriate than it did for Rousseau; not so much for the reason that states are surrounded by seas, but because even those who want to leave often find that there is simply nowhere to go: no other country will have them, and in any case what is the point of swapping one objectionable regime for another? We should, in the end, agree with Hume. The conditions for tacit consent are not met in the modern world. The state cannot be justified in these terms.

Hypothetical consent

Perhaps it is a mistake to think that the social contract theorist needs to appeal to some form of actual consent, be it historical, express, or tacit. Rather, it could be argued that the social contract is purely hypothetical: it merely tells us what we *would do*, or *would have done* in the state of nature. According to this view, the thought that if we were in the state of nature we would have contracted to bring about the state, is itself enough to show that the state is justified.

How should we understand this sort of argument? As a first step, it is worth reminding ourselves of a point mentioned in the last chapter: perhaps the best way of getting clear about your relation to something is to imagine its absence. This is a tactic often used, for example, by parents to persuade their children to eat unappetising food: you would be grateful for it if you were starving. Accordingly, then, the hypothetical contract argument tells us that if, somehow or other, we found ourselves without a state, then we would find it rational to try to bring one into existence as soon as we appreciated the nature of our plight.

So we can understand the hypothetical contract argument as running like this: even if you were not under the authority of the state, and somehow found yourself in the state of nature, then, if you were rational, you would do everything in your power to recreate the state. In particular, you would rationally and freely join in a contract to bring about the state. The hypothetical contract theorist will now plausibly ask: how can this argument *fail* to justify the state?

If it really is true that all rational individuals in the state of nature would freely make this choice, then we do seem to have a good argument here to justify the state. But we should still ask how this relates to the 'voluntaristic' assumptions of social contract theory. For if we assume that we can only acquire political obligations by our own voluntary acts of consent, and recognize that *hypothetical* acts of consent are *not* acts, it seems to follow that the hypothetical contract argument will not satisfy the demands of social contract theory.

This observation puts us in an interpretative quandary. If the hypothetical contract argument is not the sort of argument that could satisfy the social contract theorist, then what sort of argument is it? One possibility is to say that it is a way of showing that certain sorts of state are *worthy* of our consent. That is, the state has a number of desirable features—essentially that it is our best hope of peace and security—and the fact that we would consent to bring it into existence from the state of nature simply confirms that it has those features. On this interpretation it is the features of the state, and not our consent, which provide the main basis of its justification. Consent simply drops out of the picture. Ultimately, then, according to this line of argument, the hypothetical contract argument is not a form of voluntaristic defence of the state. It is much closer to the utilitarian theories which we will encounter shortly. The state is justified through its contribution to human well-being.

On the other hand, there is a way in which we might try to reconstruct hypothetical contract theory in voluntaristic terms. Consider the argument that hypothetical consent somehow indicates the presence of real consent. We should start from the thought that although almost no one ever formally expresses their consent to the state, there is nevertheless a sense in which all or most of us can be said to consent. Perhaps if we were asked, and required to think about the matter seriously and hard, we would each express our consent. So it would seem fair to say that anyone of whom this is true has a *disposition* to consent to the state. But this seems the same as saying that such people consent to the state, even if they do not realize it. Just as we can have beliefs we have never brought to consciousness (for example, for many years I must have believed that giraffes do not have nine legs, although before first writing these words I had never consciously formed this thought), we can consent to the state without realizing that we do so.

The device of the hypothetical contract can now be thought of

as a way of getting us to realize what we really think. By reflecting on how I would behave in the state of nature—running
headlong into civil society if I could—I come to realize that I do
consent to the state. The point is not that, after going through
the thought-experiment, I come to consent for the first time.
Rather, the idea is that, after going through the process, I
come to realize that I have consented all the time. On this
interpretation the point of the hypothetical contract argument is
to reveal dispositional consent: an as-yet-unexpressed attitude
of consent.

How much can be achieved with such an argument? One
difficulty is that the sense in which consent is used here is very
weak. Unexpressed, even unacknowledged, dispositions to consent are rarely considered binding in other moral or legal con-
texts. Furthermore there may well be people who go through the
hypothetical contract reasoning, and then, after deep reflection,
come to believe that they would be better off in the state of
nature, and so prefer it to the state. Perhaps they distrust cen-
tralized power. Perhaps they are more optimistic about the state
of nature than I have been here. Are there such people? It
certainly seems that there are: the anarchists and their followers
discussed in the last chapter would be good examples. Such
people cannot possibly be said to have the disposition to consent
to the state: they actively and explicitly dissent.

We might be tempted to suppose that such people are irrational. But what is so irrational about them? In any case, even
if they are irrational, this is hardly a way of showing that they
have consented. So even this weakest form of consent theory
cannot deliver what we are looking for: a universal ground of
political obligation. And if we insist that political obligations
must be undertaken voluntarily, this is a risk we always run. The
whole apple-cart can be upset by a single dissenter. As contract
theory is voluntarism *par excellence* it seems that universalism—
the thesis that everyone has political obligations—simply cannot
be delivered by contract or consent theory in any of the forms
discussed here.

Anarchism revisited

Perhaps the answer is to accept that it is impossible to show that everyone has political obligations. The insistence on a voluntaristic foundation of the state is highly plausible, and if the cost of this is that we have to accept that some individuals escape the authority of the state, then perhaps we should bite the bullet.

The argument gives renewed support to the anarchist case briefly explored in Chapter 1. If we cannot find a way of justifying the state from acceptable premises, then some sort of anarchy seems forced upon us, morally speaking at least. This critical strategy seems the anarchist's strongest weapon. No one *asked* me whether we should have a state, and the police do not request my permission to act as they do. Therefore, the anarchist argues, the state and the police act illegitimately, at least in respect of their dealings with me.

The implications of this view may be far-reaching. Most radically it could be argued that once we accept the anarchists' argument, then the only reason we have for obedience to the state is prudence, especially fear of punishment. The strong person should resist this cowardly attitude, and take no notice of the state and its agents. Or, to put this in a somewhat more moderate form, we can admit that, as we have seen, what the law requires is often independently required by morality. Hence one ought to do some things that the state decrees—refrain from murder, rape, or injury—but not because the state decrees it. Furthermore, the police often act in ways in which any citizen might: to protect the innocent, to detain and bring to justice anyone who wrongs another, and so on. So we can be grateful to the police for doing the dirty work for us. However, on this view, one should support the state and the police only in those cases where one independently agrees with the reasons for which they act. The fact that a law is a law, or the police are the police, provides no reason at all for obedience. Hence the 'philosophical anarchist' recommends that we adopt a highly critical stance towards the activities of the police and the state. Sometimes they act with moral authority, but where they do not we are right to disobey, obstruct, or ignore them.

In some respects this seems a highly enlightened picture. The responsible citizen should not blindly follow the law, but always use his or her private judgement about whether the law is justified. If it is not, then there is no moral reason to obey.

This picture has to be correct—up to a point. To argue that one should never question or disobey a law would lead one, say, to defend the persecution of Jews in Nazi Germany or to defend the recently overturned laws against mixed marriage and inter-breeding (miscegenation) in South Africa. There must be some moral limit to the obligation to obey the law. However, it is not so easy to say what this moral limit should be. At the extreme, suppose one held the view that one should not obey the law unless it accords perfectly with one's own moral judgement. Now, many people (wealthy people in particular) believe that taxation of income purely for purposes of redistribution of wealth has no moral justification. On the view about the justification of the state just canvassed, such people would be entitled to stop paying a portion of their tax. At the same time, a number of people, from a variety of social and economic backgrounds, believe that the inheritance of goods is unjust. Who inherits wealth and who does not is completely 'arbitrary from a moral point of view', to use the terminology of John Rawls (see Chapter 5). Many people think it is quite unfair that certain individuals can inherit vast fortunes, while the equally deserving get nothing. Now, if you think that there is no moral justification to inherited property, then you think that the Duke of Westminster has no more right to have you turned off 'his' inherited property than you have to exclude him, as it is not truly his. If you then add to this that one should obey the law only if it accords with your moral outlook, then you no longer have any reason (save fear of punishment) to respect much of other people's (claimed) property.

Clearly cases can be multiplied. The point is, if we accept the anarchist view just discussed, we have returned to the chaotic situation where people may follow their individual private judgement in all matters, even those of public concern. But it was for exactly this reason that Locke argued that we should move away from the state of nature. From such a perspective, the philosophical anarchist position begins to look like a very dangerous example of moral self-indulgence. Surely it is far better that we generally accept some publicly laid down and accepted set of laws, to guide our dealings with each other, than leave people to act on the basis of their own conflicting codes. In other words, having a *shared* set of laws is, within reason, much more important than anyone's private judgement about what the best laws should be.

In response, the anarchist may well argue that there is no reason to expect such a proliferation of conflicting moral views. After all, a particular moral perspective might be the correct one, and so individuals might all be brought to share the same set of basic moral principles. It is the second of these claims that carries the weight in the argument, but how plausible is it? Even if there is a single set of true moral principles, how can we ensure that everyone comes to see that truth? For those who doubt that there is any such method the anarchist position remains unattractive.

Utilitarianism

Subjects should obey Kings . . . *so long as the probable mischiefs of obedience are less than the probable mischiefs of resistance.*

(Jeremy Bentham, *Fragment on Government*, 56)

The failure of the contract arguments, combined with the unattractiveness of anarchism, makes the examination of utilitarian theory all the more pressing. The fundamental idea of utilitarianism is that the morally correct action in any situation is that which brings about the highest possible total sum of utility. Utility is variously understood as happiness, pleasure, or the satisfaction of desires or preferences. For the purposes of our discussion it does not much matter which of these options we choose, so let us speak of maximization of happiness, for convenience. Put crudely, utilitarianism requires one to perform the action that will create more happiness (or less unhappiness) in the world than any other action available at the time.

Notice that if we are to take utilitarianism seriously, we need to be able to measure and quantify happiness, so that we can determine which of several possible actions creates the most. This is often thought to be a grave difficulty. After all, if we are to compare situations we seem to need some scale by which we can measure: units of happiness, perhaps. How can we do this? Not only does the theory require us to compare one person's happiness with another's, and say who has more, but to say *how much more*. We would have to be able to make sense, it seems, of statements like: 'Fred is twice as happy as Charlie today, although yesterday he was three times as happy.' Many will think this is absurd. Trying to quantify happiness this way often seems just childish.

The problem of finding a way of comparing happiness is known as the problem of 'interpersonal comparisons of utility'. Strangely, none of the nineteenth-century founders of utilitarianism seemed to see the force of this problem, although in the last few decades a number of ingenious technical solutions have been proposed. No solution has been universally accepted and it would take us too far afield to give the issue proper consideration here. However, we should not be blind to the point that we are never at a complete loss when we are called on to make comparisons. We know of other people, say, who seem to enjoy certain foods, or forms of entertainment, far more or less than we do ourselves. More seriously, every day we see people who live in misery, while others, we know, lead wonderfully enjoyable lives. Thus we do believe that certain comparisons can be made, even if we do not know exactly how we do it. For present purposes we will simply assume that interpersonal comparisons of utility can be made, while remembering that the utilitarian owes us an account of how, precisely, this can be done.

Returning to the main issue, our question should now be, what would a utilitarian theory of political obligation look like?

According to Jeremy Bentham, as we saw above, we should obey our rulers as long as the benefits of doing so outweigh the costs. This, then, sounds like the theory that I should obey the law if, but only if, my obedience will lead to the greater happiness of society than my disobedience.

But if this is Bentham's doctrine, then a moment's thought reveals that it is a law-breaker's charter. For my happiness is, after all, part of the general happiness. So if breaking a law—say by stealing a book from a large bookshop—would increase my happiness, and I can be sure that no one would find out or suffer any noticeable loss or harm, it seems that utilitarianism would not only permit me, but require me, to carry out the theft. The more general message is that this utilitarian theory would very often sanction law-breaking.

Can this be what the utilitarian wants? It seems unlikely, and in fact there is a ready response. Consider what would happen if we all broke laws whenever we thought that doing so would lead to an increase in general happiness. In that case you could take any of my possessions whenever doing so would increase your happiness more than it would decrease mine. Possession would be extremely insecure, perhaps so uncertain that ultimately no one would work to produce anything if another could take it whenever the utilitarian calculation worked in their favour. This insecurity would lead to great overall unhappiness, rather like the insecurity in the state of nature. Paradoxically, when each of us tries to increase the general happiness together we eventually bring about general misery. This is another example of the prisoners' dilemma discussed in Chapter 1: action which individually increases happiness collectively diminishes it.

Consequently, the utilitarian can argue that we need a body of laws which will be respected, even when breaking one of these on a particular occasion would, if it were permitted, lead to an increase in happiness. This can be called *indirect* utilitarianism. The idea is that if we all reason directly in utilitarian terms things will go very badly. Hence we need to follow non-utilitarian reasoning—obey the laws—to maximize happiness.

It will help illustrate the point to make an analogy with an individual's search for happiness. A discovery made over and over again by lotus-eaters everywhere is that if you personally set out with the single goal of becoming happy, and do everything you can to become happy, more likely than not you will fail. But if you aim at something else—form and pursue an ambition, get a hobby, make some good friends—you may well find happiness as a side-effect or indirect consequence. So, it is claimed, the direct search for happiness, both individually and socially, can be self-defeating. The best we can do is set ourselves other goals, or follow other rules, in the hope or expectation that happiness will follow as a consequence. The utilitarian political philosopher should recommend a system of law which each person must follow, at least under normal circumstances. It is not, then, for the individual to consider the effect of following the law on the level of happiness within society.

This is probably Bentham's own real view: 'taking the whole body [of people] together, it is their duty to obey only when it is their interest' (*Fragment on Government*, 56). An extension of this passage provides several ideas:

1. Laws should be passed if, and only if, they contribute more to human happiness than any competing law (or the absence of law) would do.

2. Laws should be obeyed because they are laws (and will be obeyed because disobedience means punishment), and should only be disobeyed to avoid disaster.

3. Laws should be repealed and replaced if they fail to serve the proper utilitarian function.

The utilitarian message for political obligation now seems clear. The state, as provider and enforcer of a body of law, is justified if and only if it contributes more to human happiness than any feasible competing arrangement. If we think in terms of a basic contrast between the state and the state of nature, and we accept the arguments—particularly those of Hobbes—from the first chapter, it seems that the utilitarian justification of the state looks very plausible. In terms of contributing to general happiness, the state seems greatly to outperform the state of nature. Thus, for the utilitarian, the justification of the state is complete.

However, despite this success, very few political philosophers seem convinced by the utilitarian defence of the state. Many concede that the argument works very well in its own terms, but find fault with the argument's assumptions or premisses. The argument itself is very simple. In essence, it has just three premisses:

1. The morally best society is the one in which happiness is maximized.

2. The state promotes happiness better than the state of nature.

3. The state and the state of nature are the only alternatives we have.

Therefore:

4. We have a moral duty to bring about and support the state.

We saw in the first chapter that different sorts of anarchists will question premisses 2 and 3, but for the purposes of this argument, let us assume these premisses are true. The argument also seems valid in the formal sense that if the premisses are true, then the conclusion must also be true. Hence the only vulnerable part of the argument is the first premiss: the fundamental principle of utility.

And here lies the problem. Few philosophers are now prepared to accept utilitarian reasoning, for they think it has morally unacceptable consequences. In particular, it is often claimed that utilitarian morality permits, or even requires, grave injustices. A notorious difficulty, for example, is the 'scapegoat' objection: utilitarianism will permit enormous injustice in the pursuit of the general happiness.

The scapegoat objection is this. Suppose some hideous crime has been committed—perhaps a terrorist bombing in which several people are killed and many more injured. In such circumstances the police are under intense pressure to find the perpetrators. The population at large seeks vengeance, and reassurance that a similar attack will not happen again. The general happiness will certainly be served if the guilty parties are brought to justice. But opponents of utilitarianism have noticed that the general happiness will also be advanced if individuals *believed* by the population to be guilty are arrested and sentenced. As long as they are plausible suspects—have the right accents, look the part and so on—then at least the demand for vengeance will be satisfied, and we will all sleep more soundly in our beds (even if we do so only because of our false belief). Of course the innocent will suffer. But it seems plausible that the increase in happiness (or decrease in misery) of the general population will outweigh the suffering of the innocent and so make the victimization pay off in utilitarian terms. Thus, it is claimed, utilitarianism has the consequence that it can be morally correct to punish the innocent. Other examples of the same type—for instance concerning the utilitarian justification of slavery—can easily be concocted.

The point is not that it is better to punish the innocent; surely it would be better still on the utilitarian calculus to find and punish the guilty. But when everything is taken into account it seems quite likely that some miscarriages of justice are defensible in utilitarian terms. Most of the philosophical discussion is based on fictional examples, but the issue was brought to public attention in Britain in connection with the bombing of a pub by the IRA. The 'Birmingham six' had been found guilty of murder, but claimed that their confessions had been beaten out of them by the police. They attempted to bring a civil action against the police for the injuries sustained in custody. Lord Denning, in his judgement at the Court of Appeal in 1980, was addressing the question of whether the civil action against the police should be allowed to go to trial. This is what he said:

If the six men fail, it will mean that much time and money will have been expended by many people for no good purpose. If the six men win, it will mean that the police were guilty of perjury, that they were guilty of violence and threats, that the confessions were involuntary and were improperly admitted in evidence and that the convictions were erroneous. That would mean the Home Secretary would either have to recommend they be pardoned or he would have to remit the case to the Court of Appeal. This is such an appalling vista that every sensible person in the land would say: It cannot be right these actions should go any further. (Quoted in Chris Mullin, *Error of Judgement*, 216)

Denning later admitted that 'with the benefit of hindsight my comments can justly be criticised'. But the point is, so the critics of utilitarianism would say, his comments amount to a perfect application of utilitarian reasoning. It would be better to let innocent men remain in jail than to admit that the police some- times terrorize individuals into falsely confessing. And, it hardly needs to be said, so much the worse for utilitarian reasoning.

But in defence, it might seem that the utilitarian can avoid such problems by adopting the 'indirect utilitarianism' strategy outlined before. If we know that we live in the sort of society in which people can be victimized and made scapegoats, and kept in prison even if innocent, this will lead to such insecurity that it will have a greatly depressive effect on human happiness. After all, how do I know that I will not be the next utilitarian scape- goat? Accordingly the utilitarian must grant people the right not to be punished unless they are guilty. So the scapegoat objec- tion, and others like it, it is often argued, can be avoided by this more subtle utilitarian approach. And, indeed, a utilitarian con- sidering the Birmingham six might well argue that—*contra* Denning's first argument—more good than harm has been done by their release. Discredit may have been brought upon the British judicial system, but, as a result of the case and its pub- licity, better procedures for recording confessions have been adopted, for the long-term benefit and security of all.

The success of the indirect utilitarian argument seems vital for the defence of utilitarianism. If utilitarian theory can accommo- date a theory of individual rights—for example rights against victimization—then many of the standard objections to it would disappear. We have seen a sketch of how utilitarianism might accomplish this task, but there are ways to develop the objection further. For example, it can be argued that general insecurity will only be a consequence of scapegoatism if the public realize what is going on. But if the public never discover the truth then they will have nothing to worry about. (Or rather, they will have something to worry about, but as they don't know about it, they will not, in fact, worry. And so there will be no extra negative units to add to the utilitarian balance.) Thus scapegoatism is justified, on utilitarian grounds, provided it is highly efficient and secret. This, surely, is a troubling thought.

A deeper objection is that, even if the calculations work out as the utilitarian hopes, the correct result is achieved for the wrong reason. Perhaps a policy of secret victimization will not, in fact, maximize happiness. But opponents of utilitarianism argue that this is irrelevant: no one should be victimized, whatever the benefits in terms of general happiness. The Birmingham six should be released whatever the consequences. Furthermore, if utilitarians are concerned only with maximizing happiness, why should they spend so much energy trying to produce a utilitarian theory of rights? This seems to reveal a lack of faith in their own theory.

For the purposes of the present discussion we will make the assumption—one which may be overturned later—that the utilitarian theory cannot, in the end, be rescued from such criticism. I do not want to say any more about the issue now, as I will return to it in detail in Chapter 4, where I will consider John Stuart Mill's *On Liberty*, which is often understood as providing a utilitarian theory of rights. The present point is simply that, although the indirect utilitarian justification of the state seems strong, utilitarianism itself is highly suspect, even in its indirect form. Thus there are reasons to be dissatisfied with this approach to the defence of the state.

The principle of fairness

Were you to preach, in most parts of the world, that political connexions are founded altogether on voluntary consent or a mutual promise, the magistrate would soon imprison you, as seditious, for loosening the ties of obedience; if your friends did not before shut you up as delirious, for advancing such absurdities.

(Hume, 'Of the Original Contract', 470)

Whether or not individuals consent to the state, it can seem unfair of them to enjoy its benefits without also accepting the necessary burdens that help produce those benefits. So, it has been argued, anyone who gains an advantage from the state has a duty of fairness to obey its laws, to contribute taxes, and so on.

The principle underlying this view was explicitly formulated by the legal theorist and philosopher H. L. A. Hart (1907–92), who stated it thus:

When any number of persons conduct any joint enterprise according to rules, and thus restrict their liberty, those who have submitted to these restrictions when required have a right to similar submission from those who have benefited by their submission. ('Are There Any Natural Rights?', 85)

Hart's view is that this principle is, as it were, the 'rational core' of the doctrine of tacit consent. Receiving benefits does indeed bind one to the state, but not because it is a way of tacitly consenting. Rather, the force of the argument is that it is *unfair* to reap the benefits of the state, unless one is prepared to shoulder one's share of the burdens too. The benefits, of course, are the security and stability of living in a society which operates a system of enforced laws. The corresponding burdens are political obligations. A more familiar application of the same principle concerns buying rounds in a bar. If three of your friends each buy a round for the four of you, they might rightly feel aggrieved if you decide to go home just when you finish your third drink.

If we accept Hart's principle, and concede that everyone receives benefits from the state, it would seem to follow that, in fairness to everyone else, each of us should obey the laws of our country. This relies on the plausible idea that if we benefit from the laws then it is unfair and exploitative to break them for our own convenience.

Can it really be shown that everyone really does benefit from the existence of the state? Perhaps Hobbes's arguments from Chapter 1 would be enough to convince most people. But another attempt to argue for this conclusion was made by Hume. Although Hume was by no means a 'theorist of fairness' himself, we can use some of his arguments to support the claim that we all do, indeed, benefit from the state.

Hume's first step is to argue that each of us will profit if we live in a society governed by norms of justice, such as rules governing private property, and personal security. We will, of course, have to make short-term sacrifices, but justice pays in the longer term. As justice will only flourish if we all obey the law, then it turns out that obedience to the law is, in fact, in each person's individual interest.

But is it really true that obedience to the law is in the interests of each of us? If so, then, as Hume himself points out, it seems extraordinary that we should need to be forced to obedience on pain of punishment. If it is in our interests to do what the law tells us, why do we not act in that way without the need for the law to force us to do it?

Hume's answer is, in effect, that human beings are not very good at acting rationally. Suppose we have a choice between acting in one way to get a small gain now, and acting in another way which will provide a greater benefit, but in the much longer term. While it is ultimately in our interests to take the second course, Hume believes that, left to ourselves, we will generally take the first:

Tho' we may be fully convinc'd, that the latter object excels the former, we are not able to regulate our actions by this judgment; but yield to the sollicitations of our passions, which always plead in favour of whatever is near and contiguous.

This is the reason why men so often act in contradiction to their known interest; and in particular why they prefer any trivial advantage, that is present, to the maintenance of order in society, which so much depends on the observance of justice. (*Treatise of Human Nature*, 535)

Thus, in Hume's view, even though it is in our interests to obey the law, this interest is very remote and far off, and so we are likely to prefer the short-term, lesser benefit which will flow from disobedience. For, Hume supposes, if each of us follows our short-term interests, and acts unjustly, society will break down, to the great misfortune of us all. So reason tells us to seek the longer-term benefit and obey the law. However, Hume believes that although this is what our reason tells each of us, reason alone is insufficient to motivate us to act. Reason, Hume believes, is 'the slave of the passions'. And our irrational passions, our preference for immediate gratification, will swiftly overcome our rational deliberation.

So, Hume argues, as ' 'tis impossible to change or correct any thing material in our nature, the utmost we can do is to change our circumstances and situation, and render the observance of the laws of justice our nearest interest' (*Treatise of Human Nature*, 537). In other words, we need to find a way of making observance of the laws of justice contribute to our immediate interest. This is the only way in which we will be able to follow them, and thereby also bring about our long-term interests.

Accordingly, Hume argues that we should set up a system of civil magistrates, who have the power to make laws and enforce them through punishment. Obedience to the laws is already to our long-term advantage, while punishing people for disobedience makes obedience in our short-term interest too. It is necessary for us to be forced to obey the law—indeed we should welcome this—because reason is impotent as a source of human motivation. We need to be forced to act in our own rational self-interest.

Hume's purpose in making this argument was to explain the advantages of government, and to explain why we are generally prepared to accept the state, even though it is not founded on our consent. Arguing that we have any sort of moral obligation to obey is a further step, and one which Hume, strictly speaking, did not attempt. But theorists of fairness, like Hart, try to go further than Hume. We all benefit from the existence of the state, and it would be unfair to our fellow citizens to take those benefits without also accepting the burdens necessary to create them. These burdens are political obligations. Hence we have a duty of fairness to accept the duty to obey the state.

But do we really have any such duty? If we receive unsolicited benefits, must we pay for them? Reverting to the earlier example, need I buy my round, if I didn't ask for the drinks others bought me? Suppose I made clear at the start that I had no intention of buying a drink for anyone else. Can I then treat the drinks others have bought me as free gifts? The contemporary philosopher Robert Nozick, in *Anarchy, State, and Utopia* claims that unsolicited benefits create no obligations to reciprocate. He presents an example in which the other members of your neighbourhood have discovered a public address system, and decide to institute a scheme for public entertainment. Each person is assigned a day on which to broadcast—play records, tell jokes, and so on—for the benefit of all. You have enjoyed 137 days of entertainment from others, but on day 138, when your turn comes, do you have a duty to give up a day to entertain the rest? (*Anarchy, State, and Utopia*, 93). Nozick thinks it obvious that you have no moral duty to do this, but it seems to follow from the principle of fairness as stated by Hart that you do. After all, you have reaped the benefits of the public address system, and so now it is your turn to shoulder the burdens, and do your bit for the rest. So, according to the principle of fairness, you should now contribute.

Why does Nozick argue that you have no such duty? Well, you did not ask for the benefit, and you were provided with it whether you liked it or not. Perhaps you would rather have had no benefits and no burdens. But whether you want them or not, if we say that you have a duty to comply in this case it gives others a licence to force even unwanted goods on you and then demand payment, which would hardly be just.

Perhaps this counter-example can be dealt with by spelling out the theory in more detail. Perhaps one acquires a duty of fairness to contribute, only if one *accepts* (rather than merely receives) the benefits on the understanding of the costs. In the case of the public address system, you acquire a burden to tell jokes for a day only if you accept the scheme as a whole. Anyone who accepts the benefits but tries to avoid the burdens of contribution is being an exploiter or free-rider and so it is no injustice to make them pay. It seems reasonable to say that if the principle is amended to take this into account, then it generates enforceable obligations. It is unfair to accept benefits but refuse to pay.

However, once the principle is altered in this way a fresh difficulty arises. The problem now is that if the only benefits which   se to obligations are those that are accepted, then this requ.es us to be able to distinguish accepted benefits from those which are merely received. But what would count as accepting the benefits of the state? After all, how can we reject them? We get them, or most of them, whether or not we want them. In other words, we have exactly the same problems as we found with the theory of tacit consent. How can we stop the acceptance of benefits becoming purely automatic? And if we can solve this difficulty, by giving a subtle account of what it is to accept the benefits, we then have to face the possibility that some people—the anarchists and perhaps others too—might refuse to accept the benefits. Even if they appreciate the arguments of Hume and others about the advantages of the state, they see other difficulties and so prefer no benefits and no political obligations. And so they would acquire no duty of fairness to comply with the state. Consequently, on this understanding, like the consent-based arguments, the principle of fairness cannot deliver universal obligations to obey. It can only do so if we remain with Hart's original formulation in terms of 'receipt' of benefits. But as Nozick's example shows, this itself leads to problematic consequences. So, on this brief examination, it seems that the principle of fairness, although it is an improvement on consent theory, does not solve the problem of political obligation.

Conclusion

We have looked at a number of defences of political obligation, but all seem wanting in one way or another. Voluntaristic defences within the contract tradition cannot explain the obligations of those who refuse to consent. Utilitarian arguments may well have unacceptable implications, as they seem to allow us—in principle at least—to sacrifice the innocent. The fairness argument can only succeed if everyone accepts the benefits of the state, and it is unlikely that this would be the case. Does this mean that we have no political obligations?

We should first be clear that, while these arguments, taken separately, fail to demonstrate a universal obligation to obey, some of them do nevertheless have some limited success. Some people expressly consent to the state: for example those in special positions of responsibility, such as members of parliament, as well as naturalized citizens. Many more owe a duty of fairness, for most people willingly accept the benefits of the state, and it can be argued that they believe that an obligation to comply is a fair price. And if utilitarian reasoning is found acceptable then it may well be the state is entirely justified. But even if utilitarianism is rejected, if any of the other arguments start from an acceptable moral basis, then a large proportion of members of most modern societies have political obligations. Only relatively few people will escape.

What are the consequences of this? No state will be happy with the idea that some people residing within its territory have no political obligations. For one thing, the task of trying to separate those who do and do not have political obligations will provide the officers of the state with immense practical difficulties, particularly when some will exploit these difficulties and try to pass themselves off as members of the groups that escape political obligation. Thus even if the state is prepared to accept that, in theory, some people escape political obligations, in practice it would be forced to ignore this and act as if there were universal political obligations. No doubt it could make some exceptions, but probably only in special, well-defined, cases. Perhaps monks or gypsies can be allowed to escape certain taxes, or other groups can be excused compulsory military service. But no group will be able to avoid all political obligations.

However, suppose a state really did translate theory into practice, and accepted that it had no authority to interfere in the lives of certain people. Should this create difficulties for the rest of us? Not necessarily. The fact that some people avoid political obligations does not give them the right to harm anyone. These people still have a full set of moral obligations. Further, on Locke's view at least, all individuals have the right to enforce the moral law, even in the absence of government. So if governments do exist, then those of us who consider ourselves to be part of the state can call on the power of the state to protect us when threatened by independents. While the law of the land may have no special authority over independents who do not consider themselves part of the state, most moral views give us the right to self-protection by the most appropriate means: in this case by the state. Therefore the existence of some independents does not mean we cannot use the state for protection against them. We can survive well enough in the presence of some independents. Consider the example of ambassadors, and others with diplomatic immunity. In one sense, the state in which they live has no authority over them. But this does not mean that the agents of the state must permit such diplomats to act however their whims take them. A diplomat swinging an axe in a shopping mall can rightfully be disarmed by the police, just as we can rightfully restrain each other. What we cannot do, in either case, is exercise legal punishment, or use force beyond what is needed for self-defence, at least not without further authority.

But of course no state would accept that people living within its territories can escape political obligations altogether. Diplomatic immunity is a very special case, regulated by international conventions. The law will be enforced against all, even if, in some cases, the state acts illegitimately. But in acting in such an illegitimate way, the state will act with the approval of the vast majority of its citizens.

3

Who Should Rule?

Introduction

> The people of England regards itself as free; but it is
> grossly mistaken; it is free only during the election of mem-
> bers of parliament. As soon as they are elected, slavery
> overtakes it, and it is nothing. The use it makes of the short
> moments of liberty it enjoys shows indeed that it deserves
> to lose them.
>
> (Rousseau, *Social Contract*, bk. III, ch. 15, p. 266)

Whether or not we feel that the state is justified, the fact is that
we have one. And, from our current historical position, it is very
hard to see how this could ever really change. Everyone, then,
even the philosophical anarchist, has an interest in the question
of what sort of state and government we should have. What
should this government be like? Who should rule? A common
assumption is that only a democracy is ever fully justifiable.
Anything else—a tyranny, an aristocracy, an absolute monarchy—must fail. But what is a democracy? Is it really so
attractive?

Democracy, we are told, is government 'of the people, by the
people, and for the people'. Government for the people is the
idea that the government exists for the sake of its citizens, not
for the benefit of the rulers. Democratic governments rule 'in
the interests of the governed', to use Bentham's words. But then,
so could other types of government. Voltaire argued in favour of
'benevolent dictatorship', where an enlightened despot, without
the need to consult the people, would nevertheless govern in
their interest. In contrast, democracy is, most obviously, a system in which the people rule: collective self-rule. This, then, is an

account of what it means to say that democracy is government 'for the people' and 'by the people'. The first item in the original triad—government 'of the people'—seems a rather empty idea at first: what would government *not* of the people be? Anarchy? But the thought is that a democratic state has power only over the people who make up the electorate. Ruling over a subservient class, or territory, is claimed to be antithetical to the true ideals of democracy.

All contemporary theorists at least implicitly agree that democracy should ideally satisfy the three-part description. But beyond this there is enormous dispute about what democracy amounts to. In contemporary politics a general assumption exists that democracy is a 'good thing'. Democratic status is often taken to be a litmus test for the legitimacy of regimes. If a government or state is thought to be undemocratic, it is subjected to intense international criticism. Even the word 'democratic' is fought over, and has been adopted by regimes which appear quite undemocratic. When, after the Second World War, Germany divided, the Soviets who had forced the split immediately claimed the name 'German Democratic Republic' for East Germany. The Allied forces had to be satisfied with the name 'German Federal Republic' for West Germany, even though, to western commentators at least, it was clear that it was far closer to their democratic ideals.

But does democracy really deserve its contemporary reputation? After all, for most of human history democracy has been almost universally detested. It has greatly flourished in recent times, and had a brief life in Ancient Greece—albeit in a very limited form—but for the 2,000 years or so in between a democratic state was hardly seen. If democracy really is as attractive as it is often claimed to be, why should so many thinkers throughout history have rejected it?

Moreover, not all contemporary theorists find democracy so attractive. It is not so much that they doubt its value as that they deny its coherence. 'Democracy', it is sometimes said, is not the name of a political system, but a term of praise. According to this view there is no single coherent theory of democracy. There is no political system that could be approved by all those who claim to be in favour of democracy.

This type of criticism may well be an exaggeration, but there is no doubt that it has some basis. Democratic theory contains serious tensions, and it will be helpful to explore some of the most fundamental problems in formulating democratic theory before looking at arguments for and against democracy itself.

The first tension in democratic theory to which I want to draw attention is between the idea of democracy as a system of 'majority rule', and the idea of democratic 'consideration for individuals'. When someone, in protest, says that 'I thought this country was meant to be a democracy', what she would normally mean is that she supposes that she has been treated unfairly in some way. Perhaps her home has been made subject to a compulsory purchase order, for example, to make way for a road. Maybe a new airport has been planned a short distance away, or her child has been refused a place in a local state school. Whatever the details, the basis of the complaint is that an individual's interests or rights have been treated with insufficient regard. And this, it is claimed, is undemocratic.

But is it? Suppose 51 per cent of the people want the road, or the airport, or to exclude the child. Then democracy, as a principle of majority rule, seems to imply that there is nothing undemocratic at all in this treatment of her interests. The majority has ruled, against her.

Here we see a tension right at the heart of democratic theory. De Tocqueville brought out the point well, in his expression 'the tyranny of the majority'. Developing this idea, John Stuart Mill pointed out that before the large-scale establishment of democratic regimes, it was generally assumed that, if the people were ruling in their own interests, it would be impossible for political oppression to exist. For if the people governed themselves, why on earth would they pass repressive laws? But as Mill indicates, the fallacy here is to think of the people as a homogeneous mass with a single interest, each person affected in the same way by each policy. As we are not like this—we have different goals, interests, and plans; we live in different places and have different life-spans—it is quite easy to see how a majority could pass a law which has some very nasty effects for the minority. Is this undemocratic or not? Yes, if you think that a democratic state is one which must protect all individuals; no, if you think that democracy simply means majority rule.

Mill believed that steps must be taken to prevent the tyranny of the majority taking hold. We will examine his position in detail in the next chapter. The point for the moment is simply that the theorist of democracy must decide whether democracy is essentially a rather crude principle of majority rule, or whether we should follow the 'Madisonian' view (after James Madison, 1751–1804, often known as the 'father of the American Constitution') that democracy requires the protection of minorities.

A second debate concerns 'representative' and 'direct' models of democracy. In a direct democracy the electorate votes for or against laws or policies, rather than for candidates. Ideally, every major issue is put before the entire electorate, by way of referendum. A representative democracy, on the other hand, is the more familiar system in which the citizens vote to determine who will represent them at governmental level. It is these representatives who then go on to make laws. The former system, it seems, is truer to the pure spirit of democracy, yet it is virtually unknown in the modern world. Modern democracies adhere to the representative model, in which elections are used to determine who will form the government, rather than to decide the particular issues of the day. But if this representative system is thought undemocratic, then almost no democracies have ever existed on any large scale. This conclusion is drawn by many critics of contemporary 'liberal democracy'. Democracy would be a fine thing, they say, if only we had it.

These two debates—majority rule versus individual rights, and representative versus direct models—are fundamental to the formulation of a democratic theory. But they are far from exhausting the areas of controversy. For example, among the Greeks it was sometimes thought that voting for candidates was undemocratic: it gives the unpopular a less than equal chance!

Therefore rulers should be elected by a lottery. Other theorists have suggested that we should find ways of measuring and taking account of the strength of different individuals' preferences. A minority with intense preferences, on this view, should take priority over an apathetic majority. Also we should not ignore questions of deciding who is entitled to vote. In Ancient Greek democracies only a tiny proportion of the population was enfranchised: excluded were women, slaves, and foreigners, even those whose families had lived within the state's territory for generations. In the contemporary world, women were not treated on a fully equal basis in Great Britain until as late as 1928, and many countries still exclude 'guest workers' from the franchise.

On another level, we are familiar with somewhat less fundamental, if more intricate, wrangles about voting procedure. Many European countries have long debated the question of whether they should have a system of proportional representation, as until recently practised in Italy, or a system of 'first-past-the-post' elections, as in Great Britain. Such debates are, of course, of enormous importance, and the choice of system will have far-reaching consequences. For example, it is often said that Hitler was able to come to power only because Germany had a system of proportional representation. But from a more philosophical point of view the pressing tasks are to be clear about what democracy is supposed to be, and why it might be thought valuable. As a first attempt to deal with these tasks we will look at one of the most powerful anti-democratic arguments: that of Plato, in the *Republic*. By looking at this sceptical assault on the value of democracy we will begin to see whether it is worthy of the praise it so often receives.

Plato against democracy

Suppose the following to be the state of affairs on board a ship or ships. The captain is larger and stronger than any of the crew, but a bit deaf and short-sighted, and similarly limited in seamanship. The crew are all quarrelling with each other about how to navigate the ship, each thinking he ought to be at the helm; they have never learned the art of navigation and cannot say that anyone ever taught it them, or that they spent any time studying it; indeed they say it can't be taught and are ready to murder anyone who says it can. They spend all their time milling round the captain and doing all they can to get him to give them the helm. If one faction is more successful than another, their rivals may kill them and throw them overboard, lay out the honest captain with drugs or drink or in some other way, take control of the ship, help themselves to what's on board, and turn the voyage into the sort of drunken pleasure-cruise that you would expect. Finally, they reserve their admiration for the man who knows how to lend a hand in controlling the captain by force or fraud; they praise his seamanship and navigation and knowledge of the sea and condemn everyone else as useless. They have no idea that the true navigator must study the seasons of the year, the sky, the stars, the winds and all the other subjects appropriate to his profession if he is to be really fit to control a ship; and they think it's quite impossible to acquire the professional skill needed for such control (whether or not they want it exercised) and that there's no such thing as an art of navigation. With all this going on aboard aren't the sailors on any such ship bound to regard the true navigator as a word-spinner and a star-gazer, of no use to them at all?

(Plato, *Republic*, 282)

Plato's opposition to democracy exploits another apparent tension within democratic theory. Just as 'monarchy' means 'rule by the monarch', 'democracy' means 'rule by the *demos*'. But what is the *demos*? In classical Greek it can be understood both as 'the people', and as 'the mob'. On the latter understanding, then, democracy is mob rule: the rule of the rabble, the vulgar, the unwashed, the unfit.

But this insult to democracy is a mere preliminary to Plato's main anti-democratic arguments. His basic weapon is the so-called 'craft analogy'. The point is very simple. If you were ill, and wanted advice on your health, you would go to an expert—the doctor. In other words, you would want to consult someone who had been specially trained to do the job. The last thing you would do is assemble a crowd, and ask them to vote on the correct remedy.

The health of the state is a matter of no less importance than the health of any given individual. Making political decisions—decisions in the interests of the state—requires judgement and skill. It should, Plato urges, be left to the experts. Allowing the people to decide is like navigating at sea by consulting the passengers, ignoring or shunning those who are truly skilled in the art of navigation. Just as a ship so navigated will lose its way and founder, so too, Plato argues, will the ship of state.

But where are expert rulers to be found? Here Plato's answer is simple, and, to many of his likely readers, initially rather flattering. The just society is impossible unless the kings become philosophers, or the philosophers become kings. Philosophical training, Plato argues, is a necessary qualification to rule. By the idea of becoming a philosopher, Plato does not mean merely spending a few years reading and thinking about philosophy. He has a plan for an entire life of education for the 'guardians', involving in its early years not only skills of literacy, but also musical, mathematical, military, and physical education. Philosophy is not studied at all until the age of 30. Five years of philosophy are then followed by fifteen years' military service, and those who have come through this with honour are then allowed to turn permanently to philosophy: a repose interrupted only by taking one's turn in the 'weary business of politics'.

It would take us too far out of our way to consider these and other aspects of Plato's *Republic* in much detail. In particular, we cannot go into the nature and content of the knowledge Plato intends his guardians to come to possess. But let us remember the craft analogy. Ruling, like medicine, navigation, or even farming, is a skill. A special training is necessary, and not everyone is naturally capable even of acquiring the skill. Just as medicine should be left to the experts, and a medical training only given to those most suited, so should ruling, and a training to rule. Any other arrangement will lead to worse results, and consulting the populace will lead to disaster.

On the face of it, Plato's argument against democracy seems devastating. If ruling is a skill, and a skill that can only be attained by the few, then democracy seems plainly absurd or irrational. The defender of democracy must find a response to the craft analogy. But does it have a weakness?

Problems with guardianship

The first thing to be said is that Plato's own system is a form of dictatorship, and just as there are general arguments that can be used to oppose any system of democracy, there are also general arguments which can be used against dictatorship. Even if we concede to Plato that in educating the guardians he is bringing into existence a class of expert rulers, it certainly does not follow that we should concede the power to run our lives to them.

The point is not that we should never defer to experts, but that giving unchecked powers to experts is to invite catastrophe. You may choose to take a doctor's advice, or consult an architect, but who would be happy if 'doctor's orders' had the force of law, or if architects allocated houses to people? However good these people are at their jobs, why should we trust them to make decisions on our behalf? They might be good at something else too: feathering their own nests.

This objection is an old one. What is to stop the guardian—the philosopher–king—from turning the situation to his or her own advantage? It is hardly a comfort to be told that the ruler is an expert. If we expect our rulers to be corrupt, we might prefer being ruled by incompetents. At least that way the corruption might be less damaging. In Plato's system, so the objection runs, who guards the guardians?

Plato did not overlook this difficulty. His response is to argue that the guardians must be placed in a position where the opportunities for corruption are minimized. So, for example, the philosopher–kings are not allowed to own private property. There would, therefore, seem to be no scope for the sort of corruption we have so often seen in the modern world: a ruling family or clique enriching themselves at the expense of their people. Clearly this would be ruled out on Plato's system—provided that the ruling against private ownership could be enforced.

But if we do assume that it could be enforced, we seem to have backed into the opposite difficulty. If the life of the guardian is not one of great wealth, why would they agree to rule? As Plato depicts the guardians, they are philosophers who would much rather spend their time reading, talking, and thinking about philosophy. Why should they give up their time? Plato's answer is, in a way, a negative one. The guardians agree to rule, not for the intrinsic or external rewards of the role, but because they would otherwise find themselves ruled by others. Rather than allow other people—worse still, *all* other people—to rule, they grudgingly accept this necessary duty.

Still, if the guardians decide to break the laws concerning private property, or even change the laws by proper procedures, who will have the authority and power to stop them? So we cannot be fully reassured by Plato's laws designed to prevent corruption. If the answer to this is that a proper philosophical education makes a person resistant to temptation, we might reply that full and proper public scrutiny, in the face of an empowered electorate, is a far more reliable remedy.

A further worry is the question of how guardians come to be appointed. Plato believes that potential guardians can be picked out at an early age, and then undergo various rigours which will allow for the selection of the very best. This seems perfectly possible: think how generals rise from the ranks of an army. But, in the case of the guardians, we can still wonder whether their claims to rule would ever be acceptable to the population as a whole. After all, most people will not have had the benefit of a philosophical education.

If we add up these objections, what do they come to? Really not much more than the thought that we are very uncomfortable with the idea of Plato's system. Plato's society contains no guarantees that the guardians will always be able to resist temptation. And it may well be that the people do not accept their rule. But these problems with Plato's proposals hardly amount to a rousing defence of democracy. Perhaps another non-democratic system is the answer. Once more, if ruling is a skill, which can be possessed only by the few, then surely it is absurd to leave political decision-making to the rabble.

Knowledge and interests

Another kind of argument might help us to make progress. Plato claims that rulers need expert knowledge. But is such knowledge really attainable? If there really is no such thing as an expert ruler then Plato's opposition to democracy would seem to dissolve into thin air.

Some critics have argued that we should be very sceptical about the claim that there could be expert rulers who possess a special level of knowledge. After all, it is often said, no one can be absolutely certain of anything at all. Virtually all claims to knowledge—whether in politics, science, or philosophy—are fallible. And so if we leave decisions on any subject to the so-called experts, we are deceiving ourselves about their abilities.

Although it is often rather satisfying to belittle the claims to wisdom of anyone who occupies some sort of position of authority, this reply does not take us very far. For the fact, if it is a fact, that no one can know anything for certain, does not tell against the more mundane point that some people are better judges than others. Like many, for example, I am often very sceptical about the claims to knowledge made by doctors. But if I believed my leg to be broken I would turn to a doctor for help, even though I firmly believe that doctors often make mistakes, including some very serious ones. But those untrained in medicine (for example, those people sometimes exposed in the popular press as masquerading as doctors) can rationally be expected to do even worse. So even if no infallible knowledge exists it does not follow that everyone is equally skilled, or rather unskilled, in all branches of enquiry. This way of trying to defeat the craft analogy is to assert that, in effect, there are no crafts. This is too implausible to believe.

But might it not be true that there is no expert knowledge

applicable to ruling, even though expert knowledge exists on other topics? This, too, is hard to believe. Rulers today need quite subtle knowledge of economics, and of psychology and human motivation. They need (even if they do not always have) high intelligence, an enormous capacity for work, a keen memory, excellent ability to deal with detail, and skill at handling other people. It is absurd to think that no one is potentially a better ruler than anyone else. A very good case can be made that ruling is, in large part at least, a craft.

Nevertheless, there is something about this objection which may push us in a more fruitful direction. Perhaps more could be made of the point that there is something special about political decision-making, which is not like asking for a show of hands to decide whether we should amputate a diseased limb. To bring out this line of thought we should take a closer look at the nature of voting in a democratic system. Plato implies that the point of voting is to register an opinion about what is best for the state as a whole. Obviously this is often one function of voting. But Plato seems to assume that this is all voting is, and his argument comes down to the claim that it is better to leave such decisions to the experts. However, if we can argue that there is more to voting than expressing an opinion about the public good, then perhaps a more robust defence of democracy becomes possible.

Remember one of the points made at the very beginning of this chapter: democratic governments rule *for* the people, that is, in the interests of the governed. Although Plato is opposed to democracy, he shares the assumption that the rulers should have the interests of the people at heart. What he denies is that the way to achieve this is through a system of rule *by* the people. One attempt to defend democracy is to try to argue that Plato's position cannot be sustained. Rule for the people must be rule by the people.

Why might this be? Plato advocates essentially a system of benevolent dictatorship. But even if the dictator wants to advance the interests of the people, how are those interests to be known? In a democracy people show their interests, it seems, by voting: they vote for what they want. Hence voting is more than a decision-making procedure. It is a way of revealing or expressing the very information that the decision needs to take into account: what the people want. Without some sort of voting procedure, how can this be discovered?

Plato might reply that the guardians are not only benevolent, they are experts too. They have wisdom and knowledge. Plato's kings are not the bombastic, ignorant tyrants seen from time to time in the modern world. They are philosophers. But, in response to Plato, does philosophical expertise really give them a way of knowing the interests of the people? Logic and metaphysics do not tell you what the people want. Neither does ethics or even political philosophy. Philosophical knowledge and factual information seem to be two quite different things.

But is it true that political decision-making should be responsive to what the people want? Perhaps it should be responsive to the *interests* of the people—what is best for them. And could it be said that knowing the interests of the people is, indeed, the type of knowledge provided by a philosophical education? Perhaps everyone has the same interests. In that case, the philosophers' subtle powers of analysis put them in the best possible position to know the people's interests. However, whatever Plato thought about this, and whatever is true in the deepest metaphysical sense, in practical terms it must surely be false that we all have the same interests. Imagine that the building of a major road is under consideration. Some people will have an interest in that road being built. Others will have the opposite interest: for example the owner of a business situated on the existing main route. Some people will have an interest in the road taking a certain route, others will prefer a different one. The building of the road will affect people in very many different ways. So there are multiple, and competing, interests to be considered here. Reading works of philosophy will not provide the solution to this problem.

On the other hand, an example like this might make us very doubtful about the value of democracy. How should the decision be made among the competing preferences or interests? It may well be that, because there are more than two options (the road can be built along several different routes) no one option will gain majority support. But even if one does, is it obvious that we should accept the majority preference? Perhaps this would be greatly unfair to the minority (remember the Madisonian element of democratic protection of minorities). Surely what we need is a ruling by someone who knows all the relevant interests, yet, with the wisdom of Solomon, makes the fairest and most judicious decision. This is even more necessary if we accept Hume's point mentioned in Chapter 2 that people are often very poor judges of their interests when their long-term and short-term interests divide. So, at most, we have an argument for detailed opinion-polling of the population, but not necessarily yet an argument for democracy.

In fact, the position is rather worse for democracy than it looks so far. Plato claims that we need expert rulers. The defender of democracy replies that experts need to know the people's interests, and only a vote will show what these are. The response to this is that it is not only false that only a vote will reveal people's interests, but that opinion-polling may well do a more effective job. A further, and more troubling, problem is that we can never be sure that a democratic vote tells us anything at all about the preferences or interests of the people.

To see this, let us consider a rather prosaic example. Suppose a group of people are in dispute about whether smoking should be permitted in a public place which they share and control—perhaps a student house. Suppose also that they agree to be bound by a majority decision. Does this mean that the group will vote to permit smoking if and only if a majority prefer there to be public smoking? At first sight this might seem obviously so, but a moment's reflection reveals that it need not be. It will be true that some people will vote as if they are expecting to answer the question 'would you prefer there to be smoking or not?' These people will indeed vote according to their preferences. But others will vote as if the question they are answering is 'do you think that smoking *ought* to be permitted?' Accordingly some smokers will vote to deny their own pleasure, arguing that it is wrong for smokers to submit others to the adverse

effects of their behaviour. Some non-smokers, too, will vote
against their own preferences, arguing that smoking is a matter
for individual decision. In other words these people are voting in
a disinterested fashion, and so do not reveal their interests by
their vote.

In view of this, it is unsafe to assume that democracy is a way
of making individual interests or preferences known. Some
people will vote for what they most want. Others put their own
preferences or interests to one side, and vote the way they do on
moral grounds. We can never be sure what is motivating the
members of any given electorate: in fact they may not be sure
themselves.

What is the consequence of this? If people do not always vote
according to their preferences, we cannot represent the voting
process as one which automatically reveals the preferences of
the majority. So what does the vote reveal? If people are voting
from mixed motivations—some out of preference, some out of
concern for the common good—then it tells us nothing more
than that a majority of people voted for one option over another. We cannot say with confidence that a majority of people
believe the winning option to be in their interests, neither can we
say that a majority of people believe that the decision is for the
common good. Mixed-motivation voting, in short, is a mess. And
what is worse, in present-day conditions it seems to be the normal case.

Voting and the common good

The problem of mixed-motivation voting seems to force us to
decide which type of motivation voters should have. Whether
we can ensure that voters will, in practice, have that type of
motivation is a further, and perhaps more difficult, question. But
let us first consider the theoretical question.

If we do not want to accept mixed-motivation voting then it
seems we must choose between two models: one in which voters
vote in accordance with their preferences, and the other in which
voters vote in accordance with their estimates or opinions of the
common good. The problem with the former, we saw, was that

opinion-polling can be a far more sensitive way of gaining the necessary information. But perhaps the second idea—that all people should vote according to their ideas of the common good—can be used in a defence of democracy.

However, if we assume that the people are to vote according to their ideas of the common good, then we need a new argument for democracy. The last argument was that, without a vote, rulers would not be able to tell what the people want. But if people vote in accordance with their ideas of the common good then voting will not tell us this either. It will only tell us what the majority think is in the common good, not where the majority preference actually lies.

But this suggests a different defence of democracy. If we allow people to vote according to their idea of the common good, and follow the majority decision, we surely have a very good chance of being right. The argument for democracy is that it now seems an excellent way of discovering the common good.

Unfortunately, this argument seems to play right back into Plato's hands. Why should we expect a vote among the rabble to do better than leaving the matter to the specially trained experts? We may as well ask the general population to navigate ships, make medical decisions, tend sheep, and so on. What possible reason is there to believe that the people will do better than the experts?

Surprisingly enough, there is a reason. The French philosopher and political theorist, Marie Jean Antoine Nicolas Caritat, the Marquis de Condorcet (1743–94), provided a very interesting mathematical argument which appears to show the advantages of allowing people to vote on the common good. Condorcet pointed out that, if we assume that people, on average, have a better than even chance of getting the right answer, then allowing majority decision turns out to be an excellent way of getting to the right result. If a large number of people vote, then the chances of getting the right result tend towards certainty. In an electorate of 10,000, each with more chance of being right than wrong, then a majority decision is virtually certain to get the right result.

Condorcet's argument might seem a more than sufficient riposte to Plato. But it is vital to appreciate that it only works on two conditions. First, the average individual must have a better than even chance of being right (and Condorcet himself was very pessimistic about this when voting takes place on a large scale). Second, each individual must be motivated to vote according to his or her ideas of the common good, rather than out of particular interests. If the second assumption fails then we are back to the confusion of what I called mixed-motivation voting. If the first assumption fails, things are even worse. If the people are, on average, more likely to be wrong than right, then it is almost certain that majority voting will lead to the wrong result.

So we have a reply to Plato only if the two conditions can be met. Can they be? One philosopher who had a firm intuitive grasp of these points was Rousseau (even though he published his major writings on democracy twenty years before Condorcet produced his mathematical argument). Indeed, it is reasonable to see Rousseau's *Social Contract* as an attempt—among other things—to show the conditions under which democracy will be superior to guardianship. But before we look at Rousseau's position in detail, there is another, complementary, response to Plato that we should consider.

The values of democracy

So far we have considered the question of whether democracy is better than Plato's system of guardians at achieving a certain objective. In particular we have now reduced this to the question of whether democracy will be able to achieve the common good. But there is something odd about this enquiry. Many people would argue that we should favour democracy even if it turned out that democratic systems were less good than others at achieving the common good. To put this another way, we have so far looked only at the question of whether there is an instrumental justification for democracy: is it a way of achieving something else we value? But perhaps we should consider another question. Is there something *intrinsically* good about democracy? That is, could it be that democracy is good (up to a point, at least) even if it is not able always to achieve desirable consequences?

Pursuing this thought may make us reflect again about the craft analogy. The craft analogy is premissed on the idea that ruling is a skill; a skill aimed at achieving some external object. Democracy, according to Plato, is to be justified purely on the basis of how well it is able to achieve desirable consequences. But as we are aware, we value skills not just for their results but, sometimes at least, for themselves too. It might seem rather homely to bring up such an analogy in this context, but think of exercising a skill as a hobby. Even if one's hobby is something very practical, like woodworking, the hobby is rarely valued on the basis that it is the most effective way of achieving a certain object. It may be a very nice table, but when you cost the time you spent making it, no doubt there are both better and cheaper ones in the department store. Hobbies allow people to enrich and test their physical and mental powers, and develop their sense of self-worth. And this type of value is independent of the value of the goods which may be produced.

This prompts the idea that democracy should not be judged simply in terms of how well it achieves the common good, even though that is important too. So we should take another look at the craft analogy. Plato compares ruling to navigation: steering the ship of state. If we leave navigation to the mob, we can imagine what sort of chaos would ensue: a 'drunken pleasure-cruise', says Plato. We will never get where we want to go.

But need navigation always have such a clear purpose of efficient arrival at a pre-chosen destination? Consider, for example, a training voyage. In that case we might give everyone a turn at the helm. Indeed, why shouldn't a journey in the ship of state be a drunken pleasure-cruise? What is wrong with that, at least if everyone has a good time and we all get home safely?

The serious and important point to make here is that there may be values involved in political decision-making which are different from the value of achieving given objectives. Defenders of democracy will say that democracy is valuable not only, or not necessarily, because democracies make better decisions than other types of state, but because there is something valuable about democratic processes in themselves. Democracy is most commonly thought to be expressive of two values we hold dear: freedom and equality. Freedom, as understood here, is a matter of giving people a say in political decision-making; particularly those decisions that affect them. Equality lies in this freedom being given to all. For Rousseau, the problem of political order is 'to find a form of association which will defend and protect with the whole common force the person and goods of each associate, and in which each, while uniting himself with all, may still obey himself alone, and remain as free as before' (*Social Contract*, bk. I, ch. 6, p. 191). It is remarkable that Rousseau thinks he can solve this problem. How can any political system allow 'each associate [to] obey himself alone'? It is time now to turn to Rousseau and to see how he sets out to defend democracy, both on instrumental grounds (as a way of achieving the common good) and in itself (as an expression of freedom and equality).

Rousseau and the general will

> If children are brought up in common in the bosom of equality; if they are imbued with the laws of the state and the precepts of the general will; if they are taught to respect these above all things; if they are surrounded by examples and objects which constantly remind them of the tender mother who nourishes them, of the love she bears them, of the inestimable benefits they receive from her, and of the return they owe her, we cannot doubt that they will learn to cherish one another mutually as brothers, to will nothing contrary to the will of society, to substitute the actions of men and citizens for the futile and vain babbling of sophists, and to become in time defenders and fathers of the country of which they will have been so long the children.
>
> (Rousseau, *Discourse on Political Economy*, 149)

Plato, we saw, argues that ruling requires a special training or education. Rousseau does not doubt this, but he denies that it is

a training that ought to be given only to the few. Far better if
everyone acquires the appropriate skills, and then takes an active—democratic—role as part of the 'Sovereign' (the term
Rousseau uses for the body of citizens acting collectively, with
authority over themselves). A democratic state should therefore
place a high value on the education of the citizen.

Rousseau's citizens, then, are to be trained to 'will nothing
contrary to the will of society'. This is essential to the health and
preservation of the state. Citizenship, for Rousseau, also implies
active public service: 'As soon as public service ceases to be the
chief business of the citizens, and they would rather serve with
their money than with their persons, the state is not far from its
fall' (*Social Contract*, bk. III, ch. 15, p. 265). Together with
public service, Rousseau requires his citizens to play an active
role in political decision-making. By means of a form of direct
democracy, all citizens have a hand in the creation of legislation.
However, this claim needs to be made out with some care, for
there are passages in which Rousseau seems to argue against
democracy.

If we take the term in the strict sense, there never has been a real
democracy, and there never will be. It is against the natural order for
the many to govern and the few to be governed. It is unimaginable that
the people should remain continually assembled to devote their time to
public affairs, and it is clear that they cannot set up commissions for that
purpose without the form of administration being changed. (*Social
Contract*, bk. III, ch. 4, p. 239)

Thus, Rousseau concludes, 'were there a people of gods, their
government would be democratic. So perfect a government is
not for men' (*Social Contract*, bk. III, ch. 4, p. 240).

How should we understand Rousseau's position? We should
start with the difficult concept of the general will. First,
Rousseau distinguishes the will of all—the product of every
individual's particular will—from the general will. Recall the
earlier distinction between voting in one's interests, and voting
on what one thinks is right. Exercising your vote in the first
way—in your interests—is to pursue your particular will. Voting

for what is in your view the morally correct outcome, or the common good, is, for Rousseau, a matter of voting in accordance with your idea of the general will.

So what is the general will? A helpful illustration is this: suppose a company has 1,000 employees, and a fixed sum of £1 million available for wage increases. It is in each individual's interests to get as much of this money as possible, so, at the limit, we could say the particular will of each individual is to try to gain an extra £1 million. Adding these particular wills together we get the will of all: a demand for £1,000 million, which, of course, was not on offer. But suppose the employees are represented by a trade union, which acts equally in the interests of all of its members. The union can do nothing except put in a claim for the £1 million, and then share it out equally between all of its members, giving them £1,000 each. This result represents the general will: the policy equally in the interests of all the members. This is not in anyone's special interests, although it is in the common interest. Hence we see an illustration of the difference between the particular wills of all the citizens, and the general will. The general will demands the policy which is equally in everyone's interests. Thus we can think of the general will as the general interest.

Rousseau also claims that the general will must be 'general in its object as well as its essence' (*The Social Contract*, bk. II, ch. 4, p. 205). That is, it must apply equally to all citizens. By this Rousseau means that the general will must only make laws which, in principle at least, affect all the citizens, rather than executive orders targeted at particular individuals or groups. We should be ruled by laws, not rulers. The point of this, for Rousseau, is to ensure that the general will expresses a common interest. Under these circumstances, Rousseau thinks, no one has any reason to vote for an oppressive or unnecessary law, for each person is equally affected by all laws. The people, as Sovereign, make laws expressive of the general will.

How, then, are the laws to be applied? After all, they will often require action that singles out groups or even individuals. Legal punishment is the most obvious example. Rousseau's an-

swer is that application of the laws is not the business of the
Sovereign, but of the executive or government. The executive
arranges day-to-day administration, and Rousseau's view is that
it would be absurd to organize this task democratically, in the
sense of involving universal active participation. An 'elected
aristocracy'—a different sort of democracy, we might think—
seems to be Rousseau's preferred arrangement, where the 'wis-
est should govern the many, where it is assured that they will
govern for (the many's) profit, and not for its own' (*Social Contract*, bk. III, ch. 5, p. 242).

Note how Rousseau's system differs from Plato's. Even
though Rousseau describes his scheme as one in which the wis-
est govern the many, it is important to remember how restricted
a role the government or administration has. The government
does not make laws, but only applies or administers them. This
is not quite as trivial as it sounds: the government, for example,
has the right to declare war. This is a particular act—it names a
particular object—and so the people as Sovereign cannot legis-
late on the matter. All they can do is lay down the general
conditions under which war may be declared. It is then for the
government to decide whether the conditions are met, and to
take the appropriate action. So the key contrast between Plato's
philosopher–kings and Rousseau's elective aristocracy is that
Rousseau's rulers do not have the power to make laws.

So how are the laws made? Rousseau argues that the
'Sovereign cannot act save when the people is assembled' (*Social Contract*, bk. III, ch. 12, p. 261). This is how his system
differs from those of contemporary democracies. For laws are
made, not in parliament, but at popular assemblies. It is at such
assemblies that the general will is discovered:

When in popular assembly a law is proposed, what the people is asked
is not exactly whether it approves or rejects the proposal, but whether
it is in conformity with the general will, which is their will. Each man, in
giving his vote, states his opinion on that point; and the general will is
found by counting votes. When therefore the opinion that is contrary to
my own prevails, this proves neither more or less than that I was
mistaken, and that what I thought to be the general will was not so.
(*Social Contract*, bk. IV, ch. 2, p. 278)

Of course there are a number of objections to Rousseau's proposal. We might be particularly sceptical about the possibility of 'assembling the people'. But before considering these difficulties let us return to the reason why we began to look at Rousseau's position in the first place. The point was that Condorcet had demonstrated that there are conditions under which voting is an extremely good device for finding out the truth about a certain matter. If we assume that people have a better than even chance, on average, of being right, then a majority decision is very likely to get to the right answer, at least in a reasonably large electorate. But, to re-emphasize the necessary conditions for this account to apply, we have first to be sure that people are voting on their idea of the right solution—and not simply for the outcome that most favours them—and that the people do indeed, on average, have a better than even chance of being right. We introduced Rousseau as someone who had intuitively grasped the importance of these conditions, and had outlined a system which met them. Now we should examine whether this system really does so.

First, what justifies the assumption that, if the people are voting on the basis of their view of the general interest, they are likely to be right? Part of the answer must be our original observation that education was as important for Rousseau as it was for Plato. Individuals need to be educated into citizenship. But it is also vital that Rousseau wants to arrange political society in such a way that perceiving the general will should not be difficult, provided, at least, that one's vision is not clouded by particular interests. The common interest is the same for all individuals, and all are equally affected by all the laws passed.

But, we might say, how can this be? Some are rich, some are poor. Some are employers, some are employees. How can it be that everyone is equally affected by the law? Class differences surely lead to distinct, even opposed, interests. The fact that laws single no one out is hardly enough to show that all will be treated in the same way by the law. This gives rise to two lines of scepticism. Why should we think there is a general will at all—a policy that affects everyone equally? Second, even if there is one, it is unlikely to be easy to determine what it is.

Rousseau anticipated both these difficulties, and he has a radical solution to them. If his system is to be practicable, he asserts, then large inequalities must be absent. 'No citizen shall ever be rich enough to buy another, and none poor enough to be forced to sell himself' (*Social Contract*, bk. II, ch. 11, p. 225). If class differences make the formation of a general will impossible, then classes must be eliminated. All should stand on an equal footing. At the very least, no one should be so rich as to be able to purchase other people's votes, nor so poor as to be tempted to sell their own. Rousseau does not dwell on the details of how such equality is to be achieved and maintained, but it is clear that a classless society has great advantages from the point of view of democracy. It will be much more likely that everyone will be affected in the same way by the same law, and, further, the complexities of finding out what the best law is are much reduced. Rousseau, of course, accepts that even some people acting in good faith will make errors, but 'the pluses and minuses . . . cancel one another, and the general will remains as the sum of the differences' (*Social Contract*, bk. II, ch. 3, p. 203).

Even though the people meet regularly, they will not be called upon very often to make decisions. A good state needs to pass few laws. Therefore the people can use all their powers to inform themselves of what is required in the cases where they are called upon to vote.

The greatest obstacle to the emergence of the general will that Rousseau sees is not individuals' failure to perceive it, but their failure to be sufficiently motivated to act upon it. The difficulty is felt most keenly 'when intrigues and partial associations are formed at the expense of the great association' (*Social Contract*, bk. II, ch. 3, p. 203).

To see this, let us return to the example which we used to illustrate the distinction between the general will and the will of all. We imagined a sum of £1 million, to be divided between 1,000 employees. If these employees were represented by a single trade union then, assuming that there are no reasons for favouring one employee above another, the union would simply put in a request that the money should be split equally, and each should get £1,000. But suppose now that instead of one trade union there are ten, each representing 100 workers. Each of these unions would, no doubt, put in a claim for more than their 'fair share'. Membership of such a union would, in Rousseau's terms, distort one's vision. An individual would be liable to be swayed by spurious arguments 'demonstrating' why members of one's own union should get more. As Rousseau would put it, each of these unions would have a general will in respect to its members, but a particular will with respect to the whole. When 'interest groups' form, and people vote for the interest of their particular group, then there is no reason to believe that the general will would emerge from the process of voting.

Rousseau's main response to this is to recommend that either there should be no political parties, or factions, or, if there are any, there should be very many. In this way the interests of particular groups should have little influence on the decisions of the whole.

Nevertheless, this still does not do enough to explain why citizens will vote for the general will, rather than for their own particular interest. Rousseau's main solution to this problem is that individuals must be made to identify very strongly with the group as a whole. He has a number of devices to ensure this. The most obvious of these devices we have already encountered: education for civic virtue. People need to be brought up the right way so that they learn to 'cherish one another as brothers'. This cements the social bond and widens each person's view so they take an interest in the state as a whole, and hence will naturally seek to advance the general will.

We might think that this is a somewhat sinister idea: it smacks of indoctrination, despite Rousseau's obsession with the protection of the freedom of the individual and some critics claim to have noticed fascistic or totalitarian overtones in Rousseau's thinking. People are to be moulded by education to forget themselves in favour of the state. There are two things to be said in reply to this criticism. First, Rousseau assumes that there should already be bonds of custom and tradition uniting a people before it is fit to receive laws. So education is a way of formalizing and consolidating links which are already present in a community, rather than of imposing an artificial order on a diverse group of people. Second, Rousseau would not be unduly concerned to hear that some of the measures he advocates are not to the taste of modern liberals. This is even more clear in the other two devices he advocates to ensure social unity: 'censorship' and 'civil religion'.

Rousseau supposes that the state needs an 'official censor' whose role is to encourage people to act in accordance with popular morality. Rousseau does not discuss censorship in its modern sense of the suppression of speech or images, although no doubt this would be included within the censor's role. Rousseau's main concern is with enforcing and discouraging types of behaviour. In essence, the job of the censor is to ridicule, and so discourage, certain forms of anti-social behaviour. As an example, Rousseau tells us, 'Certain drunkards from Samos polluted the tribunal of the Ephors: the next day, a public edict gave Samians permission to be filthy. An actual punishment would not have been so severe an impunity' (*Social Contract*, bk. IV, ch. 8, p. 298). By such means the censor is charged with the duty of upholding, and clarifying where necessary, public morality.

As a final device to ensure social unity, Rousseau proposes that each state should be regulated by what he calls a 'civil religion'. In brief, there are three parts to Rousseau's account of religion. First, he requires that every citizen should subscribe to some religion or other, for this will 'make him love his duty'. Second, a diversity of religions should be tolerated, but only those which themselves include a principle of toleration. Otherwise some citizens will be compelled to become enemies, which is contrary to the idea of social peace. Finally, and most distinctively, in addition to private morality, each person should subscribe to the civil religion. This should have articles which are 'not exactly . . . religious dogmas, but . . . social sentiments without which a man cannot be a good citizen or a faithful subject' (*Social Contract*, bk. IV, ch. 8, p. 307).

In sum then, if Rousseau's system were in existence it would seem to have a good chance of meeting the two conditions we have set down for Condorcet's argument to apply. The conditions were that people had to vote on moral grounds, rather than in their own self-interest, and to have, on average, a better than even chance of getting the morally right answer. In Rousseau's ideal state it is plausible that these conditions will be met. Of course, it does not follow that observing Rousseau's proposals is the only way in which the conditions can be satisfied: perhaps we could devise an alternative system. But let us concentrate on Rousseau. Even if we concede that his system meets Condorcet's conditions, is it a system we should adopt?

Freedom and equality

To recall the earlier discussion, we noted, in essence, two types of response to Plato. One was to argue that democracy, in principle, is a way of achieving the 'right result' that is at least as good as, or better than, rule by experts. This instrumental form of justification, as we called it, corresponds to the argument of Rousseau we have just considered. The second type of response was to consider the intrinsic value of democracy. In essence, we can see this as the question of how well democracy expresses or advances the values of freedom and equality. Discussion of this question will have the further advantage of helping us to decide whether Rousseau's system is one which we should wish to put into practice.

First, then, how expressive of the idea of equality is Rousseau's polity? One way in which equality entered the argument was through the idea that, without rough equality of wealth, factions would form. This would not only cloud the judgement of the voters, but perhaps create an obstacle to the existence of a general will: a policy equally in the interests of all voters. For the rich would seek a set of laws which particularly benefited them, and would have the money and influence to arrange things in their own favour. So, as we noted, Rousseau assumes that genuine democracy presupposes a classless society.

The idea of the general will itself, however, is even more strongly egalitarian. The correct policy is one which benefits all citizens equally. On the face of it, then, it would be hard to devise a system which gives a greater weight to equality, particularly when combined with the democratic principle that all citizens have an equal say in the attempt to determine the nature of the general will on any given case.

Unfortunately, the appearance of equality within Rousseau's system is somewhat misleading. Rousseau always uses the masculine form to refer to the citizens. This is no accident of language. Rousseau believed that women were subordinate beings, and he simply seems to have assumed that the privilege of citizenship should be extended only to men. Thus the doctrine of the equality of citizens is rather soured by Rousseau's assumption that there would naturally be inequalities between male citizens and female non-citizens.

This inconsistency in Rousseau's system was addressed by perhaps the first major advocate of women's rights, Mary Wollstonecraft, in her *Vindication of the Rights of Women*, published in 1792. Wollstonecraft argued that there was no basis for the exclusion of women from the citizenry. But even she had a blind spot. The emancipated female citizen is assumed to have female domestic servants, and the idea that such servants should also have the vote is something which Wollstonecraft seems simply to have ignored. It was generally assumed, until relatively recently, that the only people entitled to vote were those with some property stake in the country. Those without property could not be trusted to use their votes 'responsibly'.

However, a motivation also moving Wollstonecraft, Rousseau, and, indeed, the Ancient Greeks, is the more mundane thought that those people who are active as citizens do not have the time to wash their own clothes or cook their own food. To perform one's duty as an active citizen is time-consuming, if one is both to keep oneself well informed, and attend the public forum or assembly. Anyone engaged in public life needs domestic support staff. The Greeks took for granted that democracy was consistent with slavery, Rousseau that it was consistent with sexual inequality, and Wollstonecraft that it was consistent with the disfranchisement of the poor. Two things have brought about the changes which have made universal suffrage possible. One is the (rather depressing) view that a right to vote does not bring with it an onerous responsibility to keep oneself well informed about political and economic matters; the other that in the developed world at least, household machinery has greatly eased the burdens of domestic work. It might be an exaggeration to say that the washing machine has made democracy possible, but it has certainly helped.

However, despite Rousseau's exclusion of women from the franchise, the real logic of his political thought implies that there is no good reason for this exclusion. We can, then, construct a model of genuine equality on the basis of Rousseau's proposals.

So much for equality. How about freedom? It is not difficult to detect significant limitations of freedom in Rousseau's chosen polity. The central restriction is simply the other side of the coin to the creation of the social bond. Freedom of thought is severely restricted, particularly in the area of religion. First, atheism is barred. Second, intolerant religions are not to be tolerated. Third, all must affirm the civil religion. And woe betide the hypocrite: 'If any one, after publicly recognising these dogmas (of civil religion), behaves as if he does not believe them, let him be punished by death: he has committed the worst of all crimes, that of lying before the law' (*Social Contract*, bk. IV, ch. 8, p. 307). When we add to this the existence of the office of the censor, whose role it is to enforce public or customary morality, then individuals appear to lose any freedom to be unconventional. No doubt this would also include restrictions on people conducting 'experiments of living', to use a term we will encounter again in the examination of Mill on liberty in the next chapter.

With this restrictive illiberal background in mind, we may ask how Rousseau can maintain that he has solved the problem of finding a form of association in which 'while uniting himself with all (each associate) may still obey himself alone, and remain as free as before' (*Social Contract*, bk. I, ch. 6, p. 191).

The answer is that Rousseau holds what has been called a 'positive' notion of freedom. We will look at this idea in more detail in the next chapter, but the thought is that freedom is not simply a matter of being able to follow your desires, unconstrained by others (a 'negative' notion) but instead something which requires certain types of action. Typically, theorists of positive freedom define freedom in terms of 'living the life that the rational person would choose to live'. In Rousseau's case such a life—the rational life—is available only in civil society. 'The mere impulse of appetite is slavery, while obedience to a law we prescribe to ourselves is liberty' (*Social Contract*, bk. IV, ch. 8, p. 196). The way, of course, in which we prescribe laws to ourselves is through voting as a member of the Sovereign. It is only by acting in accordance with the laws created by the Sovereign—acting on the general will—that we can be said, according to Rousseau, to be truly free.

It has been pointed out by critics that on this view one can be 'forced to be free'; in fact this is a phrase that Rousseau himself uses. Consider the case of someone who believes that the general will requires one policy (policy A), while the majority adopt another (policy B). Policy B, let us suppose, represents the general will. In that case our person will be forced to act according to policy B, and as freedom is identified with acting on the general will, then it follows that the person has been forced to be free. Rousseau would say that anything else—doing what one prefers, for example—is slavery to one's impulses, and not true freedom. Opponents of Rousseau have pointed out that on this basis even highly repressive regimes can be defended on grounds of their support of freedom. So even though we can rescue Rousseau's system from inequality, it is very unclear whether we can say—as Rousseau so wants us to say—that it advances the value of freedom.

Radical criticism of Rousseau

This criticism has been taken up and extended by certain contemporary writers, who, while being strongly influenced by Rousseau's writing, feel his ideal of the state needs to be improved and repaired in a number of ways. There are three, closely related, criticisms to be made.

The first focuses on the idea of the general will. Even if it is true that in a closely unified, highly equal society a general will can be formed and relatively easily perceived, it is not true that contemporary societies conform to this ideal; nor is it desirable that they should. Economic class is not the only obstacle to the formation of a general will; we also belong to different religions, have different moral and philosophical ideas, and come from differing cultural, ethnic, and racial backgrounds. Now this does not mean that there can never be a policy equally in the interests of all: despite our differences we all have similar basic needs. But beyond this, the fact that we value different things—economic progress or the protection of the natural environment, for example—can lead to conflict. Thus on many issues it is very unlikely that there could be any policy that is equally in the interests of all. Or, if there were, that it would be easy to discover. Perhaps then, we must simply drop Rousseau's key assumption that citizens can form their wills into a general will.

Secondly, Rousseau's treatment of those who hold a minority view is hard to admire. Dissenters are to be 'forced to be free'. Those who first affirm the principles of the civil religion and then disobey them are to be put to death. Against the background of the tight unity of the state, dissent is a crime, and crime is treason. This might be marginally defensible if the majority were always right about the general will, and dissenters therefore either mistaken or anti-social. But if there is no general will, then this argument is appalling in more than one sense.

Finally, Rousseau's critics do not accept that freedom should be equated with obedience, even 'obedience to a law one makes for oneself'. Or, to put this another way, within Rousseau's system 'making the law for oneself' is simply a matter of having some say in the decision-making procedure. But suppose, again, one is in the minority, and one's views do not become law. Then, while it may be justified to coerce such people to obey the law, it seems outrageous to say that such coercion makes them 'free', that they are being brought to obey a law that they have created for themselves. Even though the minority have taken part in the decision-making procedure, the law has been created despite them, not because of them.

The force of these criticisms can now be seen. In order for Rousseau to be able to argue that democracy is instrumentally justified—that it is a highly reliable way of achieving morally correct outcomes—he has to draw the bonds of social unity very tight. So tight, in fact, that the system becomes unacceptably repressive. So the same measures which, in Rousseau's model, make democracy defensible in instrumental terms also make it intrinsically undesirable. In an amended form it may achieve equality, but not freedom as we recognize it, nor pluralism, nor diversity. The price we have to pay for the general will is too high.

Thus Rousseau's system needs repair. And, indeed, in the light of these criticisms we can point to another oddity in Rousseau's ideal polity—an oddity which has gone unremarked so far in this discussion. This is the extent to which Rousseau allows genuine political participation. Although Rousseau's citizens are regularly called upon to vote, somewhat paradoxically he seems to discourage them from taking too active a role in politics. First, as we saw, he does not advocate a democratic assembly, and second, the assumption that only clouded perception stands in the way of unanimity leads Rousseau to conclude that 'long debates, dissensions and tumult proclaim the ascendancy of particular interests and the decline of the state' (*Social Contract*, bk. IV, ch. 2, p. 276).

However, once we drop the assumption that we can regularly and easily perceive a general will—in fact, if we drop the assumption that there is a general will altogether—then politics takes on a new cast. There now seems an urgent need to hear all voices, all arguments, and all positions. Voters can still be represented as aiming at 'the best' for the community. But perhaps what 'the best' is in any case can be a highly contested matter. Furthermore, it will probably be very controversial which policies would be most likely to achieve it.

Thus Rousseau's critics have argued that extensive political debate is not a sign of decay, but vital to the functioning of democratic politics. Furthermore, outvoted minorities have no duty to change their mind about what is correct. In general we would expect them to obey the law, but they can continue to speak up, and, if they feel strongly enough, to agitate for change. Perhaps civil disobedience can also be justified on democratic grounds. If you sincerely believe that a wrong decision has been made by the majority, then you may have not only a right but a duty to draw attention to this, by whatever means necessary. Treating conscientious disobedience as treason, in order to preserve social unity, is surely a mistake. The dissenting citizen has a place. He or she should not be silenced for the sake of peace: perhaps the majority is wrong. But even if the majority is right, attention should still be paid to dissenters.

Participatory democracy

These objections have led us to a new model of democracy, much influenced by Rousseau, but with much more respect for the individual, for debate, and for minority views. This is the theory of 'participatory democracy'. In essence, it extends Rousseau's model in three ways.

First, it claims that we must find more room for individual involvement in political discussion and decision-making than Rousseau allows, and more room and respect for dissenting voices.

Second, it supposes that Rousseau's distinction between the Sovereign and the executive needs to be rethought. It may be that we cannot all join in every political decision for practical reasons. But, once we abandon the assumption that there is a general will, there is no reason why we should restrict individual decision-making to legislation. Perhaps all citizens should be involved in deciding the most important 'particular acts' of administration, especially when we remember that declaring war is considered by Rousseau to be an action of the executive, not the Sovereign.

Many of the practical difficulties recognized by Rousseau as standing in the way of more participatory politics could easily be overcome by modern technology. There is no need to gather all the people together, whether under an oak tree or in the public square. Interactive cable television, electronic mail, and other aspects of information technology can all be pressed into service as alternatives to the town meeting. Any citizen can post political speeches on electronic bulletin boards. Voting can be executed at the touch of a button. One can do one's democratic duty from the comfort of a favourite armchair!

Finally, advocates of the idea of participatory democracy have argued that political decision-making should, in effect, go 'all the way down'. People should be consulted not only in the matter of legislation, but in all decisions which affect them. Hence, it is proposed, we should follow democratic principles of decision-making not only in the public forum, but in the workplace, the family, and the other institutions of civil society. For what use is a vote on issues of industrial policy when matters of most immediate concern—the nature of one's working environment, whether one even has a job tomorrow—depend on the absolute decisions of another person, one's boss. As Marx observed, and as women have learnt to their cost, equal political rights are worth fighting for, but they are of little value if one is still treated unequally in day-to-day life. The removal of legal impediments or restrictions does not necessarily lead to an improvement in anyone's position.

Theorists of participatory politics claim that only active, democratic involvement in all matters of concern can achieve real freedom and equality for all. Only when we are involved in making the decisions which structure our lives in all spheres are we really free, they argue. And, to put this in the context of the discussion of political obligation from the last chapter, only in a participatory democracy are the voluntaristic assumptions of social contract theory satisfied. In such a society we can genuinely be thought of as voluntarily contributing members of society. And so, on this view, it is only under these conditions that we even acquire an obligation to obey the state.

The idea of a participatory politics is, on the face of it, very attractive. We are the subjects of national and local decision-making—we have to obey the rules—so surely we should play our part as authors of those decisions. Only when we truly make the laws to which we are subject can we genuinely reconcile freedom and authority. But it is not difficult to find fault with the scheme as proposed. Any fully participatory model would be afflicted by grave difficulties, and this is probably why Rousseau proposed the limits to his system that he did.

The first difficulty is that fully participatory politics is barely conceivable, and, to the extent that it is conceivable, it is likely to be extraordinarily inefficient. John Stuart Mill pointed out that, while groups of people are much better than a single individual at deliberation, individuals are much better than groups at action. Thus if a group wishes to have its decisions implemented, it must always delegate this to an individual.

In response, it will be said that no one has really proposed that somehow 'the whole people' is to carry out its own instructions. Of course administrators must be appointed. But the whole people, or at least all those affected, will be involved in making the decisions. But again, although deliberation is better done in groups than by individuals, it does not follow that the bigger the group the better the deliberation. Indeed, it is likely that a small, well-selected group will deliberate better than a large one. Large groups create noise, digressions, and confusion. The best arguments might never be heard. So surely there is room for expert deliberators within a democracy, and a fully participatory politics might find it hard to give such people a proper role.

The second problem is somewhat more subtle, but still obvious enough. In the computerized political fantasy we come home to find a list of questions for the day. But why should we find ourselves voting on one set of issues and not another? Who, in other words, sets the agenda? This is not a trivial question. Often the most powerful person is not the one who decides yes or no, but the person who puts the question in the first place. Participatory politics becomes far less appealing if the agenda is to be set by appointed officials.

In reply, it will be said that 'the people' can set the agenda. They will vote on which issues are to be voted on. But how will the agenda for this preliminary meeting be set? By vote? And so on. The idea that we could have participatory politics at every level is beginning to look naïve and even incoherent.

No doubt there are ways around this. Perhaps we could appoint, by lot, a 'president for the day', who gets to set the day's agenda. On reflection, though, the lack of continuity in such a system looks like a recipe for disaster. Rousseau's view that society will function better when fewer decisions need to be made by the people as a whole begins to look much more attractive. But even Rousseau had little to say about the problem of agenda-setting. The best he could do was propose that those who draft the laws upon which a vote is to be taken should themselves be excluded from the franchise. This seems like a way of arguing for a powerful, independent, apolitical civil service: an idea far removed from the goal of participation.

Finally, the most obvious problem has already been pointed out by Rousseau. Oscar Wilde said that 'the trouble with Socialism is that it would take up too many evenings'. Many critics of participatory democracy have quoted these words as being even more appropriate in that context. The point is that, while we care about actively involving ourselves in decisions that concern us, we also care about many other things too. It is very unclear whether we should give up the other things we value— listening to music, talking to our friends and families, even watching television—for the sake of a say in every decision that affects us. And once we extend political participation to the workplace, participation takes up not only our evenings but much of our days too. In clamouring for all to play an active, equal role in politics, we risk, if not starving to death, then at least having far less productive working days.

In sum, while the idea of participatory democracy is a very attractive one, it is very hard to see that it can be made to work in a way that is worth the effort. Even if a participatory society is best from the point of view of preserving freedom and equality, it seems to do less well from the point of view of advancing prosperity and allowing the fulfilment of life plans. Can we do better?

Representative democracy

> Participation should be as great as the general degree of improvement of the community will allow; and that nothing less can be ultimately desirable than the admission of all to a share in the sovereign power of the state. But since all cannot, in a community exceeding a single small town, participate personally in any but some very minor portions of the public business, it follows that the ideal type of a perfect government must be representative.
>
> (Mill, *Representative Government*, 217–18)

Any system of government—even the most radical participatory democracy—needs administrators to execute policy. Carrying out the decisions of the people cannot be done by the people as a whole. The further question is what powers these administrators should be given. In the standard model of participatory democracy, the presumption is that administrators should be given very little power, with as much as possible being reserved for the people. In Plato's system, at the other extreme, the people have no role at all and the administrators—the guardians—have complete power. Rousseau decided the matter a third way: the people make the laws, and the administrators carry them out. But another, more familiar, model is available too. The people elect representatives who then both make laws and put them into practice. This is the idea of representative democracy, as defended by Mill.

For Mill, representative democracy is the only means by which democracy can survive in the modern world. To understand why Mill says this we should enquire, first, what he took the proper function of governments to be. What are the purposes of governments? For Mill, they are twofold: to 'improve' the citizens, and to manage their public affairs. Thus governments are to be judged by their effects on individuals, whether

they improve them morally and intellectually, and by their efficiency in dealing with matters of public concern. In this latter
respect Mill recognizes that there are many branches of government—jurisprudence, civil and penal legislation, financial and
commercial policy—each with its own standards of success and
failure. Although for Mill the ultimate standard for each of them
is the same—how well it advances general happiness—this further claim is not essential to the main argument so far.

It is no surprise to be told that governments are required to
manage society's affairs effectively. But Mill's conception of the
other proper function of governments is more controversial. Do
governments have any duty, or even any right, to concern themselves with the moral well-being of their citizens? One major
theme of modern liberalism is that the moral welfare of the
citizens is none of the government's business. And so it is odd
to find Mill—one of the founders of modern liberal theory—
making the claim he does. But we will leave this to one side for
now, as we shall return to it in far more depth in both the next
and the final chapter.

Mill thinks it is easy to show the advantages of his system over
what he calls good despotism, or absolute monarchy, and this
would also include Plato's guardianship. The management function of government he concedes could be carried out by a despot, though, so he claims, less well than by a democracy. But his
main argument against despotism is the type of human beings it
is likely to create.

Mill's claim is that despotism leads to passivity and inaction,
for it produces a people who have no need to inform or educate
themselves in the business of the state. This affects not only the
individuals themselves, but also the likely prosperity of the state.
'Let a person have nothing to do for his country and he will not
care for it' (*Representative Government*, 204). Or, if the subjects
do inform and educate themselves, and take an active interest in
the affairs of the state, then they will not for long be content with
their subjection.

If further proof of the advantages of democracy were needed,
Mill asks us to

Contrast the free states of the world, while their freedom lasted, with the contemporary subjects of monarchical or oligarchical despotism: the Greek cities with the Persian satrapies; the Italian republics and the free towns of Flanders and Germany, with the feudal monarchies of Europe; Switzerland, Holland and England, with Austria and ante-revolutionary France. Their superior prosperity was too obvious ever to have been gainsaid: while their superiority in good government and social relations is proved by the prosperity, and is manifest besides in every page in history. (*Representative Government*, 210)

Mill's key assumption is that human beings flourish only under conditions of independence. They need to be self-protecting and self-dependent if they are to avoid oppression and make their lives worthwhile. Thus Mill feels confident that all citizens must play their role in the exercise of sovereignty.

But what should the exercise of sovereignty come to? Not, Mill argues, direct democracy. He might, if pushed, concede that direct democracy would be the best way of improving the citizens, both morally and intellectually, but in terms of its efficiency as a form of government it is a disaster. One argument is that modern societies are simply too large to make direct democracy possible. But, more importantly, in words not far from Plato's, he argues that things will go badly wrong if we let the people exert great influence over their appointed expert administrators.

At its best, it is inexperience sitting in judgment on experience, ignorance on knowledge: ignorance which never suspecting the existence of what it does not know, is equally careless and supercilious, making light of, if not resenting, all pretensions to have a judgment better worth attending to than its own. (*Representative Government*, 232)

However, critics of representative democracy argue that it is not so much a welcome move from direct democracy in the direction of realism, as an unhealthy move away from democracy altogether. This is clearly Rousseau's view (remember his comments about the 'people of England'). Is representative democracy any more than a sham, behind which lurks elective dictatorship? If so, it can hardly be recommended as a system of equal power, nor as a system which presupposes and extends the moral and intellectual development of the citizens.

Mill would accept that representative democracy can fail to achieve its purposes. But he is keen to propose a system that will do better. In particular he emphasizes the importance of educating the citizens for citizenship. The most significant means of doing this is by participation in public business. Although, of course, this cannot mean participation in national government for everyone, there are other possibilities. So, for example, Mill emphasizes the importance of jury service and participation in local government, for this requires citizens to acquire a range of skills not likely to be available to those 'who have done nothing in their lives but drive a quill, or sell goods over a counter' (*Representative Government*, 217).

Such participation alone, however, is not enough to secure the advantages of representative democracy. Mill identifies a number of threats to democracy. One is the possibility that the system will encourage unworthy or unfit people to stand for election. Mill agrees with Plato that the people best equipped to rule us are those least likely to want to. Or, to make the point the other way round, the qualities most likely to lead to success in politics—flattery, duplicity, manipulation—are the ones we would least wish to have in our rulers.

Thus representative democracy must face the problem we saw with Plato's guardianship: how to protect ourselves from unsavoury leaders who may obtain power. This problem was considered in detail in *The Federalist Papers*, written by James Madison, Alexander Hamilton (1757–1804), and John Jay (1745–1829), and published under the pseudonym 'Publius' over a series of ten months in 1787 and 1788 in a number of New York city newspapers. The papers were written with a view to convincing the New York state voters to ratify the new Constitution of the United States. The Federalists supported what they called a 'republic', by which they broadly meant what we have been calling a representative democracy. Certain anti-Federalists, on the other hand, instead favoured participatory styles of democracy, and presented the Federalists with the problem of

showing how to safeguard representative democracy from falling into an elected tyranny. The Federalists' main proposal on
this score was to take over the idea of the 'separation of powers',
found in John Locke and Charles-Louis de Secondat, Baron de
Montesquieu (1689–1755), who had proposed that the legisla-
tive, executive, and judicial functions of government should be
placed in independent hands. In theory this meant that the
activities of any branch of government would be checked by the
other two, and this would safeguard the people against the corruption of its rulers.

Mill accepts that power should be dispersed throughout the
agencies of the state, to effect a system of 'checks and balances',
so that the over-ambitious have little chance to exploit their
power. But he also suggests further measures to prevent abuse
of the democratic process. He proposes that there should be a
limitation on the money people may spend on their election
campaign. How can we trust anyone prepared to pay a large sum
of money to gain election? Surely they would seek a return on
their investment. Secondly, Mill argues, somewhat surprisingly,
that members of the government should not be paid. For otherwise a seat in the chamber 'would become an object of desire to
adventurers of a low class' (*Representative Government*, 311).
Those not of independent means, but obviously suitable
and able, can be supported by private donations from their
constituents.

The greatest obstacle to representative government, however,
is the possible behaviour of the voters. For Mill it is vital that
voters should vote in accordance with their ideas of the general
interest; that is, they should vote for whichever candidates they
feel most likely to improve the citizens and efficiently manage
the affairs of the country in the interests of all. Here he uses an
analogy with jury service:

[The citizen's] vote is not a thing in which he has an option; it has no
more to do with his personal wishes than the verdict of a juryman. It is
strictly a matter of duty; he is bound to give it according to his best and
most conscientious opinion of the public good. (*Representative Government*, 299)

Hence we see the extra importance of real jury service as a form of participation. It educates voters by giving them a highly distilled and concentrated training for democracy.

Mill's worry is that a voter may give a 'base and mischievous vote ... from the voter's personal interest, or class interest, or some mean feeling in his own mind' (*Representative Government*, 302). Or it may also be that the voters are too ignorant to perceive the public good correctly.

One remedy Mill sees to the first of these problems is to have an open vote, rather than a secret ballot. As people have a duty to vote for the public good, it is reasonable that they should be held accountable for their vote. Therefore it should be a matter of public record. Thus public disapproval would be a force to keep people from exercising their vote out of self-interested reasons. The danger in this, Mill recognizes, is the danger of coercion. Secret ballots were introduced because powerful local individuals would press individuals—particularly their employees—to vote a particular way, with the threat of a loss of job, or of other favours, for failing to carry out the instruction. A secret ballot makes this threat empty: no one can know who has voted for which candidate. Mill naïvely believes that this is a lesser danger than the possibility of 'base' or self-interested voting, which would distort the poll. Mill's position, surely, is highly questionable.

Mill's other remedy—to prevent the distorting effects of class and personal interests—will, he hopes, also have the effect of neutralizing the influence of stupidity and ignorance. He argues that certain people, at least temporarily, are to be excluded from the franchise. This includes those unable to 'read, write, and, I will add, perform the common operations of arithmetic'. And he goes on:

I regard it as required by first principles that the receipt of parish relief should be a peremptory disqualification for the franchise. He who cannot by his labour suffice for his own support has no claim to the privilege of helping himself to the money of others. By becoming dependent on the remaining members of the community for actual subsistence, he abdicates his claim to equal rights with them in other respects. (*Representative Government*, 282)

The other side of the coin to this is that, although everyone who meets Mill's conditions is entitled to a voice, 'that every one should have an equal voice is a totally different proposition' (*Representative Government*, 283). Mill argues that certain people who are especially well qualified to exercise their judgement should be given more than one vote. He feels that the particularly intelligent or well educated should be favoured with two or more votes (he doesn't give final details).

Mill's most pressing concern is that the uneducated poor—the numerical majority—will, out of a combination of ignorance and class interest, make a terrible mistake. They will elect a government which will attempt to improve the position of labourers by raising the taxes of the wealthy, protecting home industries from competition, reducing uncertainty of employment, and so on. Mill's argument against this is that it will make everyone—including the workers—worse off by relaxing industry and economic activity, and discouraging saving and investment. Thus, Mill argues, the workers are mistaken about where their interests lie, and so, being in the majority, might tilt the country towards disaster.

We will return to the issue of the just distribution of property in Chapter 5. The details of the case do not really matter for the present argument. The point is simply that Mill wants to ensure that representative democracy contains certain safeguards to prevent it from being dictated to by stupidity and class interest. Mill's main approach to democracy is to defend it on instrumental grounds, and to identify the steps to be taken if there is a danger that it might lead to undesirable consequences.

Would plural voting and partial disfranchisement achieve the goal Mill wanted? Perhaps, but there is something of a tension in his thought here. To protect industry we could bias the ballot in favour either of the rich or (so Mill thinks) the educated. He prefers the latter option for it is vital that those with only one vote should be able to accept the reasoning which favours others with more than one. Thus each of the uneducated will accept that the educated 'understand the subject better than himself, that the other's opinion should be counted for more than his own accords with his expectations, and with the course of things which in all other areas of life he is accustomed to acquiesce in' (*Representative Government*, 284). But contrast this argument with another,

I may remark, that if the voter acquiesces in this estimate of his capabilities, and really wishes to have the choice made for him by a person in whom he places reliance, there is no need of any constitutional provision for the purpose; he has only to ask the confidential person privately what candidate he had better vote for. (*Representative Government*, 294)

This remark, made just ten pages after the first, occurs in the context of the discussion of a proposal that we should have two stages of election. We vote for a group of electors, who then go on to elect members of parliament. Mill has little time for this suggestion. He thinks that the only possible justification for it would be that perhaps we ought to leave such important decisions as electing our rulers to those whom we recognize as wise. Mill's response is that, if we think such people are wise, we need only ask them how to vote, and follow their instructions. Exactly the same reply has been made by Mill's critics to his proposal about plural voting. If the uneducated revere the educated then we need not give the latter extra votes, for the uneducated can simply seek out their opinions. But if they do not respect such opinions then they would not accept plural voting. Plural voting is either unnecessary or unjustified.

Protecting the minority

Although the case just discussed is one where, Mill claims, the ignorant majority will end up doing themselves harm by pursuing what they wrongly see as their own class interest, this type of example raises perhaps the main problem that troubled Mill about democracy: the place of the outvoted minority. Mill, we have seen, was particularly concerned to prevent the 'tyranny of the majority'. Most of us, of course, can accept being on the losing side from time to time. But sometimes an entrenched majority will win vote after vote, leaving the minority group permanently outvoted and ignored. So, in *Representative Government*, Mill takes great pains to ensure the representation of minorities in parliament. He declares his approval of a very complicated, elaborate (and possibly incoherent) system of proportional representation, involving the possibility of transferring one's vote to a candidate in another constituency, should one's favoured candidate fail. By such, or similar, means we ought to be able to ensure the representation of many minorities in parliament.

Nevertheless, representation is one thing, protection another. A represented minority could still be outvoted in parliament. So the measures so far proposed will not have the effects we might hope for. Class, race, or religious oppression remain possible under the system of majority rule, even when the minority are represented. The only way of guaranteeing that this could not happen, within the democratic system, is by giving the morally highly enlightened very many votes. But this returns us close to Plato.

In fact, Mill's solution to this—as we shall see in the next chapter—is to restrict the legitimate sphere of government activity. Certain things are just not the business of the government or of the majority. Thus the government cannot interfere in certain areas of people's lives, and people have certain rights and liberties, with which the government may not interfere.

However, to pass final judgement on Mill's model of democracy, we can see that it contains a form of the same tension that afflicted Rousseau's. The problem with Rousseau's view was that democracy could only be relied upon to produce decisions that were in accordance with the general will if it severely restricted the freedom of the citizens. In other words, if democracy is to be instrumentally justified, it cannot achieve the twin virtues of freedom and equality to which it aspires. For Mill, it is not freedom that is sacrificed but equality. Certain citizens are to be excluded from the franchise, on educational or economic grounds, while others are given more than one vote. Mill's system leans more closely towards Plato than he is prepared to admit. Perhaps Mill should have had more faith in the abilities and virtue of the uneducated poor. Or perhaps any democratic system is bound to be compromised.

Conclusion

One upshot of the discussion so far is that we are very unlikely to be able to find an instrumental defence of democracy which also builds the values of equality and freedom into a feasible system. And however we restrict freedom and equality, there is no reason to think that democracies necessarily make better decisions than other types of systems. Indeed, we can conceive of systems combining extensive market research and wise administrators which are almost bound to do better. Nevertheless, few people are prepared to abandon democracy on this basis. Why not?

Clearly the answer must be that democracy, for us, is not valued purely as a decision-making procedure, but for at least one other reason. What reason could that be? As a case study, consider the South African election of 1994. This election—the fact of it, even more than the result—was celebrated the world over. Black South Africans were enfranchised for the first time, but why was this seen as so significant? Surely the cause for celebration was not simply that black South Africans were more likely to be treated with justice than they had been in the past, although this was no doubt part of the reason for rejoicing. Rather, it seems, the main idea was that the mere fact that they now had the vote was a way of recording that black South Africans were at last treated as worthy of respect. That people are included in the franchise has a certain symbolic or expressive value. In this case it symbolizes that, in some way at least, black and white South Africans stand together as political equals. Having a vote, then, seems to be important irrespective of what people do with the vote when they have it.

To think of this in another context, consider the argument commonly used in the early part of this century to deny women the vote. It was often said that women did not need to vote, because the interests of married women would be the same as those of their husbands, and of unmarried women the same as those of their fathers. There are so many things wrong with this argument it is hard to know where to start. To make just a few objections, first, even if the claim about common interests is true, why should it not be the case that the interest is registered for every person who holds it? Second, again, even if it is true, why is this a reason for giving men the vote and denying it to women, rather than the other way round? Third, it may well not be true. Why assume that women have the same interests as their husbands or their fathers? But the fourth objection is the most decisive. Whether or not women's interests are the same as men's, it is insulting and demeaning to give men a vote while denying it to women. Universal suffrage is a way of expressing the idea that we believe women, just as much as men, are owed respect as citizens.

It is one thing to say that all the holders of the franchise are to be respected as citizens. But need we also say that everyone is owed equal respect, or is to be respected as equals? We have just seen one proposal that, while all should, in principle, have a say, sometimes this should be denied for certain people, while others should have more than one vote: John Stuart Mill's plural voting scheme. It is interesting to note that no major thinker seems to have agreed with Mill on this issue. Few have even felt it necessary to give arguments to support their opposition. Why not? Simply because Mill's proposal violates the idea that democracy is a way of expressing *equal* respect for all. This, perhaps, is why we withdraw the vote from criminals: by their behaviour they forfeit the right to equal respect.

Is there anything else we can say in defence of the type of democratic system we now have? Perhaps the best we can add is this. In the contemporary world, we have to accept that we cannot survive without coercive authority structures. But if we have such structures, we need to have people to occupy the roles within them: rulers, in other words. In past centuries human beings may have been prepared to accept that certain people had a natural right to rule. Perhaps they were thought to have been appointed by God. But this is not a line of reasoning we are now prepared to accept. We will accept that individuals have a right to rule only if they have been appointed by the people, and are recallable by the people. That is, only democracy allows us an answer we can accept to the question 'why should these people rule?', or 'what makes their rule legitimate?' By democratic means we can, of course, also exercise some measure of control over the rulers' behaviour. Perhaps this is the best we can hope for, both in terms of political structure and as a last-ditch defence of modern democracy.

4

The Place of Liberty

Mill on liberty

> The only purpose for which power can be rightfully exer-
> cised over any member of a civilized community, against
> his will, is to prevent harm to others. His own good, either
> physical or moral, is not a sufficient warrant.
>
> (Mill, *On Liberty*, 135)

One simple principle

Once democracy is in place, what work is there left for the
political philosopher? An optimistic view is that, as soon as we
have a democratic decision-making procedure, the fundamental
work of political philosophy is over. All decisions can now be
left to the fair process of the electoral machine. Sadly, as we
observed in the last chapter, even if democracy is the best system
we can think of, it is not a cure-all. And Mill suggests it has its
own dangers: the threat of the tyranny of the majority. It is naïve
to think that the existence of democracy rules out injustice. The
fact that 'the people' make the laws does not rule out the possibility that the majority will pass laws which oppress, or are
otherwise unfair to, the minority. Somehow the minority must
be protected.

Mill's way out of this problem may seem surprising. After
arguing for the virtues of representative democracy, the next
thing he proposes is that we should severely limit its powers. His
work *On Liberty* (in fact, published earlier than *On Representative Government*) is concerned with the question of 'the nature
and limits of the power which can be legitimately exercised by
society over the individual' (*On Liberty*, 126). Mill argues that
we should reserve considerable powers for the individual. There

are limits to state intervention, and also limits to the proper use of public opinion as a way of moulding beliefs and behaviour.

How much power should the state have? We have seen that a range of views is possible. At one extreme, the anarchist claims that the state has no justified power at all. This seems equivalent to the view that there is no acceptable limit to the liberty of the individual, or, at least, not a limit that the state may impose. At the other extreme, defenders of absolute government, such as Hobbes, argue that the state has no obligation to pay any regard at all to the liberties of its subjects. It may enforce whatever rules and restrictions it wishes.

Between these two poles, a spectrum of possibilities exists. Finding neither anarchy nor absolutism acceptable, Mill took it to be his task to define his position on this spectrum. Why, as a champion of liberty, did Mill reject anarchy, which many feel is the highest realization of individual liberty? As we saw in Chapter 2, Mill takes the view that if people are given complete freedom then some will surely abuse it, using the absence of government to exploit others. Hence he writes: 'All that makes existence valuable to any one depends on the enforcement of restraints upon the actions of other people' (*On Liberty*, 130). Anarchy means living without the law, and, according to Mill, our lives would then hardly be worth living. Mill takes it for granted that tyranny is no longer to be considered a serious option, and so sets out to determine the correct mix of freedom and authority.

On what grounds may the state interfere to prohibit people from acting as they wish, or force them to act against their wishes? Different societies, Mill observes, have 'solved' this problem in different ways. Some, for example, have prevented the practice of certain religions or even suppressed religion completely. Others have imposed censorship on the press and other media. Many have outlawed certain sexual practices. Homosexual acts between men were illegal until as recently as the 1960s in Great Britain, and while prostitution is not illegal in Britain, it remains against the law for a prostitute to solicit for customers. All these are limitations of people's liberty, carried out through the exercise of state power. But does the state have the right to interfere in people's lives and liberties in any of these ways?

Mill seeks a principle, or set of principles, that will allow us to decide each case on its real merits, rather than abandoning the matter to arbitrary custom and popular morality—Mill's greatest enemy. His answer is both radical and refreshingly simple. Mill's Liberty Principle (cited at the start of this chapter) announces that you may justifiably limit a person's freedom of action only if they threaten harm to another. To many modern readers this principle (also known as the 'Harm Principle') may seem blindingly obvious. But it has not been obvious through most of history. For centuries people have been persecuted for worshipping the wrong god, or for not worshipping at all. But what harm did they do to anyone, or anything, except perhaps to their own immortal souls? Mill's view should not even be obvious to us now. Suppose a friend is falling into drug addiction. May you forcibly interfere to stop her only if she is likely to cause harm to others? This example opens up serious issues regarding both the interpretation and plausibility of Mill's principle. Probably no society, past or present, has ever lived by the principle as Mill intended it to be understood. Indeed, as we shall also see, Mill himself shied away from some of its most unconventional consequences.

Before going any further, however, it is worth returning to one element in the statement of Mill's Liberty Principle. He says that it is to apply to 'any member of a civilized community'. So does he intend to accept restrictions on the liberty of the uncivilized? As a matter of fact, he does. He explicitly states that the principle is meant to apply only to people in 'the maturity of their faculties' (*On Liberty*, 135). Children and 'barbarians' are excluded, for 'Liberty, as a principle, has no application to any state of things anterior to the time when mankind have become capable of being improved through free and equal discussion' (*On Liberty*, 136).

Mill's point here is that liberty is only valuable under certain conditions. If those conditions do not apply, then liberty can do

a great deal of harm. Children should not be free to decide
whether or not to learn to read, and Mill shared the Victorian
view that certain peoples were 'backward' and thus should also
be treated as children. What is important here is not whether
Mill was right or wrong about barbarians, but the condition he
laid down for the application of the Liberty Principle. Liberty is
 valuable as a means to improvement—moral progress. Under
some circumstances liberty will, just as likely, have the opposite
effect, and so progress will have to be effected by some other
means. But Mill is in no doubt that when society is in its maturity—when we have progressed to a civilized level—state
interference in individual action should be regulated by the
Liberty Principle.

An illustration: freedom of thought

One of Mill's most cherished beliefs was that there should be
complete freedom of thought and discussion. He devotes almost
a third of *On Liberty* to these vital freedoms, while accepting
that there should sometimes be limits to what one is permitted to
say in public.

The first thing to note, for Mill, is that the fact a view is
unpopular is no reason at all to silence it: 'If all mankind minus
one were of one opinion, and only one person were of the
contrary opinion, mankind would be no more justified in silencing that one person, than he, if he had the power, would be
justified in silencing mankind' (*On Liberty*, 142). In fact, Mill
argues, we have very good reason to welcome the advocacy even
of unpopular views. To suppress them would be to 'rob the
human race, posterity as well as the existing generation'. How
so? Well, Mill argues that, whether the controversial view is
true, false, or a mix of the two, we will never gain by refusing it
a voice. If we suppress a true view (or one that is partially true)
then we lose the chance to exchange error, whole or partial, for
truth. But if we suppress a false view we lose in a different way:
to challenge, reconsider, and perhaps reaffirm, our true views.
So there is nothing to gain by suppression, whatever the truth of
the view in question.

Is there really harm in suppressing a false view? We must first ask how we can be so sure that it is false. Even if the would-be censor claims to be certain of the truth of the customary opinion, there is quite a gulf, as Mill points out, between *our being certain of* a view, and *the view being certain*. Not to recognize this is to assume infallibility, but history provides enough evidence of how mistaken this assumption is. Many beliefs that were once held as certainties have been considered by later generations not only to be false, but to be absurd. Think, for example, of those people who now claim to hold the once widespread belief that the earth is flat.

More dramatically Mill reminds us of the cases of Socrates and Jesus, the first executed for impiety and immorality, the second for blasphemy. Both were tried by honest judges, acting in good faith. But both perished in societies where the assumption of infallibility led to laws prohibiting the advocacy of views contrary to established traditions. Of course, in western democracies we are unlikely to execute people for their views now. The point, however, is that the moral systems of both Socratic philosophy and Christianity were suppressed because they conflicted with established views 'known for certain' to be true. This illustrates the thought that the human race is capable of monumental error. Never, thinks Mill, have we the right to claim infallibility.

One further example may illustrate and extend Mill's point. The ancient Alexandrian library, one of the treasures of the ancient world, was reputed, at its height, to contain over 700,000 volumes. But in the year AD 640 Alexandria was captured by the Arabs, under the leadership of 'Amr, and this, according to the tale of the much later writer Abulfaragius (apparently a highly unreliable source) is what happened to the library:

John the Grammarian, a famous Peripatetic philosopher, being in Alexandria at the time of its capture, and in high favour with 'Amr begged that he would give him the royal library. 'Amr told him that it was not in his power to grant such a request, but promised to write to the caliph for his consent. Omar, on hearing the request of his general, is said to have replied that if these books contained the same doctrine

as the Koran, they could be of no use, since the Koran contained all
necessary truths; but if they contained anything contrary to that book,
they ought to be destroyed; and therefore, whatever their contents
were, he ordered them to be burnt. Pursuant to this order, they were
distributed among the public baths, of which there was a large number
of the city, where, for six months, they served to supply the fires.
(quoted in *Encyclopedia Britannica*, 11th edn., 1910–11, i–ii. 570)

It is a pity that the Arabs did not have *On Liberty* available to
them, for they would have done well to take pause, and heed
Mill's point that: 'There is the greatest difference between pre-
suming an opinion to be true, because, with every opportunity
for contesting it, it has not been refuted, and assuming its truth
for the purpose of not permitting its refutation' (*On Liberty*,
145).

But before we feel too smug, we should note Rousseau's
comments on the story of the library:

[Omar's] reasoning has been cited by our men of letters as the height of
absurdity; but if Gregory the Great had been in the place of Omar and
the Gospel in the place of the [Koran], the library would still have been
burnt, and it would have been perhaps the finest action of his life.
(*Discourse on the Arts and Sciences*, 26 n.)

The *Discourse on the Arts and Sciences* was written by Rousseau
in 1750, for a competition set by the Academy of Dijon on the
question 'Whether the restoration of the Sciences and the Arts
has had a purifying effect on morals'. Why would book-burning
have been the finest act of Gregory the Great's life? Rousseau
reports that the truth on such matters came to him on the road
between Paris and Vincennes, on the way to visit Diderot, who
had been imprisoned for sedition. He realized, so he says, that
developments in the arts and sciences, so far from aiding human
progress, had caused more unhappiness than happiness, and,
furthermore, had corrupted public morals. Unable to complete
his journey, he sat down and scribbled out a draft of this highly
controversial thesis, with which he won the prize. It is hard to
imagine a view further from Mill's. Rousseau suggests that we
offer up a prayer: 'Almighty God! Thou who holdest in Thy

hand the minds of men, deliver us from the fatal arts and sciences . . . give us back ignorance, innocence, and poverty, which
alone can make us happy and are precious in Thy sight' (*Discourse on the Arts and Sciences*, 27). Beneath Rousseau's rhet-
oric is a very serious objection to Mill's project. Can it be right to
assume that it is always better to know the truth than to remain
in ignorance? Mill's argument appears implicitly to assume that
knowledge will lead to happiness, but why should we believe
that? Just as an individual may sometimes lead a happier life in
blissful ignorance of what his or her acquaintances really think
of them, presumably there are times when society profits too by
ignorance or false belief. Perhaps the truth is too hard to bear, or
will dissolve the bonds of society. This is often said about belief
in God and the afterlife. That is, so the argument goes, the
reason why people should believe is not because there is a God
and an afterlife—there may or may not be—but because unless
these beliefs are widely held society will fall into selfishness and
immorality. Therefore we should not allow the propagation of
atheism, for, if it catches on, society will disintegrate. Whether
or not we accept that argument, it does not take much imagination to come to the conclusion that human beings would have
been better off if we had never discovered certain scientific
truths: those, for example, which led to the development of
nuclear weapons.

   Should we then sometimes oppose freedom of thought? The
argument that we should rests not on the truth of the received
opinion, but on its utility, its importance to society. On this view,
we can have good reason to suppress an opinion even if it is true.
This argument against freedom of thought seems very strong,
but so is Mill's reply. Everything depends on the theory that a
certain view is necessary for social peace, and that its contrary
will be destructive of that peace. But what makes us so sure that,
say, disbelief in God will lead society into dissolution? Or that
knowing about the structure of the atom will lead to more harm
than good? We are just as fallible on that issue as we are on any.
As Mill puts the point:

The usefulness of an opinion is itself matter of opinion: as disputable, as open to discussion, and requiring discussion as much as the opinion itself. There is the same need of an infallible judge of opinions to decide an opinion to be noxious as to decide it to be false. (*On Liberty*, 148)

Indeed, Mill reminds us, Christianity itself was suppressed by the Romans, on the grounds of the harm it would do to the preservation of society.

Still, the position is not quite as clear as Mill makes out. If we cannot know for certain whether believing the truth is more likely to lead to happiness or to harm, then we have no more reason, on this argument, to permit freedom of thought than to ban it. Thus Mill must be making the assumption that, in general at least, believing the truth is a way of achieving happiness.

If that is so, what harm can be done by suppressing a false view? In fact, there are very strong reasons against doing so, Mill argues, even if we could know it to be false. If we do not consider challenges to our opinion, then 'however true it may be, if it is not fully, frequently, and fearlessly discussed, it will be held as a dead dogma, not a living truth' (*On Liberty*, 161). As Mill says, we 'go to sleep at [the] post as soon as there is no enemy in the field' (*On Liberty*, 170). One danger here is that the real meaning of the view might be lost or enfeebled if it is not constantly challenged and defended, and so becomes 'deprived of its vital effect on the character and conduct, the dogma becoming a mere formal profession, inefficacious for good' (*On Liberty*, 181). But perhaps the great danger is that when challenged by a sparkling presentation of the opposite, false, view, the champions of the received truth will be unable to defend themselves. Not only will they look foolish, but the false view may gain a popularity it does not merit, sometimes with disastrous consequences.

This, according to some accounts, is what has happened to evolutionary theory in the United States. Believers in Darwinism, while realizing the theory has some apparent flaws, nevertheless did not take seriously the thought that any intelligent, scientifically trained person could fail to accept the broad truth of evolutionary theory in some form or other. Consequently, when well-organized and skilful religious fundamentalists started packaging and deliberately mixing up sophisticated and plausible objections to Darwinism with their own advocacy of 'creation science'—the literal belief in the Old Testament— the Darwinian establishment was not ready to meet the challenge. And so the creationists developed a following way out of proportion to the scientific merits (nil) of their theory. Many Americans—in certain southern states a majority—still believe that evolutionary theory should not be taught in schools.

Two types of case have been considered so far: where the new view is true and where it is false. In each case, allowing the expression of the view will do good, not harm. There is a third case where this is even more obvious: where there is partial truth on both sides of the issue. This is the most common case of all. The only way in which truth might finally emerge is by allowing full and free discussion of all sides of the issue. So, Mill concludes, in all cases mankind will benefit from the expression of views opposed to the current orthodoxy, and so there is never a case for censorship.

Harm to others

While there is never a case for censorship, Mill accepts that there are occasions on which it is right to limit freedom of expression. An example he suggests is this:

An opinion that corn-dealers are starvers of the poor, or that private property is robbery, ought to be unmolested when simply circulated through the press, but may justly incur punishment when delivered orally to an excited mob assembled before the house of a corn-dealer, or when handed about among the same mob in the form of a placard. (*On Liberty*, 184)

The fact that freedom of expression, in this case, is almost certain to lead to harm to others is enough, Mill thinks, to bring it within the scope of activities that can properly be regulated by governments.

Now we have seen that, according to Mill, we may interfere with the liberty of an adult only to prevent harm, or threat of harm, to others. In severe cases, we can, with justification, use the force of law, while in other cases social pressure is the more appropriate restraint. But what does Mill mean by 'harm'? Suppose that a group of people want to set up a new religion, and worship in private. Mill's view is that as long as they do not attempt to coerce anyone into membership, then the rest of society has no business interfering. Why not? Because this behaviour does no harm to anyone else. But immediately the zealot of another, established, religion will object: of course they are causing me harm. First, their heathen behaviour causes me great offence and anguish. Second, they are thwarting my plans to convert the whole world to my religion. It is simply not true that they do no harm.

This objection can be put another way. We can divide actions into two classes: purely self-regarding actions and other-regarding actions. Other-regarding actions affect or involve at least one other person. Purely self-regarding actions concern only the agent, or if they do involve others it is with their free consent. Mill's Liberty Principle, then, comes down to the claim that, while we may regulate and supervise other-regarding actions, we have no business interfering in self-regarding actions. So far so good. But now Mill's critic asks for an example of a purely self-regarding action to fall into this protected realm. And, pretty much whatever we offer, the critic will be able to find some third party affected by the action. For example, whether I decide to wear black shoes or brown shoes today looks like a self-regarding action, if any action is. But then the makers of brown shoe-polish would clearly prefer me to wear brown shoes. Furthermore, my friends of highly refined sensibilities might suffer distress and embarrassment on my behalf if it turns out I am wearing the wrong shoes for the occasion. So even a trivial example like this seems to turn out to be other-regarding. If we try very hard we might find some examples of purely self-regarding action. For example, if I live alone it is perhaps hard to see how my decision whether to sleep on my front or my back could affect anyone else (although the pillow-making industry may have an opinion, as may the health service if I am more likely to avoid back pain one way or another). But if we have to resort to such examples then Mill is lost. If we interpret the Liberty Principle as giving the individual freedom, but only over self-regarding actions understood this way, then it is left without a serious range of application.

Thus it is clear that Mill could not have intended to be understood in this manner. He was determined that the sphere of liberty was not to be left to the 'likings and dislikings' of society. So it is obvious that he must distinguish between those actions which society, or its members, dislike, or find annoying or offensive, and those actions which cause *harm*. Mere offence, or dislike, for Mill, is no harm. So what did Mill mean by harm?

Mill often uses the terminology of 'interests' in his statements of the Liberty Principle. So, for example, he says that his view authorizes 'the subjection of individual spontaneity to external control, only in respect to those actions of each, which concern the interest of other people' (*On Liberty*, 136). Harm, then, is sometimes read as 'damage to interests'. Understood in this way, the Liberty Principle essentially reads 'act as you like, so long as you do not harm the interests of another person'.

This gives us some help, but unfortunately no one seems to have been able to give an adequate definition of 'interests' in this sense. The term is most commonly used in connection with financial interests. If someone has a financial interest in a scheme, then they stand to gain or lose money depending on the success of that venture. However, Mill was not exclusively concerned with people's financial well-being, and so we must add that individuals have, at least, an interest in their personal safety and security. Therefore murder, assault, rape, theft, and fraud would all count as actions which harm the interests of the person attacked or defrauded. The Liberty Principle then would, quite rightly, allow us to restrict individuals' freedom of action to prevent them carrying out such acts.

But we must be careful here. Mill does not say that society may rightly interfere with someone's freedom of action whenever he or she threatens to harm your interests. We have already seen an example which illustrates this. My decision to wear black shoes may, in some small way, harm the interests of the brown

shoe-polish manufacturers, but Mill gives them no right to intervene. In fact Mill himself points out many much more serious
examples of this: 'Whoever succeeds in an overcrowded profession, or in a competitive examination; whoever is preferred to
another in any contest for an object which both desire, reaps
benefit from the loss of others, from their wasted exertion and
their disappointment' (*On Liberty*, 227). Mill intends that none
of these forms of competition will be ruled out by the Liberty
Principle, despite the fact that they are capable of doing severe
harm to the interests of the losers. Clearly, then, we have not yet
got to the bottom of the Liberty Principle. In Mill's view, harming another's interests is not enough (not a sufficient condition)
to justify constraint. Indeed, we will later see reason to question
whether Mill even thinks it is a necessary condition. To make
further progress we must broaden our view.

Justifying the Liberty Principle

[Each person] should be bound to observe a certain line of
conduct towards the rest. This conduct consists . . . in not
injuring the interests of one another; or rather certain interests which, either by express legal provision or by tacit
understanding, ought to be considered as rights.

(*On Liberty*, 205)

Liberty, rights, and utility

In the passage just quoted Mill appeals to a new idea: interests
which ought to be considered as rights, or 'rights-based interests'. Perhaps this can help us understand the Liberty Principle.
For example, while there are laws which enforce my right to
keep my property against your attempts to take it by force, I
have no similar right to be protected against economic competition. Indeed there are many interests which do not normally
seem to give rise to claims of right. When my rich aunt strikes me
out of her will, my interests may suffer, but she does not infringe
my rights.

This may seem a promising approach, but there are two serious matters to consider. First, how do we know what rights we have? Suppose I claim a right for my business to be protected against competitors. What can Mill say to show me that I have no such right? Second, it is very odd to see Mill using the concept of rights at such a crucial point in the argument. For early in the essay he writes (or should we say boasts?): 'It is proper to state that I forego any advantage which could be derived to my argument from the idea of abstract right, as a thing independent of utility' (*On Liberty*, 136). But how is this consistent with the appeal to the idea of 'rights-based interest'? This statement of intent apparently contradicts the explicit appeal to rights in the passage just noted.

Perhaps it will be thought that the most charitable thing to do would be simply to ignore Mill's statement that he will refrain from appeal to the notion of an 'abstract right'. But this would not really do. Mill has very good reasons for making this statement, as we can see if we look, for a moment, at the idea of a right.

Within liberal circles it is often taken as a fundamental axiom that people have certain basic rights. Normally included are the right to life, free speech, free assembly, and freedom of movement, together with rights to vote and stand for office. Some theorists, although not all, add rights to a decent standard of living (shelter, food, and health-care). Most often these rights would now be collected together under the name of 'human rights' or 'universal human rights'. In the past they would have been called 'the rights of man' or 'natural rights'. Anything—particularly any action by a government—that violates a human or natural right is morally wrong, and should be remedied. It is a familiar and comforting notion that we all have rights, and that these must be respected. Countries which ignore the rights of their citizens are often the subject of intense international criticism.

Nevertheless, the idea of a natural right is highly problematic. In fact, one of the features which makes a theory of natural rights initially so attractive turns out to be one of its main weaknesses. That is, the theory claims that natural rights are basic, fundamental, or axiomatic: they are the ultimate ground of all further decisions. This is attractive because it makes the theory seem so rigorous and principled. But the disadvantage is that we are left with nothing more fundamental to say in defence of these rights. Suppose an opponent doubts that there are any natural rights. How can we reply? Short of saying that the opponent must be insincere or confused, there seems nowhere left to turn. Using the terminology of natural rights may be a successful tactic in disputes between those who agree that there are such things, but otherwise it seems to leave us dangling and exposed.

A further, related, difficulty is that, if natural rights have a fundamental status, and so are not arrived at on the basis of some other argument, how do we know what rights we have? This difficulty was exploited by Bentham, who pointed out that if it is 'self-evident' that people have natural rights, why do different theorists have different ideas about what those rights should be? There are major inconsistencies between the accounts given by different political philosophers. This raises not only the question of how to adjudicate between different accounts, but also leads to the troubling thought that a statement of what natural rights we have often seems little more than one person's opinion.

Bentham's best-known attack on the idea of natural rights starts with the observation that a right seems to be a legal idea. We think of rights and duties as being distributed by laws. The laws give you rights to vote, to receive welfare benefits, to protection by the police, and so on. In Bentham's view this is all there is to a right: 'Right is with me the child of law . . . A natural right is a son that never had a father' (*Anarchical Fallacies*, 73). If this is correct then it makes the idea of a natural right—a right independent of the law of the land—'nonsense on stilts' (*Anarchical Fallacies*, 53). There just cannot be such a thing.

Of course not everyone will accept Bentham's argument. Theorists like Locke simply deny Bentham's major assumption: that rights can only be created by legal decree. But Mill favoured Bentham's view, and was very suspicious of the idea of natural rights. This is what he means by saying that he intends to make no use of the idea of abstract right. But how, then, can he use the notion of rights-based interests? Does he mean 'those interests *already respected* by the law as rights'? A moment's thought is enough to dismiss this idea. After all, Mill saw himself as putting forward a doctrine with radical, reforming consequences, critical of the current state of affairs. To accept the present system of rights would be to put oneself back into the hands of custom and prejudice, and this is precisely what Mill wanted to avoid.

If Mill can neither accept natural rights nor rely on conventional rights, then what is left for him? The answer lies in how he completes the passage where he declares his opposition to abstract rights, partially cited above. After saying that he will make no use of the idea of abstract right, as a 'thing independent of utility', he adds: 'I regard utility as the ultimate appeal on all ethical questions; but it must be utility in the largest sense, grounded on the permanent interests of a man as a progressive being' (*On Liberty*, 136).

Mill intends to defend a view of rights which makes them not natural or fundamental, nor a simple echo of whatever happen to be the laws of the land, but derived from the theory of utilitarianism. We took a preliminary look at utilitarian theory in Chapter 2, and we also saw the 'indirect utilitarian' argument used to justify rights. It is worth, briefly, going over the main lines again, before showing how this theory can illuminate Mill's doctrine of liberty.

Mill explains and defends the utilitarian system in his work *Utilitarianism*. As he defines it, utilitarianism is the theory which: 'holds that actions are right in proportion as they tend to promote happiness, wrong as they tend to produce the reverse of happiness. By happiness is intended pleasure and the absence of pain; by unhappiness pain and the privation of pleasure' (*Utilitarianism*, 257). Broadly we might summarize the view as saying that utilitarianism requires us to maximize the sum total of happiness or pleasure in the world. (This will not quite do as a summary of Mill's view, as he claims that some pleasures—of the intellect, for example—are qualitatively more valuable than other more bodily pleasures. But we can ignore this complication.)

How can we connect the idea of a right with utility? This connection is made explicit in *Utilitarianism*: 'To have a right, then, is, I conceive, to have something which society ought to defend me in the possession of. If the objector goes on to ask, why it ought? I can give him no other reason than general utility' (*Utilitarianism*, 309).

In brief, the basic idea is to lay out a system of rights which will maximize the general happiness. That is, we grant people certain rights so that more happiness can be achieved within the structure of those rights than would be possible under any alternative system. Perhaps the best way of thinking about this is to put yourself in the position of a utilitarian legislator. Suppose you are responsible for setting out the legal system, and you want to set it up in such a way that laws maximize happiness. Naïvely, it might be thought that under such circumstances you should make just one law: 'Act to maximize happiness.' But this is not so obvious.

We must remember a distinction made in Chapter 2 between direct and indirect utilitarianism. A direct utilitarian believes that an individual should perform an action whenever that action will lead to more happiness than any available alternative. On this view, we saw, it is sometimes said that it is acceptable to punish someone who is innocent if that will placate an angry mob and defuse a potentially disastrous situation. The direct utilitarian must weigh up the distress to the innocent victim, the likelihood that the deception will become public, the likely effects of allowing the mob to try to find the guilty party, and any other factors that might affect the balance of pain and pleasure that will flow from the situation. If the sums say that we will maximize happiness by punishing the innocent, then this is what we should do.

The indirect utilitarian follows a more subtle strategy. On this view, it is accepted that the goal of law and morality is that happiness should be maximized, but it is claimed that this goal will not be achieved by allowing individuals to seek to maximize happiness themselves. Consider the last example. Suppose it is true that utility is sometimes advanced by making some people scapegoats. Suppose, too, that everyone knows this. Everyone, then, realizes that there is a possibility that they will be picked on and victimized. Knowing this is likely to cause an atmosphere of anxiety and gloom. The possibility of scapegoating would be detrimental to the general happiness. Therefore the indirect utilitarian might calculate that the general happiness will best be served by ensuring that no one is punished unless they are proved guilty. Although there might be a few, very special, occasions when we might profit from scapegoating, in the long term we do much better in utilitarian terms by giving everyone immunity—a right—against victimization. This, then, is a sketch of how to derive a utilitarian theory of rights. While it is true that, in the short term, we might do better to violate a right, when we take long-term effects into account utilitarianism suggests that rights are to be obeyed.

Indeed indirect utilitarianism can be taken one step further, although Mill did not do this himself. Henry Sidgwick (1838–1900), the most thoughtful and sophisticated of the early utilitarians, suggested that, while utilitarianism is the correct moral theory, it might sometimes be better if this were kept secret. Perhaps most people should be given some very straightforward, simple maxims to follow: do not lie, do not murder, do not cheat, and so on. His reason for this is that, should ordinary people know the truth of utilitarianism, they would be likely to attempt to calculate in direct utilitarian terms. Not only would this be a bad thing for the reasons already given; most people would also make poor calculations through lack of care, or ability, or through the magnification of their own interests. (Compare Hume on our powers of reasoning in Chapter 2.) It is much better, thought Sidgwick, to keep utilitarianism as an esoteric doctrine, revealed only to the enlightened élite. (This view has been called 'government house utilitarianism' by its opponents. It treats citizens in the patronizing fashion that European powers treated their colonial subjects in the days of empire.)

As I said, Mill did not go this far, and, it is true, his own indirect utilitarianism is implicit in his view rather than explicitly stated. But once we have appreciated the idea of indirect utilitarianism, we have seen how a utilitarian theory of rights is possible. This, then, will inform the utilitarian legislator. The insight of indirect utilitarianism is to note that, instead of setting out a single law—maximize happiness—the utilitarian legislator might do much better, in terms of the general happiness, to set out a larger body of law, which guarantees and respects secure rights of individuals. Indeed, it may well be that Bentham and Mill thought of themselves as primarily addressing law-makers, rather than the public. After all, Bentham's major book on the topic is called *An Introduction to the Principles of Morals and Legislation*.

And now we can begin to see how the pieces fit together. According to Mill, the greatest happiness will be achieved by giving people a private sphere of interests where no intervention is permitted, while allowing a public sphere where intervention is possible, but only on utilitarian grounds.

How does this solve the question of where to draw the line between the private and public spheres? Mill himself is not explicit, but there is a ready answer. First we acknowledge that the private sphere is identified with the sphere of 'rights-based interests'. Then we raise the difficult question of what makes the difference between rights-based interests (my interest in personal safety) and other interests (my interest in not being struck out of my aunt's will)? The answer to this question is given by the theory of utilitarianism. It will serve the general happiness if we pass a law which protects people's interests in walking down the street free from attack, but it will diminish general happiness if we set out restrictions about whether aunts can or cannot strike their nephews out of their wills.

Other examples might help to make this clearer. As we saw in detail, Mill wants to protect freedom of thought. Why? Because this is most likely to achieve the truth, and (Mill implies) knowledge of the truth increases happiness. So we are assumed to have a rights-based interest in freedom of thought. But Mill does not want to protect an individual's business against fair competition. Why not? Because according to Mill the utilitarian advantages of free trade mean that no other system can advance happiness to the same extent. (The feudal system, for example, in which individuals purchased licences to be the monopoly supplier of a particular good, led to enormous inefficiencies.) Therefore people are to be given rights to compete in business, not rights which protect their financial interests against competition. The position is somewhat complex, because, of course, Mill accepts that we have to have certain rights in our property which protects it from theft and fraud. But indirect utilitarianism, in Mill's view, does not extend to protection against economic competition.

This utilitarian defence of the Liberty Principle seems very plausible. The utilitarian theory of rights supplies exactly what is missing: a doctrine of rights which does not rest on the false foundation of natural rights theory, nor on the shifting sands of convention. It appears to allow us to make perfect sense of Mill's proposal. Yet the idea that a utilitarian defence can be given of Mill's Liberty Principle has met with strong criticism. And it is not difficult to find examples where utility and liberty seem to conflict. As one critic has said: 'A drug addict who has success-fully kicked the habit is thoroughly justified on utilitarian grounds in stopping some incautious young experimenter from taking the first steps down a road which may prove to have no turning' (R. P. Wolff, *The Poverty of Liberalism*, 29). In other words, utilitarianism would seem to encourage exactly the type of paternalistic intervention that the Liberty Principle ex-pressly rules out: remember that the Liberty Principle does not permit anyone to interfere with another even for their own good. So, it is thought, liberal rights cannot be justified in utili-tarian terms.

This objection brings out that even if it is possible to construct a utilitarian theory of rights, it does not yet follow that the utilitarian theory would be a liberal theory. Why should we think that, in the long term, there would be more happiness in Mill's society than in the society, governed by customary morality, that he sought to replace? Or in some other society in which enlightened, experienced elders are given the right to direct the lives of its younger members?

To appreciate Mill's response to this problem we need to take yet another look at the wording of the passage in *On Liberty* where Mill declares his allegiance to utility: 'I regard utility as the ultimate appeal on all ethical questions; but it must be utility in the largest sense, grounded on the permanent interests of a man as a progressive being' (*On Liberty*, 136). 'Utility in the largest sense' presumably means that we should include all sorts of pleasures and forms of happiness—intellectual and emotional as well as bodily—in the calculation. But why does he add 'grounded on the permanent interests of a man as a progressive being'? There are some further aspects of Mill's view that we will have to understand before everything falls into place.

Individuality and progress

The key to solving this problem lies in chapter 3 of *On Liberty*, entitled 'On Individuality, as one of the Elements of Well-being'. It is here that Mill tries to show that the general happiness will be best advanced by assigning people a large private sphere of rights to non-interference. In this chapter Mill argues that freedom is essential to originality and individuality of character. And, Mill claims, 'the free development of individuality is one of the leading essentials of well-being' (*On Liberty*, 185). Here Mill wants to make several points, and it may be helpful to set them in the context of a criticism made by one of Mill's earliest and more impressive critics, James Fitzjames Stephen (1829–94), in his book *Liberty, Equality, Fraternity*, first published in 1873.

Stephen argued that is it absurd to think that liberty is always good in itself. Rather, he claims, it is like fire. It would be irrational to ask whether fire is good in itself; it all depends on the purpose to which it is put. And Stephen has chosen his analogy well. Controlled fire has given us many of our most important technological achievements—the internal combustion engine, for example—but uncontrolled fire is a great fear and, often, a great disaster. This, supposes Stephen, is the case for liberty too.

Mill is prepared to accept that liberty does not always lead to 'improvement'. But he stresses, 'the only unfailing and permanent source of improvement is liberty' (*On Liberty*, 200). Advancing liberty contributes much more to human happiness than any other possible competing policy might. Mill has several reasons for saying this.

First, he argues that, even though people do make mistakes, individuals are still *more likely* to be right about what would make them happy than anyone else. After all, they pay more attention to the issue, and give it more thought than anyone else is likely to. Nevertheless, Mill recognizes that people could exercise liberty far more than they do at present, for he notes that people commonly abuse this power, and before acting ask: 'what is suitable to my position? what is usually done by persons of my station and pecuniary circumstances? or (worse still) what is usually done by persons of a station and circumstances superior to mine?' (*On Liberty*, 190). Independence of judgement, Mill claims, will surely lead to superior consequences. But he does not mean that no one should ever try to influence other people's behaviour. On the contrary, he is keen to emphasize that each of us has a duty to try to convince others of their mistakes, if we feel that they are embarking on foolish or damaging courses of action. We may reason and plead with people. But this is all we may do. Force is out of the question:

Considerations to aid [another's] judgment, exhortations to strengthen his will, may be offered to him, even obtruded on him, by others: but he himself is the final judge. All errors which he is likely to commit against advice and warning are far outweighed by the evil of allowing others to constrain him to what they deem his good. (*On Liberty*, 207)

Such measures must, in Mill's view, nevertheless fall short of concerted social pressure, although how in practice we can draw this distinction he does not make clear. But overall Mill's position is that leaving people to themselves will tend to make them happier than if we insist that they follow society's recommendations.

A second reason for liberty is that it will not only lead to better decisions in the long run, but also that the exercise of freedom of choice is itself vital to the full development of human nature. Those who are slaves to custom, Mill suggests, will never develop into rounded, flourishing individuals; not necessarily because they will be unhappy, but because they will fail to develop one of their most distinctively human capacities, the capacity for choice.

Mill's third—and most important—reason for championing liberty and individuality is this:

> As it is useful that while mankind are imperfect there should be different opinions, so it is that there should be different experiments of living; that free scope should be given to varieties of character, short of injury to others; and that the worth of different modes of life should be proved practically. . . . [This is] quite the chief ingredient of individual and social progress. (*On Liberty*, 185)

Thus, Mill claims: 'In proportion to the development of his individuality, each person becomes more valuable to himself, and is therefore capable of being more valuable to others' (*On Liberty*, 192). Mill's idea is that human progress is best served by giving individuals the licence to engage in 'experiments of living'. Those who take up this opportunity may well conduct 'successful' experiments, and so arrive at styles of life which others can choose to follow. In other words, role models can show others how to live (or not to live) their own lives, and from these role models the less creative can take up various new possibilities for themselves.

It is at this point that we see Mill at perhaps his most optimistic, and we see the point of his appeal to 'utility in the largest sense, grounded on the permanent interests of a man as a progressive being'. Mill's view is that mankind is progressive, in the sense that human beings are capable of learning from experience, to the long-term benefit of all. Through the experiments of some individuals we may learn things of great value, for the permanent benefit of mankind. Those of us too timid to conduct experiments of our own may nevertheless learn from the more adventurous. It is by observing, and trying out, the various possibilities that we are presented with that mankind will be able to learn what sorts of lives will lead to genuine human flourishing. Liberty is vital as a condition of experimentation. This, it seems, is the primary reason why Mill is convinced that liberty will—in the long run—secure the greatest possible happiness for human kind.

Is Mill too optimistic? That was certainly the opinion of James Fitzjames Stephen. His immediate criticism is that Mill was wrong to think that giving people liberty is likely to lead to vigorous experimentation. Freedom from the interference of others is just as likely to lead to idleness, and lack of interest in life. But a deeper point can also be made, one far more threatening to Mill's project.

In the interpretation of Mill I have presented, the great weight of his position comes down on his assumption that human beings are progressive, capable of learning from experience. Does the experience of the twentieth century give the lie to this view? If so, then the heart drops out of Mill's position. Humankind keeps on repeating its mistakes. If people will not learn from others' experience, then we lose Mill's reason for encouraging experiments in living. What is the point of other people demonstrating new lifestyles to us, if we are not prepared to learn? Without some such defence of experiments of living, there is far less justification for individuality and liberty, on the arguments Mill gives. Indeed some have said that human beings, generally, are in the state Mill reserved for 'children and barbarians': incapable of being improved by free and equal discussion. And, as Mill himself argues, such people are not fit recipients of liberty, at least, not according to the utilitarian calculus. Perhaps this pessimism about the possibility of human improvement is a great exaggeration. But if the truth lies somewhere in the middle, if humans are less capable of improvement than Mill imagines, the utilitarian case for liberty is correspondingly weakened. Progress is the cornerstone of Mill's doctrine.

Liberty as an intrinsic good

Could it be that Mill was wrong to attempt to defend the Liberty Principle in utilitarian terms? In effect Mill has presented liberty as *instrumentally* valuable: it is valuable as a way of achieving the greatest possible happiness for society. But perhaps he should have argued that liberty is intrinsically good, good in itself. If we take such a view, as many contemporary liberals claim to, then we avoid the problem that maximizing happiness perhaps requires a non-liberal society. Liberty is valuable, whatever its consequences.

Some will object that there are no intrinsic goods: everything is valued for something else, rather than for itself. But note that even Mill must accept that there is at least one intrinsic good: happiness. Utilitarians claim that happiness is the only intrinsic good. Everything must be justified in terms of its contribution to the total sum of happiness. But then, why shouldn't we say that there are *two* (or more) intrinsic goods, happiness and liberty? In fact, some commentators have been tempted to say that this is Mill's real view, even though he denied it!

Mill would reject this interpretation of his views. He is clear that liberty is good primarily as a means to improvement, and where it fails to have that effect—in the case of children and barbarians—there is no case for liberty. Liberty is intrinsically good only when it adds to our happiness, but then it is 'part of happiness' rather than an independent value. Furthermore, unconstrained liberty would lead to anarchy. Utilitarianism provides an account of what liberties we should have, and which we should not have. For example, Mill argues that we should be free to compete in trade, but not free to use another's property without their consent. Thus his position allows us to set out limits to liberty, while paying it great respect.

This is not a conclusive argument for Mill's approach. It is not true that only utilitarianism can set out restrictions to liberty:

perhaps liberty can be restricted for the sake of liberty, or fairness. And there are other ways of defending liberty without relying on utilitarianism (we will see John Rawls's non-utilitarian approach in the next chapter). Thus Mill's argument is only one way of trying to defend liberalism. Yet the Liberty Principle gives us a reasonable, if problematic, statement of a liberal political philosophy. Is it one we should accept? Not everyone thinks so.

Problems with liberalism

> Euthanasia or the killing of another at his own request, suicide, attempted suicide and suicide pacts, duelling, abortion, incest between brother and sister, are all acts which can be done in private and without offence to others and need not involve the corruption or exploitation of others.

> (Lord Devlin, 'Morals and the Criminal Law', 7)

Poison, drunkenness, and indecency

What would life be like if we tried to regulate society according to the Liberty Principle? As I mentioned early on in this chapter, Mill himself falls short of endorsing some of the most shocking implications of his view. In his final chapter Mill sets out some of the 'obvious limitations' of the Liberty Principle. One limitation concerns certain restrictions on liberty that are justifiable to prevent crime. So, for example, Mill argues that if the only reason why people bought poison was to commit murder, then society would be entirely justified in banning its production and sale. The fact is, however, that most poisons have other functions too, and so Mill recommends that the law should require chemists to keep a register, recording full details of sales, including the name of the purchaser, and their declared purpose. Accordingly if someone is later found poisoned, the police will already have a list of prime suspects. Strictly, a purchaser, with innocent intent, might complain that this arrangement is intrusive, and in violation of personal liberty. But Mill's view is that the violation is trivial in the light of the benefits of the system, and so this is an obvious exception to the generality of the Liberty Principle.

Another exception is that, while drunkenness, ordinarily, is no crime, anyone who has been convicted of violence to others when drunk should, according to Mill, be prohibited from drinking. Here, for Mill, the danger of harm outweighs an individual's right to drink alcohol.

Although certain liberals might worry that these cases—particularly the latter one—are overly restrictive of human liberty, Mill's point is that restrictions are justified to ward off serious harm, even if that harm is a fairly remote possibility. A further example, however, raises much more serious issues of principle:

there are many acts which, being directly injurious only to the agents themselves, ought not to be legally interdicted, but which, if done publicly, are a violation of good manners, and coming thus within the category of offences against others, may rightly be prohibited. Of this kind are offences against decency; on which it is unnecessary to dwell, the rather as they are only connected indirectly with our subject, the objection to publicity being equally strong in the case of many actions not in themselves condemnable, nor supposed to be. (*On Liberty*, 230–1)

Mill's prose, on this delicate subject, does not have its usual clarity, but the intention of the passage is clear. Certain actions—sexual intercourse between husband and wife, for example—would be condemned by no moral code if performed in private, but would be acceptable to very few people (and certainly not to Mill) if performed publicly.

But how can Mill make this view consistent with the Liberty Principle? What harm does 'public indecency' do? After all, Mill insists that mere offence is no harm. Here Mill, without being explicit, seems to allow customary morality to override his adherence to the Liberty Principle. Few, perhaps, would criticize his choice of policy. But it is hard to see how he can render this consistent with his other views: indeed, he appears to make no serious attempt to do so.

Once we begin to consider examples of this kind we begin to

understand that following Mill's 'one simple principle' would lead to a society of a kind never seen before, and, perhaps, one which we would never wish to see. Some of the apparent inconsistencies in the liberal position were brought out very well by Lord Justice Devlin, in his essay 'Morals and the Criminal Law', published partly as a response to the Wolfenden Report of 1957, which recommended the decriminalization of homosexual acts between consenting adults. The Wolfenden Report also argued that prostitution should not be made illegal. These recommendations seem fully in accord with the Liberty Principle. Yet, as Devlin observes, many of the laws of contemporary societies are very hard to defend in terms of the Liberty Principle. Some examples are laws against duelling, incest between siblings, and euthanasia.

To make his point, Devlin focuses on the question of prostitution. Why is the liberal prepared to permit it to exist? The standard answer might be that it is simply none of the law's business: prostitution is a matter of concern only for the prostitute and the customer. But then, asks Devlin:

If prostitution is . . . not the law's business, what concern has the law with the ponce or the brothel-keeper . . . ? The Report recommends that the laws which make these activities criminal offences should be maintained . . . and brings them . . . under the head of exploitation. . . . But in general a ponce exploits a prostitute no more than an impresario exploits an actress. ('Morals and the Criminal Law', 12)

Devlin's own view is that we can understand these matters only by assuming that society holds certain moral principles, which it enforces through the criminal law. If anyone breaks these principles they are thought of as offending society as a whole.

While Mill would certainly deny Devlin's claim that the law ought always to uphold customary morality, there is no doubt that he would have felt uncomfortable if faced with Devlin's examples. This is not to say that liberals like Mill could never find grounds for objecting to euthanasia or brothel-keeping. The real question is that, if the Liberty Principle is intended as seriously as Mill suggests, why should the liberal be concerned if it comes into conflict with customary morality? Mill's pretended adherence to 'one simple principle' does not reflect how complicated his beliefs really are.

Marxist objections to liberalism

Criticism of a quite different sort comes from the Marxist tradition. Marx's own writings on this topic appear most famously in his early essay 'On the Jewish Question', published in 1844, when Marx was 26. In 1816, laws were passed in Prussia which granted Jews far inferior rights to those of Christians. Marx's own father, Heinrich, for example, converted to Christianity the year after the anti-Jewish laws made it impossible for him to remain both a lawyer and a Jew. The Rhenish parliament had voted for Jewish emancipation in 1843, but the king vetoed the proposed legislation. Hence the Jewish Question was a matter of intense debate among liberals and intellectuals in Prussia.

'On the Jewish Question' was written in response to Marx's friend and colleague Bruno Bauer, who had written against Jewish emancipation from an atheist perspective. Bauer's position was that religion stood in the way of both Christians and Jews. If the people of Germany were to gain emancipation then both the state and its citizens had to be emancipated from religion. Religion had to be abolished.

Marx claims to disagree with Bauer, although what he really does is to set Bauer's remarks in a deeper, more theoretical context. According to Marx, Bauer overlooks a crucial distinction: between political emancipation and human emancipation. This goes hand in hand with a failure to recognize the distinction between what Marx calls 'the state' and 'civil society'.

The demand for political emancipation is the demand for equal rights. In the context of religious emancipation, the emancipated state is one whose laws contain no religious barriers or privileges. For Marx, the USA was an example in which political emancipation was nearly complete. The laws of most of the American states, even in 1844, took people to be equals irrespective of their religion. Yet discrimination can exist at another level. Even if the laws of the state are 'religion-blind', individuals can remain full of religious bigotry and hatred. In consequence, members of some religions suffer discrimination in employment, education, and other areas. In the private world of day-to-day activity, of economic life—civil society—discrimination exists even in a politically emancipated state. Thus, Marx asserts, 'a state can liberate itself from a limitation without man himself being truly free of it' ('On the Jewish Question', 44). Political emancipation is not human emancipation.

This sets the scene for Marx's critique of liberalism. Liberalism seeks a regime of rights to equality, liberty, security, and property: political emancipation. Yet not only does the possession of such rights fall short of human emancipation; liberal rights are actually an obstacle to it. For liberal rights are egoistic rights of separation: rights which, according to Marx, encourage each individual to view others as limitations to his or her freedom. Marx's idea is that the genuinely emancipated society is one in which individuals see themselves, and act, as fully co-operating members of a community of equals. Liberalism parodies this by setting out, at the level of the state, a sham community of 'equal' citizens, which cloaks the egoistic day-to-day activity of competition between unequals in civil society, where man 'treats other men as means, degrades himself to a means, and becomes the plaything of alien powers' ('On the Jewish Question', 46). The rights granted to the citizen reinforce the egoism and antagonism of civil society.

For Marx political emancipation—liberalism—is a great advance over the hierarchical, discriminatory state that preceded it. But it is a long way from his ideal, a communist society in which emancipation extends all the way down to civil society. This change, of course, Marx believes can only be accomplished by revolutionary action. Liberalism, by contrast, appears to Marx to be a shallow, superficial doctrine.

Communitarianism and liberalism

Is Marx right? Few theorists now have any confidence that Marx has given us much understanding of what he really means by human emancipation, or how it is to be achieved. However, the underlying point of his critique has been taken up in a quite different way by certain contemporary critics of liberalism, who call themselves not communists but communitarians. Communitarians share Marx's opposition to what they see as the atomism or individualism of liberalism. But, unlike Marx, they see the remedy for this not in some imagined community of the future, but in the culture and traditions of existing society.

Liberalism, it is said by communitarians, conceives of people as isolated individuals who, in their own little protected sphere, pursue their own good in what they take to be their own way. Liberal individuals see themselves as having no special attachment to the customs, culture, traditions, and conventions of their own societies. Communitarians argue, in response, that we are thoroughly social beings, and that our identities and self-understandings are bound up with the communities in which we are placed. If we did not find ourselves in our particular, local, social settings, with our commitments and allegiances, we would, quite literally, be different people. Mill, himself, in *Utilitarianism* pays lip-service to this view, suggesting that:

The social state is at once so natural, so necessary, and so habitual to man, that, except in some unusual circumstances or by an effort of voluntary abstraction, he never conceives himself otherwise than as a member of a body; and this association is riveted more and more, as mankind are further removed from the state of savage independence. Any condition, therefore, which is essential to a state of society, becomes more and more an inseparable part of every person's conception of the state of things which he is born into, and which is the destiny of a human being. (*Utilitarianism*, 284–5)

Yet communitarians would charge that Mill has not understood the significance of his own words. Only in the contrary, isolated individualist, view, does liberty seem so valuable. For Mill, liberty allows us to throw off the crushing weight of the bonds of custom and conformity. But, the communitarian argues, not only does this presuppose a false view of human nature (that it is *possible* for us to throw off these 'bonds'); it also has most dangerous consequences. By denying the importance of our community we set out on a path which will lead to individual alienation, and, ultimately, the dislocation of society. To over-come this we must acknowledge the importance of customary morality—the bond which holds society together. We must also acknowledge that no one can expect to be given the right to do anything which will seriously undermine that morality. Of course, we need not see customary morality as static and un-changing—there can surely be disputes about what it is. But the room for moral reform is constrained by the customs and traditions of one's society.

A likely reply to the communitarians is that they are propos-ing a highly repressive form of society which gives little place to individual freedom or liberty. But communitarians also argue that liberals are mistaken about the nature of real liberty. Liber-als assume a 'negative' definition of liberty: one is free to the extent that one is able to make one's own choices about how to live. But, communitarians argue, this is a crude, and indeed false, view. You do not make people free by leaving them alone. On the contrary, it is necessary to bring people to a position where they can make the *right* choices about how to live: the choices that the rational person would make.

On this alternative view of 'positive liberty', thorough socialization is a preliminary to the development of freedom, and this will inevitably involve education about one's 'real inter-ests'. But no one has an interest in anything that undermines their society, and with it their identity. And so, it is said, it follows that your (positive) freedom is in no way limited if you are not permitted to engage in actions which compromise impor-tant parts of customary morality. This is similar to Rousseau's view, discussed in Chapter 3, that obedience to the general will advances, rather than restricts, an individual's liberty.

Mill and the communitarian will view each other's doctrine of liberty with mutual suspicion. If Mill's negative definition leads to isolation and alienation, then the communitarian's positive definition leads to repression in the name of freedom. But the dispute between Mill and the communitarian really seems to come to this: which would be a happier society—one that follows a (modified) form of the Liberty Principle, or one that follows a (modified) form of the customs and traditions of society? In fact we can see that the views might even meet in the middle: perhaps a compromise between the two will be best of all. (We will look at a similar debate in more detail in the final chapter.)

Conclusion

It is, I think, fair to say that Mill was right to value (negative) liberty, and to believe that a liberal society is likely to be happier than many illiberal ones. But, as we have seen, his own defence of liberty rests very heavily on the idea that human beings are capable of making moral progress. That, for Mill, was an article of faith. But if he was wrong it may well be that a communitarian society would be preferable to a liberal one on utilitarian grounds: perhaps experiments in living will do more harm than good if no one will learn from them. Defenders of liberty, then, must either show that people are capable of making moral progress, or find an alternative foundation for their view.

I cannot resist ending this chapter with an anecdote. In the mid-1980s I met a Spanish lawyer who had studied law and philosophy during the highly autocratic Franco era. I asked him whether it had been possible to study political philosophy, and he said that he had indeed taken such a course. For most of the year they studied the Ancient Greeks, but in the last few weeks they had also covered the moderns. After studying Hobbes, Locke, and Rousseau, they spent some time on Hegel, and then had a two-hour seminar on Marx. But they were given only a few minutes on John Stuart Mill. It was Mill, not Marx, that Franco's regime chose to censor. This makes perfect sense. The doctrines of Karl Marx were unlikely to turn the heads of affluent provincial law students. But John Stuart Mill on free speech and liberty was quite another thing.

5

The Distribution
of Property

The problem of distributive justice

We shall suppose that a creature, possessed of reason, but
unacquainted with human nature, deliberates with himself
what rules of justice or property would best promote public
interest, and establish peace and security among mankind:
His most obvious thought would be, to assign the largest
possessions to the most extensive virtue, and give every
one the power of doing good, proportioned to his incli-
nation. . . . But were mankind to execute such a law . . . the
total dissolution of society must be the immediate
consequence.

(Hume, *An Enquiry Concerning the
Principle of Morals*, 192–3)

Liberty and property

How should property be distributed? As Hume indicates, this is
a topic fraught with difficulties. Obvious answers to the question
might be disastrously naïve.

The liberty of the citizen, in Mill's view, requires the protection of each person from harm. For Mill one form of harm is
harm to property: theft, fraud, or damage. But, he argues, we
have no right to protection from the effects of a normal functioning market, no rights to protection from economic competition.
Mill favours *laissez-faire* capitalism—at least for as long as individuals are in their present state of moral imperfection. (In a late
work, *Chapters on Socialism*, he suggests that socialism would be
a more appropriate form of economic organization for the morally perfected beings of the future.) Mill also supposes that the

individual has a duty to pay his or her share of the expenses of running the government, and should also be taxed to support those unable (or unwilling) to support themselves.

To what extent is a commitment to these policies a consequence of accepting the value of liberty? And what other values are relevant in assessing the justice of a system of property? In fact, in defending his views of distributive justice Mill makes a fairly direct appeal to utilitarianism. Others, such as Locke, have thought that in deriving a just system of property we should appeal to natural property rights. And others again have given a more fundamental role to the idea of equality.

Let us consider, for a moment, whether accepting the value of liberty has any consequences for the question of distributive justice. How should a liberal society distribute property? Opinions differ widely. One tradition, following Locke, supposes that valuing liberty requires the recognition of very strong natural rights to property. In the libertarian development of this view—the most eloquent presentation of which is *Anarchy, State, and Utopia*, published in 1974 by the Harvard philosopher Robert Nozick—these rights are so powerful that the government has no business interfering with them. The government in Nozick's 'minimal state' has the duty to enforce individual property rights, but may not tax individuals beyond the level required for the defence of the citizens against each other and foreign aggressors. In particular, on this view the state violates individual rights to property if it attempts to transfer property from some (the rich) to others (the poor). Distribution is to be left to the unimpeded free market, gifts, and voluntary charitable donations.

The libertarian, then, tries to argue from the value of the liberty of the individual to a very pure form of capitalism. In effect, this places an individual's property within his or her 'protected sphere' of rights, where no one else, government or individual, may interfere without consent.

An opposing view points out that libertarianism is bound to lead to vast inequalities of property, which in turn will have a detrimental effect on the liberties—or at least the opportunities—of the poor. This view, welfare liberalism, argues that property must be redistributed from the wealthy to the less fortunate to ensure equal liberty for all. Property remains outside an individual's protected sphere, and the government has the duty to supervise and intervene where necessary (subject to the laws of the land) to protect liberty and justice. The most important variant of welfare liberalism is contained in *A Theory of Justice*, published in 1971 (three years before Nozick's book) by Nozick's Harvard colleague, John Rawls. In fact much of contemporary political philosophy has been inspired by Rawls's work, whether in defence of it, or, like Nozick, in opposition.

Nozick and Rawls, then, give different answers to the question of distributive justice. A fully worked out view requires responses to a number of questions. Are there natural property rights? What place is there for the free market? Should we tolerate large inequalities of wealth? What should the government's role be? There is no shortage of answers to these questions. But which answer is right?

The income parade

It is hard to jump right into these questions without some aids to reflection. The problem of distributive justice is the problem of how goods should be distributed. And, it seems, one excellent way of prompting thought about 'how things should be' is to consider how they are. So perhaps we should start with some facts.

Raw income statistics, while no doubt useful, often fail to sink in. It is all very well to be told that the top few per cent of the population hold so much of the wealth, but it is often hard to appreciate the significance of such dryly presented figures. For this reason a Dutch economist, Jan Pen, in his 1971 book *Income Distribution*, decided to present the facts about the income distribution in the United Kingdom in a rather different way.

Pen invites us to imagine a Grand Parade of everyone in the UK economy who earns a wage of any sort, including those who receive social security. The Grand Parade is in single file, with people ordered by income, the lowest earners in the front, and the highest at the back. We are to suppose that the entire parade passes us by in one hour. The peculiar feature of the parade is that everyone's height is determined by their pre-tax income. That is, the more one earns, the taller one is. Those who earn the average wage will be of average height, those who earn double will be twice the size, and so on. Suppose that, as spectators, we are of average height, and watch the parade go by. What would it look like?

First, for a few seconds we see extraordinary people of negative height. These are individuals who own loss-making businesses. But these are soon replaced by people the size of a matchstick or a cigarette: housewives who have worked for a week or so, and so do not have an annual income, schoolchildren doing paper rounds or odd jobs, and so on.

These folk take five minutes to pass, and after ten minutes people about 3 feet tall—the height of a 2-year-old child—begin to come through. These include many unemployed people, old-age pensioners, divorced women, some young people, and owners of shops doing badly. Next follow ordinary workers in the lowest-paid sectors. Dustmen, transport workers, some miners, unskilled clerks, and unskilled manual workers. There are many black and Asian workers within this group. After fifteen minutes the marchers finally reach 4 feet tall. And for the next fifteen minutes there is very little change in height, as skilled industrial workers with considerable training and office workers pass by.

Pen comments at this point: 'We know that the parade will last an hour and perhaps we expected that after half-an-hour we would be able to look the marchers straight in the eye, but that is not so. We are still looking down on the top of their heads' (*Income Distribution*, 51). It is forty-five minutes before we see people of average height. These people include teachers, executive civil servants, shopkeepers, foremen, and a few farmers.

In the last six minutes the parade becomes sensational, with the arrival of the top 10 per cent. At around 6′ 6″ we see headmasters, youngish university graduates in various jobs, more farmers, and departmental heads, most of whom had no idea that they were in the top 10 per cent. Then, in the last few minutes, 'giants suddenly loom up'. A lawyer, not exceptionally successful, 18 feet tall. The first doctors, 7, 8, 9 yards. The first accountants. In the very last minute university professors appear, 9 yards tall, managing directors, 10 yards, a permanent secretary, 13 yards, high court judges, accountants, eye surgeons—20 yards or more.

For the last few seconds we see people the size of tower blocks; businessmen, managing directors of major companies, film stars, members of the royal family. Prince Philip is 60 yards tall, the singer Tom Jones nearly a mile high. At the back comes John Paul Getty: between 10 and 20 miles tall.

These figures are, of course, rather old. An up-to-date version would see the last few minutes dominated by lawyers, accountants, bankers, stockbrokers, and company directors, with public sector employees (especially university professors!) rather further back. But though they are dated, presented this way the statistics are quite startling. It is hard to read through the account without thinking that there *must* be something wrong with any society so unequal. But is such a reaction justified? Other types of response are just as possible. One is to say that the parade simply does not give us enough information to allow us to give a properly considered judgement. Another, complementary, reaction is to say that the parade is seriously misleading. Developing this last point, the claim could be advanced that this pretended 'scientific' presentation of bare data is 'value-laden', in the sense that the selection of data would only be made by someone who wishes to persuade us that current society is unjust.

It is true that a defender of the current system would hardly choose to present it in this way. So if the parade is misleading, how? What does it exaggerate, distort, or leave out? Pen himself questions the nature of the 'reference unit'. That is, the parade includes everyone in the economy who earns any sort of income. Accordingly some spectacular effects of the parade are the result of admitting children with spare-time jobs, women who worked for just a few weeks or a few hours each week, and others who do not attempt to live solely off their own wages. These people, generally, are members of families where the family's combined income may be more substantial. So it is obvious that if we take families, or households, as the basic unit of comparison then many of the lowest incomes will be eliminated.

A more philosophical objection is that the data presented this way simply ignore many pertinent facts. For example they do not tell us whether some people obtained money by honest trade or by theft or fraud; by working hard or by exploiting others. How can we assess the justice of a society without knowing these things?

Property and markets

> The first man who, having enclosed a piece of ground, bethought himself of saying 'This is mine', and found people simple enough to believe him, was the true founder of civil society. From how many crimes, wars, and murders, from how many horrors and misfortunes might not any one have saved mankind by pulling up the stakes or filling up the ditch and crying to his fellows: 'Beware of listening to this impostor; you are undone if you once forget that the fruits of the earth belong to us all, and the earth itself belongs to nobody.'
>
> (Rousseau, *Discourse on the Origin of Inequality*, 84)

Locke on property

One way of arguing that a society is just, despite its inequalities, would be to show that the individuals in that society who hold property have moral rights to that property. Can such a theory of property rights be constructed?

According to Nozick, a theory of property rights needs three different principles: 'justice in initial acquisition'; 'justice in transfer'; and 'justice in rectification'. John Locke, whose ideas we looked at in Chapters 1 and 2, addressed himself primarily to the first question in his writings on property: how can an individual form a right to property appropriated from its natural state?

This is a very puzzling issue. Every object now owned by someone was either once owned by no one, or is ultimately made from something that was owned by no one. This book is made from paper. Most paper is made from wood. The trees from which that wood came might have been deliberately planted as a crop, but those saplings came from seeds, and those seeds were descended from trees which once belonged to no one. Thus at some point an object, be it tree or seed, which belonged to no one became someone's individual property. How could that be? How could someone gain the right to exclude others from the use of that object? This question is even more pressing in the case of land. Anyone may use unowned land. As soon as it becomes private property no one may use it without the permission of the owner. How can someone come to have the right to exclude others in this way? To answer these questions requires an account of justice in initial acquisition.

Locke's *Second Treatise* contains a chapter on property, and in it are several arguments designed to show that justified initial acquisition is possible. Locke takes for granted that if you are the rightful owner of property you have various rights over that property. Not only can you use it, but you can also transfer it to others by sale or gift. And this includes bequeathing the property to your heirs. Thus Locke seeks to justify property rights broadly as we understand them in contemporary society.

There is still great scholarly disagreement about how we ought to read Locke's arguments. Not even Locke could have thought that they are clearly expressed. But there is no doubt that for Locke labour is all-important in the appropriation of property. On one reading of the text we can discern at least four strands of argument in Locke's defence of initial appropriation of property. How many arguments Locke thought he was making is another matter.

The first idea is the argument from survival. Locke assumes that initially the world was owned in common by all human beings. How, then, could anyone come to own anything as individual private property? Locke first relies on the 'fundamental law of nature' discussed in Chapter 1 of this book: mankind is to be preserved as much as possible. If no one could take anything we would all die. So we must be permitted to take what we need in order to survive. Locke gives this a further theological defence. Not to permit human beings, put on earth by God, to survive would be to offend against God's rationality. Nevertheless, our appropriation from nature must be constrained by two conditions—the 'Lockean provisos'—if it is to be justified: we must not take more than we can make use of (the non-wastage proviso); and we must leave 'enough and as good' for others. These two provisos apply not just to the survival argument for property, but to all of Locke's arguments.

While eminently reasonable, the survival argument has some obvious limitations. First, it justifies the appropriation only of objects we need to consume in order to survive—fruits and nuts, for example—rather than land itself. Second, it does not specify how exactly objects are to be taken into private ownership. Both these flaws are remedied by Locke's next argument, contained in the famous chapter on property in the *Second Treatise*:

Though the Earth, and all inferior Creatures be common to all Men, yet every Man has a *Property* in his own *Person*. This no Body has any Right to but himself. The *Labour* of his Body, and the *Work* of his Hands, we may say, are properly his. Whatsoever then he removes out of the state that Nature hath provided and left it in, he hath mixed his *Labour* with, and joyned to it something that is his own, and thereby makes it his *Property*. It being by him removed from the common state Nature placed it in, it hath by the *labour something annexed to it*, that excludes the common right of other Men. For this Labour being the unquestionable Property of the Labourer, no Man but he can have a right to what is once joyned to, at least where there is enough, and as good left in common for others. (*Second Treatise*, s. 27, pp. 287–8)

Locke here starts from two premises: you own your own labour; and in labouring on an object you 'mix your labour' with that object. Thereby, so long as that object is not already justly claimed by another, you come to own the object on which you have laboured (provided you leave enough and as good for others). Not surprisingly this is commonly known as Locke's 'labour-mixing' argument. The great advantage of this argument over the previous one is that it seems it can justify the appropriation of land, as well as nuts and berries.

The basic thought behind this argument is very attractive. Those who are the first to work on a plot of land should be entitled to keep it. We are reminded of wild-west pioneers, staking their claim on the frontier, and working the land to prove their title. One common adverse reaction is that this seems very hard on those unable to work. But Robert Nozick has pointed out a more fundamental flaw. The argument that mixing your labour with land entitles you to the land seems to rely on a missing premiss: if you own something and mix it with something else that is presently unowned (or owned in common by all), then you come to own that other thing. But this premiss is surely false, and Nozick provides a counter-example: 'If I own a can of tomato juice and spill it in the sea so that its molecules (made radioactive, so that I can check this) mingle evenly throughout the sea, do I thereby come to own the sea, or have I foolishly dissipated my tomato juice?' (*Anarchy, State, and Utopia*, 175).

How can we save the labour-mixing argument? Perhaps we should take Locke's key idea to be not *mixing*, but *labour*. That is to say, mixing labour is not analogous to mixing tomato juice, for there is something special about labour. But what? Here we encounter Locke's third argument: the 'value-added' argument. Consider the amount of food that could be gathered from a plot of uncultivated land. Now consider the amount that could be provided by a plot of the same size under cultivation. Locke suggests that the cultivated plot will be perhaps a hundred times as productive. From this Locke concludes that 'labour . . . puts the difference of value on every thing' (*Second Treatise*, s. 40, p. 296). In other words, in labouring on land one massively increases its value. This is why labouring entitles the labourer to appropriate cultivated land.

But this argument too has an obvious difficulty. We might be persuaded that labouring entitles you to keep the *added* value.

But the land is not part of the added value: it was there before you came, and, in normal circumstances, would still have been there had you never laboured. So this is an argument, at best, for keeping the fruits of production. It seems to give no right to keep the land worked on. Is there anything that could yield that consequence?

A fourth argument might help. Locke says that God gave the earth to the use of the:

Industrious and Rational . . . not to the Fancy and Covetousness of the Quarrelsom and Contentious. He that had as good left for his Improvement, as was already taken up, needed not complain, ought not to meddle with what was already improved by another's Labour: If he did, 'tis plain he desired the benefit of another's Pains, which he had no right to, and not the Ground which God had given him in common with others to labour on. (*Second Treatise*, s. 34, p. 291)

In this passage Locke wants us to consider someone who has appropriated and improved land (Industrious) and another person (Quarrelsom) who makes a claim for the land Industrious has worked on. Provided that there is plenty of land left, Quarrelsom's only reason for wanting Industrious's land is laziness: not being prepared to put in the work that Industrious has. But this is no good reason, and so no good reason to complain about Industrious's appropriation. Behind this, I suggest, is an implicit appeal to the notion of desert. If Industrious has worked hard, she deserves the fruits of her labour. At least no one else has a valid claim.

Unfortunately this argument shares the defects of the earlier ones. The fruits of labour may be deserved, but the land would have been there anyway. Perhaps the argument justifies a temporary title to the land—it is yours to use for as long as you are making good use of it, but for no longer. Yet property rights are rarely thought of as conditional in this way: certainly Locke did not think so. This argument gives you no right to sell your land, or to leave it to your children. Furthermore those unable to fend for themselves will rightly feel aggrieved if labouring is made a necessary condition of acquiring property. However strongly we feel the attraction of the view that labouring on land should entitle one to it, it is very hard to explain why this should be so, at least within Locke's framework.

A further and related problem concerns the 'enough and as good' proviso. Perhaps Locke is right to suppose that there is no good reason to object to another's appropriation if there is plenty of equally good land left. But what should we say once land becomes scarce? The logic of Locke's position would seem to suggest that property rights dissolve at this point. But of course he says no such thing. Probably his view was that as long as people are better off working on other people's land than they would have been in the state of nature, then they have no justified complaint about another's property rights. And in 'proof' of the benefits brought by labour and property rights Locke claims that a king of a large and fruitful territory in America (where little of the land had been transformed by labour) 'feeds, lodges, and is clad worse than a day Labourer in England' (*Second Treatise*, s. 41, p. 297).

However, unless we read the 'enough and as good' proviso literally—that there really is enough and as good land left for others to take—Locke's defence of property rights is far less persuasive. For if land is scarce then it will be taken by those first to stake their claim by labour. Those born to a later generation, unable to find land of their own, will complain that they have been unjustly treated in comparison with those who have inherited land: not because they are quarrelsome and contentious, but because they will feel that they have been denied something given to others. Why should you have land and I have none, if the only difference between us is that your ancestors were industrious and mine not? And what can be said in response?

Surely some sort of response, or new argument, is needed to defend property rights. After all, virtually the entire non-liquid surface of the earth is now claimed as the private property of individuals, firms or nations. And so it seems that either these holdings are illegitimate, or that there must be justified ways of coming to acquire property. In fact, however, virtually no progress has been made in improving upon Locke's argument.

It is easy to see why not. We noted earlier that before an item of property comes to be appropriated by an individual or group, everyone is at liberty to use that item. Once it becomes an individual's property, this liberty of non-owners is cancelled. Others can use it only with the owner's permission. What could I possibly do to a piece of land, or other object, which could have such powerful effects? Why should anything *I* do to an object overturn *your* previous liberty to use it? It is very hard to find an answer: thus it is very hard to find a satisfactory principle of justice in acquisition. Perhaps it is impossible.

Does this mean that property is theft (in Proudhon's famous formulation)? That would be too simplistic a conclusion. A more modest response is to suppose that there may be something wrong with the schema we set up at the beginning. That is, perhaps it is wrong to focus on the issue of justice in acquisition as a separable element in a theory of distributive justice. Possibly we could argue for a system of distributive justice which included ownership of private property as one element of the system. That way we might be able to justify private property as an intrinsic part of a theory of justice without worrying too much how property was originally appropriated from nature. And this is just what many defenders of the free market try to do.

The free market

One alternative to Locke would be to attempt a utilitarian justification of property rights. We can see how such an argument would go: allowing people to appropriate property and to trade it and leave it to their descendants will encourage them to make the most productive use of their resources. Accordingly this would make a greater contribution to human happiness than any alternative arrangement. Such an argument is already implicit in Mill's view, outlined above.

This utilitarian argument concerns itself less with the process by which people come to acquire property than with the benefits of trade and inheritance. It is part of the argument that individuals should hold property, but it is less important *how* they come to hold that property. To put this another way, for the utilitarian the issue of justice in transfer takes priority over the issue of justice in initial acquisition. And many utilitarians stress the importance of the capitalist free market as a mechanism of transfer.

The 'pure model' of a capitalist free market includes a number of essential features. First, property in land, raw materials, and other goods (including labour) is held by individuals or firms, under a system of secure property rights. Second, goods are produced for profit, rather than to satisfy the consumption needs of the producer, or of other needy people. Third, all goods are distributed by voluntary exchange on a market regulated by laws of supply and demand. Finally, free competition exists: anyone may produce and offer for sale any good.

This is the pure model. No real economy perfectly incorporates all these features: generally all are modified in some way. For example, in many countries the state owns and runs certain enterprises. Second, most countries have a significant 'voluntary' sector, producing goods and services on a partly charitable basis. Third, some goods cannot legally be traded on the open market (plutonium, heroin). And fourth, various state-enforced monopolies exist (the post office, for example) which prevent newcomers from entering a particular industry. However, it is also clear that most countries now approximate to this model to a greater or lesser extent. Are they right to do so?

What is the alternative to the capitalist free market model? As we have just seen, it can be modified by restricting the type of exchanges people can make. But the most radical alternative is the planned economy. It contrasts with the free market in all essential features. Here the state, in the name of the people as a whole, controls all property. Second, production is not for profit, but to satisfy the needs of the citizens. Third, distribution is by central allocation, rather than by trade. Finally, the state has ultimate control over who may produce how much of each good. Thus enterprise is carried out in accordance with a central plan, allocating resources to various industries.

The free market looks less autocratic than the planned economy, but, superficially at least, less rational. The free mar-

ket leaves all decisions to individuals. How, then, do they co-
ordinate? How can we make sure that there will be enough of
each good provided? How can we avoid wasteful over-
production in certain sectors? Planning from the centre will, it
seems, ensure that enough of each good is produced to satisfy
the demands of all. Marx's collaborator, Friedrich Engels (1820–
95) wrote:

Since we know how much, on the average, a person needs, it is easy to
calculate how much is needed by a given number of individuals, and
since production is no longer in the hands of private producers but in
those of the community and its administrative bodies it is a trifling
matter to regulate production according to needs. (*Speeches in
Elberfeld*, 10)

But, according to many commentators, arguments like this
have led to one of the most costly mistakes of the twentieth
century. Despite the rational appeal of planning, all attempts to
put a planned economy in place have failed—and they would
have failed much sooner if they had not been supplemented by
extensive, illegal, black markets. The market has been able to
achieve a far higher level of efficiency and well-being for its
citizens than the planned economy, despite its 'anarchic', unco-
ordinated, nature. But why should that be so?

The best answer was provided by the Austrian economist and
social theorist F. A. von Hayek (1899–1992). To understand his
reasoning we must take a brief look at how the free market can
be expected to function. Suppose that a certain good—garlic,
say—costs a certain price: 50 pence per bulb. Then a respected
scientist publishes a report indicating that consuming a bulb of
garlic a day wards off cancer and heart disease. Accordingly
demand for garlic soars. Garlic retailers sell out rapidly, and
prices spiral. Huge profits are made in the garlic industry.

The prospect of such profits will prompt new producers to
enter the garlic market. Supply begins to rise, and as it does the
price falls again, until a new equilibrium is established. Eventually demand equals supply at a price where garlic producers
achieve the same profit levels as are available elsewhere in the
economy.

This rather banal example of economic life shows the remarkable powers of markets. First, the price system is a way of signalling and transmitting information. The fact that the price of a good rises indicates that the good is in short supply; if the price falls then it is oversupplied. Second, the profit motive gives people a reason to respond to that information. If prices rise in a sector because of increasing demand, this normally means that larger than average profits are to be made, and so new producers rush in. If prices fall, because of falling demand, generally profits fall, and so some firms will leave the industry. In both cases an equilibrium will eventually be established, where the rate of profit for the industry is roughly equivalent to the average rate of profit for the economy as a whole.

These are the two key features of the market: it signals information, and it gives people an incentive to respond to that information by changing production patterns. Nor should we forget the importance of competition in driving down prices, and driving up quality. In combination these factors lead to the consequence that, broadly, in markets people (with money) get what they want from other people. And the position of the consumer is almost always improving. But not because others are being altruistic. As Adam Smith (1723–90) pointed out:

It is not from the benevolence of the butcher, the brewer, or the baker that we expect our dinner, but from their regard to their own interest. We address ourselves, not to their humanity but to their self-love, and never talk to them of our own necessities but of their advantages. (*The Wealth of Nations*, 119)

Many theorists accept that the market can distribute goods to individuals in a way in which no planned economy could match. If I want a certain good and if I have the money I can go and buy it. I can express my preferences in my purchasing behaviour, and others try to make as much profit as they can by responding to them. In the planned economy there are two problems. How will the planner know what I want? It might be common knowledge that people like ice cream, and need socks, but how can the planner know that I prefer vanilla ice cream to chocolate, or plain socks to patterned ones? And why should the planner take the trouble to make sure I get what I want? Real planned economies have been plagued by chronic shortages of some goods, such as winter tights, over-production of others such as low-grade vodka, and a depressing lack of quality and variety in those goods that are available. In order to run an economy as efficiently as the free market, the planner needs a level of omniscience, omnipotence, and benevolence rarely attributed to mere human beings.

This is essentially a utilitarian argument for the free market: it will advance human happiness to a level that could not be achieved by the planned economy. Arguments based on liberty have also been offered. The planned economy involves restrictions on individual behaviour. In his important study, *The Economics of Feasible Socialism*, first published in 1983 and now translated into a score or more of languages, Alec Nove quotes a passage from a novel by Vasili Grossman:

I wanted since childhood to open a shop, so that any folk could come in and buy. Along with it would be a snack-bar, so that the customers could have a bit of roast meat, if they like, or a drink. I would serve them cheap, too. I'd let them have real village food. Baked potato! Bacon-fat with garlic! Sauerkraut! I'd give them bone-marrow as a starter, a measure of vodka, a marrow-bone, and black bread of course, and salt. Leather chairs, so that lice don't breed. The customer could sit and rest and be served. If I were to say all this out loud, I'd have been sent straight to Siberia. And yet, say I, what harm would I do to people? (*The Economics of Feasible Socialism*, 110)

Robert Nozick puts essentially the same point more succinctly: 'The socialist society would have to forbid capitalist acts between consenting adults' (*Anarchy, State, and Utopia*, 163).

It will be better to postpone discussion of the liberty argument for the free market until later: it comes out in sharpest focus as a criticism of Rawls's views, which will be discussed shortly. First we should take stock. So far the main discussion has shown some substantial utilitarian advantages of the free market over the fully planned economy. But from this comparison it does not, of course, follow that the free market is the best possible system. It is easy to derive improvements under a utilitarian analysis. This can clearly be seen in cases of 'market failure' for goods with 'externalities'.

Externalities come in two types: positive and negative. A negative externality is something you get for nothing, but would rather not have: polluted air, or noise, for example. A positive externality is again something you get for nothing, but in this case are pleased to have it: for instance, a pleasant view over your neighbour's front lawn. One important category of goods with positive externalities are 'public goods'. These are goods which, if provided, benefit all, whether or not the recipient has contributed to their production. Consider street lights. The benefits of street lights cannot be restricted only to those who have helped pay for them: thus they are public goods in this sense.

The free market will tend to oversupply goods with negative externalities, and undersupply goods with positive externalities. It is easy to see why. Creating a negative externality is often a way of dumping your costs on another: literally. If it is cheaper to use a noisy production process than a quiet one, other people are inadvertently 'subsidizing' my use of the noisy process by bearing the cost of being disturbed by the noise. Public goods, on the other hand, are subject to the free-rider problem. Why should I contribute to supply street lights if I will get the benefit whether or not I contribute? But if everyone thinks like this— and the market encourages this type of reasoning—no lighting will be provided. It is normally assumed that the solution to these problems is to make the state the supplier of public goods, taxing citizens to pay for them. Similarly the state can make pollution illegal, returning the costs to the polluter. More recently other approaches have been considered, and some enacted: giving those people who suffer from negative externalities the right to recover damages, and those individuals who supply goods with positive externalities the right to charge those who benefit.

Thus we can see that there are utilitarian arguments for modifying the market, whether by state intervention or the creation of new legal rights. But is modification enough? Are there deeper problems with the market? The most powerful objections come from the Marxist and socialist tradition: the market is wasteful; it alienates the worker; it is exploitative; and it leads to unjust inequalities. Let us consider these in turn.

Arguments against the market

In his *Speeches in Elberfeld*, quoted above, Engels complains that the free market is extraordinarily wasteful. This is essentially a utilitarian argument against the free market, and Engels has two main charges. The first is that the free market inevitably leads to crisis after crisis, in which individuals are thrown out of work, and businesses are ruined as goods are wasted or sold at a loss. Engels was one of the first theorists to point out that the capitalist market is punctuated by a 'trade cycle' of boom and bust. Try as they might, economists and politicians have never been able to work out a method by which capitalism can avoid this destructive cycle. Engels's second argument is that capitalist society contains an enormous number of people who perform no productive role. A communist planned economy could incorporate these people into production, improving efficiency and reducing the working day. These people include not only the unemployed, but members of the police and armed forces, the clergy, domestic servants, and, most despised of all, 'speculating, swindling superfluous middlemen, who have forced themselves in between the producer and the consumer' (*Speeches in Elberfeld*, 11). It is interesting that defenders of the market see middlemen as heroes of enterprise, essential to the efficient running of an economy by moving goods from where they are oversupplied to areas where they are over-demanded. For Marx and Engels they are bloodsucking parasites.

Suppose Engels is right. How convincing is his case against the market? Well, what would be better? We can no longer share his confidence in the self-evident rationality of the planned economy. A modified market, as outlined above, despite its flaws, may well be more efficient than anything else that has been proposed.

But the market is wasteful in another sense: wasteful of the potential of the worker. This is the second criticism of the market: that it leads to alienation. The central thought here is that in the capitalist free market the nature of work is degraded and unfitting for human beings. The profit motive requires capitalists to adopt the most efficient methods of production available. This generally means incorporating a highly developed form of the division of labour, in which each worker performs a highly specialized, boring, and repetitive task. In essence, then, the nature of work under capitalism is alienating in that the worker becomes subordinate to a machine 'and from a man becomes an abstract activity and a stomach' (Karl Marx, *Early Writings*, 285). The potential of the worker as an intelligent, creative human being is frustrated. It has been said that under capitalism for many workers the day's most skilled activity is driving to and from work.

The question for critics of the market, however, is whether alienation is a consequence specifically of the capitalist form of production, or whether it is a consequence of modern technology more generally. Can we really conceive of a form of production which will produce enough to satisfy our needs, but will not depend on an alienating system of production? If there is one, it has not yet been discovered.

A third criticism is that capitalists exploit workers in the free market. For Marx exploitation is essentially the extraction of surplus labour. The worker is paid for a day's work. In that work the worker creates profits for the capitalist which are in no way proportional to the work the capitalist puts in. Indeed, shareholders take a portion of profits but do no work at all. At bottom, then, the thought is that those who receive rewards in the market without putting in a proportional level of work are exploiters. Those who receive less than they create are exploited.

The most natural defence of the free market is to claim that capitalists in fact receive fair return for the use of their property, or for the risk of their money. After all, labour alone produces nothing. Someone must supply raw materials, machinery, factories, and so on. The debate about exploitation, then, comes down to the question of whether capitalists are entitled to earn a reward for using their property. But are they morally entitled to own this property? So it seems that we cannot address the question of whether the free market leads to exploitation without settling first the more basic issue of the justification of private property rights.

Finally, the most common criticism of the market made by Marxists, socialists, and many liberals is that it is bound to lead to great inequalities and such inequalities are unjust. Unconstrained, the free market can lead to devastating poverty. Consider Engels's description of the area of St Giles, in central London, in 1844:

All this is nothing in comparison with the dwellings in the narrow courts and alleys between the streets, entered by covered passages between the houses, in which the filth and tottering ruin surpass description. Scarcely a whole windowpane can be found, the walls are crumbling, door-posts and window-frames loose and broken, doors of old boards nailed together, or altogether wanting in this thieves' quarter, where no doors are needed, there being nothing to steal. Heaps of garbage and ashes lie in all directions, and the foul liquids emptied before the doors gather in stinking pools. Here live the poorest of the poor, the worst paid workers with thieves and the victims of prostitution indiscriminately huddled together . . . and those who have not yet sunk in the whirlpool of moral ruin which surrounds them, sinking daily deeper, losing daily more and more of their power to resist the demoralising influence of want, filth and evil surroundings. (*The Condition of the Working Class in England*, 60–1)

All advanced countries have accepted that society has a duty to protect people from such a fate and so various welfare provisions are made—some more effective than others. Unemployment and disability benefits, income supplements, and other grants now allow the vast majority of individuals in western societies to obtain a level of income which provides them with a minimal standard of living.

Is the level of inequality generated by the market, even as modified by the welfare state, acceptable? Such a society is depicted by the income parade discussed above. Is it just? Arguably the considerations presented here demonstrate that societies so characterized can be given a utilitarian justification. This contention might seem surprising. It is often supposed that utilitarianism would recommend a roughly equal distribution of resources, rather than the inequalities of the income parade. The central assumption in the utilitarian argument for equality is that people have 'diminishing marginal returns' for goods. The utility or pleasure derived from eating a first chocolate biscuit is much more than that derived from the second. So if there are two of us, and two biscuits, then utilitarianism is likely to recommend one each. Similarly a given sum of money provides much more utility for the poor than for the rich. To maximize utility we must share things out, and so redistribution from the rich to the poor maximizes utility.

The weakness in the argument just given is that it seems to assume that *how goods are distributed* does not affect the *quantity of goods available for distribution*. But it is often supposed that an egalitarian distribution will suppress initiative and enterprise: why work hard, or try to develop new products, if doing so will make a negligible impact on your income? Allowing at least some inequalities, on the other hand, will produce incentives for people to innovate and to work more productively. Thus it seems that an unequal society may well produce more than an equal one, and so it is possible that it will do better in utilitarian terms, even if we accept that most goods have diminishing marginal returns. Thus utilitarian defenders of the free market claim that the market makes a far stronger contribution to human happiness than the planned economy or equality could do. But the market can be improved by allowing governments to provide public goods, and to introduce legislation to reduce the supply of 'public bads' (goods with negative externalities). The government should also introduce some form of welfare provision to eliminate the worst aspects of poverty. Such a system might be the best we can do in utilitarian terms. Is this enough to show that such an economy is just? Many are not convinced. Rawls's theory of justice is the most powerful recent attempt to try to do better.

Rawls's theory of justice

> Certain principles of justice are justified because they
> would be agreed to in an initial situation of equality.
>
> (Rawls, A Theory of Justice, 21)

A hypothetical contract

What is the just society? How could we know? Let us, to get
started, think about a fairly simple example in which a question
of justice seems to arise. Suppose two people—you and I—are
playing poker. I deal, and you pick up and look at your cards.
Before picking up my own hand I notice a card—the Ace of
Spades—lying face up on the floor. Seeing this I propose that we
throw in the hand and that I should deal again. But you argue
that we should play the hand out. So we disagree. What should
we do?

Ultimately, of course, one of us might bow to superior pressure, even physical force. But before we come to blows we should
realize that several strategies are open to us to try, if we wish, to
resolve the issue by determining what the fair or just outcome
should be. One, for example, might be that we have already
made an agreement which covers the case. Before sitting down
we might have drawn up a lengthy document outlining what to
do in just this eventuality and many others like it. Presumably
reference to such an agreement would decisively settle the dispute. More realistically, we might have made a verbal agreement
to play by a certain well-known set of rules of the game. Again
reference to the rules settles the matter.

But perhaps, as is more likely, there is no actual agreement we
can refer to. What else can we do? A second thought is to ask the
advice of an 'impartial spectator'. There might be an onlooker
we both respect, or, if we are playing in a club, a referee. Or if we
are children—brother and sister, say—we might ask our mother
for a decision. Again, by this method we ought to be able to
come to a definitive ruling.

But what if there is no one like this around either? A third
strategy would be to conjure someone up in the imagination—a

hypothetical spectator. 'What would your father say if he were here?' Admittedly this does not guarantee a resolution; we might have the same dispute again over what he *would* say. But it is not unheard of for someone to realize that he or she is in the wrong by reflecting on how an impartial person would view the situation. So this tactic can, in some cases, yield a helpful answer.

Finally, we could appeal to a hypothetical agreement. We might, in our imaginations, consider the questions of what agreement we would have made if one or other of us had raised the issue before the game started. Perhaps I can convince you that, if we had discussed the matter, we would have agreed to throw the hand in under these conditions. You only disagree because you are distracted by the actual hand you have been dealt. Maybe it is the first good hand you have been dealt all evening. This blinds you to the justice of the situation. Imagining what you would have agreed to before you were dealt this hand is a way of trying to filter out the bias caused by your own special interests. And it is this idea that Rawls adopts in his attempt to argue for his principles of justice.

It is clear that, if we are to use the hypothetical agreement method to solve problems of justice, we must suppose that the hypothetical contract will take place under some sort of special conditions. For consider again the card game: we cannot use the method if we suppose the hypothetically contracting parties (you and I) are placed exactly as they are in real life. For in real life we have a dispute—I want a re-deal, you do not—and the hope is that we can find a method to resolve this dispute. If we are to reach a hypothetical agreement we must abstract from real life. In the card game this is easy enough. We imagine what agreement we would have made before the cards were dealt. So we assume some ignorance. Neither of us knows what hand we have. If we can successfully imagine this then we will be in a position where we cannot be biased by our particular interests; that is, by whether we have a good hand or a bad one. If we do not make this abstraction then the chances that we can find a hypothetical agreement are very slim.

Rawls, then, uses a hypothetical contract argument to justify his principles of justice. Accordingly we can divide Rawls's project into three elements. The first is the definition of the conditions under which the hypothetical agreement is to take place; the second is the argument that his principles of justice would be chosen under such conditions; and the third is the claim that this shows that they are the correct principles of justice, at least for modern democratic regimes. Let us consider the first of these elements, the conditions of the contract, which Rawls calls the 'original position'. What ignorance or knowledge do we need to attribute to the contractors if an agreement about social justice is to be possible?

Were we to try to imagine a hypothetical contract between everyone in a modern society we would fail. There are no terms to which literally everyone would agree (or if there are some, these would hardly amount to a complete conception of justice). We can expect some rich people, for example, to be strongly opposed to taxation, while some poor people will want the rich to be taxed more than they are at present, in order to increase welfare benefits. Hence we have a dispute, and the point of a theory of justice is to attempt to resolve such disputes.

Rawls supposes that people's views of justice are often biased, in part, by their own particular interests. Because they already know what social cards they have been dealt—intelligence, strength, and so on—people will often fail to take a properly impartial stance as required by a concern for justice. Rawls's leading thought is that, while justice requires impartiality, impartiality can be modelled by assuming ignorance. This opens the way for a hypothetical contract argument. To make this clearer, consider the following example (not, by the way, one of Rawls's own).

Suppose, in the not-too-distant future, the supply of soccer referees dries up. (Imagine they are so disillusioned by the abuse they get from the players that they all take up archery.) For many games it becomes impossible to find a neutral referee. Suppose that this is true of the game between United and City, and suppose, too, that the only qualified referee at the match is the manager of United. Understandably City object to the proposal that he should referee the game. However, the Soccer Association are aware that this difficulty arises from time to time, and so they have invented a drug. If you take this drug you behave perfectly normally, except in one respect. You have a highly selective loss of memory. You are unable to remember which football team you manage (and cannot hear anyone who tries to remind you). Having taken this drug how should the manager of United referee the game?

The answer is that he may as well be impartial. He knows he manages one of the teams, but not which one. Accordingly if he randomly picks one of the teams to favour he may find himself doing his own team harm. If we assume that he does not want to run the risk of unfairly damaging his own team's prospects, then all he can do is act as fairly as he is able, and let the game run according to the rules. Ignorance spawns impartiality.

With this in mind, we can consider Rawls's construction of the original position. People in the original position—the hypothetical contractors—are placed behind a 'veil of ignorance' which makes them unaware of their particular circumstances. Because of this ignorance they do not know how to be biased in their own favour, and they are apparently forced to act impartially.

The people in the original position, Rawls says, do not know their place in society or their class position. They are ignorant of their social status, their gender, and their race. Importantly they are also ignorant of their possession of 'natural assets'—their abilities and strengths. In all these respects they do not know which cards they have been dealt.

Is this enough to allow them to come to an agreement? It would be, were it the case that the only thing dividing people on questions of justice were personal interest. But Rawls recognizes that this is a crude and insulting over-simplification. People also disagree because they value different things. They have different 'conceptions of the good', that is, different ideas about what makes life worthwhile. People have different moral, religious, and philosophical views, and different aims and ambitions. They also have different views about what the good society should be like. Rawls excludes all this information too. People in the original position do not know their own conception of the good, and neither, says Rawls, do they know their 'special psychological propensities'.

To illustrate the power of this method, the suppositions so far seem to be enough to explain why people in the original position would agree to what Rawls calls the Liberty Principle—that each person is to have an equal and extensive set of basic liberties. To choose a different principle to regulate liberty would, in effect, be to discriminate against a certain group, or to accept diminished liberty for all. But who would agree to do this if they did not know which group or groups they belonged to? Who would choose to discriminate against a particular race if they did not know their own race? And why would anyone choose to limit everyone's liberty? The Liberty Principle seems an obviously rational choice.

On the other hand, an objection is that individuals might choose lesser or unequal liberty if this would make everyone better off. Rawls denies this, and we will look at his reasons shortly. But a more subtle objection is that people as so far described would simply be unable to make any choices or decisions. They do not know what they are like, nor what types of things they like. How, then, can they make any sort of decision about how society ought to be? Without a conception of the good, how can they even know that they value liberty?

Rawls's answer is to presuppose a certain type of motivation. The parties in the original position, he stipulates, are assumed to possess a 'thin theory of the good'. The first, and most important, element of the thin theory of the good is that agents in the original position know that they want what Rawls calls 'primary goods'. These are liberties, opportunities, wealth, income, and the rather mysterious 'social bases of self-respect'. What these have in common, Rawls supposes, is that they are what people should rationally want, whatever else they want. That is, whether your conception of the good is a life of unadulterated pleasure, monastic virtue, hunting, shooting, and fishing, consciousness-raising, or whatever, Rawls's primary goods are desirable. You always want liberty, opportunity, and money, supposes Rawls, as all-purpose means to your personal ends in life. Thus agents in the original position know that they want primary goods.

Rawls adds that they prefer more of these primary goods to fewer, and that the agents are rational, in the sense that they will take the most efficient means to achieve their ends. Also they are not envious, and so will not be resentful of anyone else's good fortune. Finally, they are 'mutually disinterested'. They take no interest in the plight, whether positive or negative, of anyone else.

It is important to try to keep clear that Rawls is *not* saying that this is what people in the world are really like. People are often envious, or irrational, and we certainly often do care very much about how other people's lives go. Rather, he is creating a hypothetical—fictional—model of a person who will take part in the original position. In the card game, in order to come up with a fair, hypothetical agreement, we supposed that the players had not been dealt their hand, even though they had. Similarly, in the case of the original position we suppose a far more radical level of ignorance and knowledge to ensure impartiality between the contracting parties. We end up with a view of people in the original position who are very unlike real people. But this is not a criticism of the theory. The conditions of the original position, behind the veil of ignorance, are not meant to describe the nature of a person, but to act as a methodological device; a device which helps us come to a view about the correct principles of justice.

There are just a few more pieces to add before the picture of the original position is complete. Rawls assumes that people are ignorant of certain facts about their society. They do not know its economic and political situation, its level of civilization or culture, or the generation to which they belong. However, they do know that people—real people, people in society—have a sense of justice and are capable of having a conception of the good.

They also know that their society is in what Hume called 'the circumstances of justice'. Hume pointed out that in certain conditions the idea of justice seems not to apply. If we are in a condition of dire scarcity, so bad that we cannot even ensure everyone's survival, then the idea that we should criticize anyone's actions as unjust seems absurd. If just to stay alive you must take what you can from others, then considerations of justice look completely irrelevant. At the other extreme, if we were in a situation of such abundance that we could all have as much as we desired, then conflicts of justice would not arise. If you have what I want, why should I dispute with you about it if I could get another just like it, without any difficulty? Accordingly, the circumstances of justice are 'between scarcity and abundance', and Rawls assumes that his parties know that they are deciding on principles to regulate a society placed in such conditions.

Choosing principles of justice

Having constructed the original position, what principles of justice would be the outcome? Rawls says that any of us can think our way into the original position at any time. If we do, we will see for ourselves whether or not we would, in fact, choose his principles of justice. The principles we would choose, says Rawls, are:

  1. Each person is to have an equal right to the most extensive total system of equal basic liberties compatible with a similar system of liberty for all.
  2. Social and economic inequalities are to be arranged so that they are both:
    (a) To the greatest benefit of the least advantaged ... and
    (b) Attached to offices and positions open to all under conditions of fair equality of opportunity. (*A Theory of Justice*, 302)

Principle 1 is the Liberty Principle, 2(*a*) the Difference Principle, and 2(*b*) the Fair Opportunity Principle. According to Rawls the Liberty Principle has 'lexical priority' over the other two, as does the Fair Opportunity Principle over the Difference Principle. What this means, for Rawls, is that, once we have reached a certain level of well-being, considerations of liberty should have absolute priority over matters of economic well-being or equality of opportunity. On this account, for example, it is no defence of slavery that it makes the slaves better off than they would be with their freedom. The fact is that enforced slavery is inconsistent with recognizing equal liberty, and so must give way even if it has economic advantages for the slaves. Similar things can be said about the priority of the Fair Opportunity Principle over the Difference Principle.

The main object of our interest in this chapter is the Difference Principle. Note that it is a broadly egalitarian principle in the sense that, for Rawls, there is a general presumption in favour of an equal distribution of goods among all citizens. However, Rawls takes notice of an argument discussed earlier which often seems to generate a powerful criticism of egalitarianism: that it leaves no room for incentive. That is, some people will work much harder if they know that they will get extra rewards for doing so. But the hard work of the highly productive is capable of benefiting us all: either directly through new job and consumption opportunities, or indirectly through raised tax revenues. Now, if an inequality benefits everyone then what can be the objection against it? After all, who does it harm? On these grounds egalitarianism is sometimes accused of being both inefficient and irrational.

Rawls accepts the conditional statement that *if* an inequality is necessary to make everyone better off, and, in particular, to make the worst off better off than they would otherwise be, then it should be permitted. This idea yields the Difference Principle. However, *whether* incentives are necessary in the manner outlined is a question not for philosophers, but for psychologists and economists.

In the last section I suggested that a utilitarian political philosophy would probably yield a free market with a welfare state. Such a system would allow far greater inequalities than the Difference Principle could justify. But how can Rawls show that the Difference Principle is to be preferred on grounds of justice? His answer is to use the device of a hypothetical contract. From the original position people would choose his principles of justice in preference to utilitarianism. But why would they do that? Why not choose utilitarian principles?

It may help to consider an adaptation of the original position. Suppose you have just woken up in a hospital bed. First you realize that you are suffering from an extensive memory loss. Looking down you see that you are swaddled from head to toe in bandages. You don't remember your name, sex, or race, nor can you discover these by self-inspection (the tag on your bandaged wrist has only a number). Facts about your family, occupation, class, strengths, skills, and so on are all lost to you. You do recall some general theories you once learnt in economics and sociology classes, but you cannot remember anything from your history lessons. In fact, you could not even say what century it was. Then into the ward walks a man in a white coat. 'Good morning', he says, 'I am Professor John Rawls. Tomorrow your memory will return, your bandages will be removed, and you will be free to leave. So we don't have much time. What we need you to do is to tell us how you would like society to be designed, bearing in mind that, from tomorrow, you will be living in the society you have chosen. We want you to design society purely in your own interests. Although you do not know what your actual interests are, I can tell you that you want as many primary goods as possible—liberties, opportunities, wealth, and income—and you should not consider the fortunes of anyone else. I will come back this evening to see what you have decided.' Under these circumstances what would it be rational to choose?

Note, in passing, that we have slipped into talk of 'choice' of principle rather than the idea of 'agreement' we started with. In practice this makes no difference. People in the original position are assumed to be the same. Therefore they will all reason in the same way, and so we may as well concentrate on the choice of just one person. This does no harm, and it makes the argument easier to handle.

So would you choose the Liberty Principle? We have already seen the main reason why you should. As you do not know which group or groups you belong to it would be irrational to discriminate against one portion of society. For all you know you would be discriminating against yourself. This is a reason for choosing equal liberty. But why the *most extensive* equal liberty? This seems to follow from Rawls's assumption that people not only want Primary Goods, they also want as much of as many of them as possible. From behind the veil of ignorance, or from your hospital bed, the Liberty Principle seems an obvious and automatic choice. (No doubt similar things can also be said about the Fair Opportunity Principle.)

Remember, though, that Rawls argues that people will not only adopt the Liberty Principle, but also that they will give it 'lexical priority' to the other principles. According to this view we cannot sacrifice liberty for the sake of anything else. But it could be argued that giving such an absolute priority to liberty is hardly rational. There are times when liberty should be sacrificed for the sake of security—think of wartime blackouts and curfews. Or in times of great economic hardship and scarcity we might accept a restriction on political and civil liberties if this is the only way we will get fed. How, then, can we accept the priority of liberty?

Rawls deliberately ignores cases of emergency, like wars, wanting to understand the more 'central' cases of justice before looking at these less common problems. And he has also said that we can assume that we are choosing principles of justice for a society placed in 'the circumstances of justice'. That is, we already know that resources in our society are not in dire scarcity, and so we need not concern ourselves with such problem cases. Rawls's plausible view—although one that could be questioned—is that, given moderate prosperity, liberty should always be preferred to further material advances.

So now we turn to the derivation of the Difference Principle. This, of course, is the principle which says that the distribution of wealth and income in society should be equal, unless an inequality will be to everyone's advantage. In particular it must be to the advantage of the worst off. Why should such a principle be chosen?

In effect we are now addressing an example of the problem of rational choice under uncertainty. To decide what principles of justice it would be rational to select, we first need to know what principles of rational choice it would be appropriate to use in this case. Seeing matters in this way means that we can help solve the problem by tapping into the resources of 'rational choice theory'.

To see the type of issue in play, let us start with a very simple case as an example. Suppose you are sitting down to a meal in a restaurant, and are faced with having to choose a first course. It is a fixed-price menu, so you need not worry about the relative costs of the items. Also ignore any dietary or religious concerns you may have. The choice is a reasonably simple one. There are only two items on the menu, mussels and melon. Melon is a safe option. This is a good restaurant, so they would only serve ripe melons of high quality. You can be sure that you will find it enjoyable. Mussels, however, are more of a gamble. Normally they give you great pleasure—very much more than melon—but a bad mussel can spoil your whole week. From past experience you can assume, let us say, that one dish of mussels in ten will have a bad effect. Given these facts, what should you choose?

It will help to bring things out if we set this information in tabular form. The numbers are supposed to represent the relative amounts of utility—'pleasure' and 'displeasure'—you get from the options.

Melon   **5** (whether good or bad)
Mussels   **20** (If good—90% chance)   **– 100** (If bad —10% chance)

One theory of rational choice says that we should 'maximize expected utility', or 'maximize average value'. What this means is that we derive an 'average' figure for what each option is worth, and then choose the option with the highest average. This average figure is the expected utility. Of course calculating the average utility of the melon is trivial; whatever happens you will get 5. Calculating the expected utility of the mussels is slightly harder work. What we do is take the utility of each possible outcome and multiply it by its probability. Then we add together each of these amounts and so arrive at our average figure. So we begin by multiplying 20 (the utility of good mussels) by 0.9 (the probability that they will be good) and obtain 18. We then multiply −100 (the utility of bad mussels) by its probability and obtain −10. Adding these together (18 and −10) gives us 8, which is the expected utility of the mussels.

Another way of seeing this is to imagine that you are in a long-run series of this 'game'. Suppose you eat at this restaurant 100 times, and each time order mussels. If the probabilities run true, then you would have had ninety 'good' experiences and ten 'bad' ones. Each good experience is worth 20, so totalling these gives 1,800. Each bad experience is worth −100, yielding a total of −1,000. Consequently 100 dishes of mussels will yield a 'profit' of 800, and so the average profit—the expected utility— is 8. It is important to realize that calling this 'expected utility' does not mean that this is what you would actually expect to get. In fact you will never get 8, you will either get 20 or −100: expected utility is an average figure.

If you are to maximize expected utility then you will choose the mussels. Is this the most rational thing to do? Some people, no doubt, would strongly disagree. Mussels, although in some sense a good bet, remain very risky. It is foolish to take such a risk, some will say, when there is a perfectly decent alternative. The melon is a good, safe option, and, for some people at least, this makes it the more rational choice. Nothing can go wrong. Those who reason this way can often be represented as adopting the 'maximin' principle of rational choice. This instructs us to make sure that the worst possible outcome is as good as possible: maximize the minimum. Used in real life, this is a principle for pessimists. It tells you that you should not rush across the road (you might get killed), but wait for the traffic signals to show that it is safe to cross. Maximiners will do this, even if the chance of death is very slight, and the inconvenience of not crossing very high. Maximiners, then, will choose the melon.

So far we have two candidate principles of rational choice: maximize expected utility and maximin. In fact there is no limit

to possible principles of rational choice. To illustrate a third—
maximax—consider an extension to the original example. Suppose the waiter, before taking your order, says 'and today's
special is fish eggs'. On further enquiry he reveals that this is a
novelty dish prepared by the chef, who, at the beginning of the
meal lays out fifty plates, one of which contains caviar, while the
other forty-nine contain lumpfish roe. Accordingly, there is a 2
per cent (1 in 50) chance of getting caviar, and a 98 per cent
chance of lumpfish roe. You are also assured that if you do strike
lucky and get the caviar it will be served up with great ceremony,
and so you will certainly know that you have got it, whether or
not you can actually taste the difference.

   You calculate that if you do get the caviar it will be such a
thrill that it will be worth 50 to you. On the other hand, if you get
the lumpfish roe (pasteurized, of course) it will not do any harm,
but you will get no pleasure out of it. Probably you will leave
most of it. So you value it at zero. Now, if you were playing
maximin you would stick with the melon. This still has the 'best
worst' outcome: 5 is better than 0. Similarly, maximization of
expectations still dictates the mussels. (Fish eggs have an expectation of 1, as can easily be calculated.) But some will argue that
it is rational here to go for the fish eggs. After all, if the gamble
comes off, the pay-off is very large indeed. Someone reasoning
this way might well be implicitly relying on the 'maximax' principle, which tells us to choose the option which has the 'best best'
outcome (however unlikely): maximize the maximum, a principle for risk taking optimists. As fish eggs is the option with the
best possible outcome (even if this outcome is very unlikely to
occur) it is the one that should be chosen.

   Maximax is really a joke principle; it is not a serious idea.
Whoever would choose fish eggs in this example surely would
not continue to do so if, should the gamble be lost, instead of
lumpfish roe, they were to be taken out to the back of the
restaurant and shot. Probably those who think of themselves as
maximaxers follow the more complex principle of 'maximax
constrained by disaster avoidance'. But let us leave this to one
side. The point so far is that, in the restaurant example, we have

identified three different principles of choice, and each issues in a different decision. Having now identified and illustrated these principles we can return our attention to the social case, and rational choice from the original position or the poor unfortunate in the hospital bed.

It may not be easy to see immediately, but selecting a principle of rational choice for use in the original position turns out to be vitally important. For each of the three principles we have identified yields a different model of the just society. Those who choose to maximize expectations are looking for the outcome with the highest average score. Accordingly, from the hospital bed they should choose some version of the average utilitarian theory of justice: we should make the average position in society as good as possible. Maximaxers, by contrast, have their eyes only on the best outcomes. So they are likely to choose a highly unequal form of society with a privileged, wealthy, and powerful ruling class. Finally, maximiners look only to the worst off, wanting to make the worst off in society as well off as possible. In other words, they would choose Rawls's Difference Principle.

We can now see that the burden of Rawls's argument comes down to the claim that the rational principle of choice in the original position is maximin. This is not to say that Rawls believes maximin to be a suitable principle of choice for every case of decision under uncertainty. Melon is not the uncontroversially rational choice on the menu. Sometimes it seems more rational to take some risk. However, Rawls claims that the very special circumstances of the original position make maximin the only rational choice in this case. We need now to examine his arguments for this.

Reasons for maximin

What, then, is the rational principle of choice to use in the original position, or hospital bed? Before attempting to answer this a few more remarks about the nature of the choice need to be made. First, we might ask, why not choose a principle like 'everyone should live in a palace'? That way I would be sure to be well off. But, of course, Rawls would reply that you cannot know that your society would be able to sustain such a situation; almost certainly it would not. Your society is in the 'circumstances of justice'—between scarcity and abundance—and you must choose a principle that will be suitable for all levels of productivity between the two extremes. So, we might say, there are *physical constraints* on your choice.

And, we need hardly add, there are *logical constraints* too. Whatever you choose must be logically possible. So you cannot choose the principle 'everyone should have slaves', or 'everyone should be richer than everyone else'.

More importantly, Rawls claims that there are also *formal constraints* which reflect the idea of a hypothetical *contract* model of justification. The thought is that certain formal conditions need to be met if people are correctly to be said to have entered a contract, and Rawls imports these conditions as further constraints on choice. One is that the terms must be known, or at least knowable, to all the parties. There is no contract if its terms are deliberately concealed from one or more of the contracting parties. This is the constraint of *publicity* and it is enough to rule out the sort of 'two-level' or 'government house' style of utilitarianism we saw advocated by Sidgwick in the last chapter.

A second formal constraint is that of *finality*. If a contract is made in good faith then the parties will not seek to have it revoked just because things turn out badly. Many contracts have terms to cover unlikely contingencies. For example, one party may contract to compensate the other in the event of non-delivery. If you enter such a contract then you must be prepared to bear these 'strains of commitment'. So, in this example, if I know in advance that I will not, in fact, compensate you if I fail to deliver, then I have not entered the contract in good faith. The upshot of this idea for the Rawlsian contract is that I must not make a choice that I would want to go back on if things turned out badly. Suppose that, from my hospital bed, I choose a very unequal society, and then find that, in actual society I do badly by these arrangements, and find myself near the bottom of the heap. If I am then discontented and want the system changed, then I have not made my choice in good faith, as I am not prepared to bear the strains of commitment. This idea is clearly important if we think that the just society should also be stable in the long term. We will shortly see the work to which Rawls puts this idea.

We are, then, looking for a principle of rational choice which yields a decision which is physically and logically possible, and does not violate the constraints of publicity and finality. This is not yet enough to determine the choice of a single principle, for it seems that choosing either on the basis of the maximization of expectations (average utilitarianism), or of maximin (the Difference Principle) both remain possible. So what do we do now?

It might be helpful to proceed in the other direction. Under what circumstances would maximization of expectations be a rational principle of choice? Within economic theory maximization of expectations is virtually taken to be the definition of rationality. Why should this be? The answer is that in a long-run series of decisions, which are discrete in the sense that what happens in one does not depend on what has happened or will happen in another, you almost certainly do better by being a maximizer of expectations than by following any other policy. Suppose, for example, at the end of each day's work you were given wages of £50, but also told that you could gamble those wages for a 50 per cent chance of £150. Thus the expected value of this gamble is £75. If you were offered this gamble every day, and were sure that the person offering it was honest, then it would simply be stupid to follow a regular policy of playing safe. Should you do so you would ensure a wage of £250 for a five-day week, whereas gambling will bring you in, on average, £375. So in such a long-run series maximization of expectations is surely the rational strategy—and economic theory assumes that individuals are indeed faced with many such choices and decisions (albeit of less regularity and predictability than in the case described).

Now it is important for Rawls that the choice from the original position is not the first in a long-run series of choices. It is a one-off, unrepeatable offer! If things go badly you do not have another chance. So maximization of expectations is not so obviously the rational policy, for it involves taking risks (remember the dish of mussels). Might this mean that the choice is a matter of temperament, rather than rationality?

On the contrary, Rawls argues that the use of the maximin principle, and, therefore, the selection of the Difference Principle, is the more rational decision because of the special circumstances of the choice. He has a number of arguments, not all of them entirely convincing, but the best one is that alternative principles of choice involve taking risks so grave that to do so would be foolish in the extreme. If you decide to gamble, and you lose, you are stuck. There is no second chance. The original position will not be replayed. If you choose to maximize expectations, and so select utilitarianism, there is always the possibility that you will have the misfortune to end up very badly off.

Admittedly we have already assumed that the Liberty Principle would be chosen—people should not gamble with their liberty—so you will not end up as someone's slave. But you might be very poor, unemployed, and homeless. Perhaps the existence of such disadvantaged people is an inevitable side-effect of a particularly efficient type of market economy. Why take the risk of this if something better can be guaranteed by use of the maximin principle? And, Rawls adds, perhaps unfairly, if the gamble failed how would you justify your taking such a risk to your descendants, whose life prospects would also be diminished by your choice?

As a follow-up, Rawls argues that, if you did decide to take the gamble, and ended up in poverty, then you would not consider such a society just, and may well press for change. But this would be, in a sense, to 'go back' on your initial agreement. In other words, if the gamble failed you would not be able to bear the 'strains of commitment'. Accordingly you have not made the contract in good faith, and so have violated the 'constraint of finality'.

This further argument seems to depend on taking the idea of a contract very literally; perhaps more seriously than we ought.

But the argument doing the real work is simply that maximin is to be preferred because alternative principles of rational choice involve taking chances that are just too risky to be rational in the circumstances, given that this is a once-only choice with no going back. And this certainly seems to be a good reason for rejecting the principle of maximization of expectations.

But is it a strong enough reason to use maximin? Perhaps Rawls has not played fair by making his main comparison one between maximin and maximization of expectations. A defeat for utility maximization is not automatically a victory for maximin. There may be other, intermediate principles, which share some of the advantages of both. Consider the choice situation in which you are told that if you open Box B you will receive 5 units, and if you open Box A you have a 50 per cent chance of 4 units, and a 50 per cent chance of 10 units. In this situation if you were to use the maximin principle then you would be required to choose B, for this has the higher minimum result: 5. Yet one has to think of a very special case in which option B would be the rational one, whether we are talking about pounds, millions of pounds, or just pennies. (Perhaps you need exactly £5,000 for a life-saving operation.) So, thinking again, can we come up with a new principle of choice which allows one to choose A over B, but avoids the grave risks associated with maximization of expectations (or indeed maximax).

One answer is to select the principle of 'constrained maximization'. That is, one should use a principle which says, roughly, 'maximize expectations, but exclude any option which contains a very bad possibility'. This is a principle that allows one to gamble, but does not permit one to risk everything. And such a principle seems nicely to overcome the problem of avoiding grave risks, but without endorsing the 'boring' maximin principle. Anyone using such a principle of 'maximization constrained by a safety net', as we might call it, might well be prepared to choose a society of great inequality if it boosts the average position in society, provided that no one is left too badly off. In other words there would be a minimum income, provided, if necessary by the government, to make sure that no one is left in too desperate a plight. We might even think that contemporary western societies largely fit this model: the free market modified by the welfare state.

Rawls thinks that the argument for constrained maximization fails. The problem, he believes, is that from the standpoint of the original position it would be impossible to set the social minimum in a non-arbitrary way. As we do not know the actual circumstances of our society we cannot decide that, say, 'everyone should get at least £100 per week'. Given how society actually turns out, that might not be enough for someone to be kept fed, clothed, and housed. Or it might turn out not to be economically possible. A more general principle is needed: one that is applicable however society turns out. How about 'no one should get less than half the average income'? But why half? Why not a quarter? Why not three-quarters? And how can we be sure that any of these would be sufficient to guarantee an acceptable standard of life? Rawls suggests that the contracting parties, in trying to set a social minimum, would finally settle for this suggestion: 'make the worst off as well off as possible'. But that is simply the Difference Principle, and so, it seems, this form of constrained maximization collapses back into maximin.

Some suspect that Rawls has not been imaginative enough in trying to set the social minimum in a non-arbitrary fashion. Why not set it, for example, so as to overcome the 'strains of commitment'? Rawls's case is far from made. Still, there is some plausibility in the idea that the Difference Principle would be chosen from behind the veil of ignorance, in the original position. And we have already accepted that the Liberty Principle and the Fair Opportunity Principle would also be selected, although it is less clear that they should be afforded the priority Rawls gives them. Thus far, then, Rawls's project seems a (qualified) success.

But the argument is not over yet. For even if Rawls is correct that his principles would be chosen, what does that prove? Why is that supposed to be a justification of the principles? After all, we are not, now, in the original position, and so why should we care what people in such a position would do? What, in other words, justifies Rawls's method? This is our next topic.

Rawls and his critics

A hypothetical contract is not simply a pale form of an actual contract; it is no contract at all.

(Dworkin, 'The Original Position', 18)

The hypothetical contract method

Why, then, should we take Rawls's argument seriously? Here is one bad reason. Rawls has presented a hypothetical contract argument. Whatever can be shown to be the result of a hypothetical contract is just. Therefore the outcome of Rawls's method is just.

The weakness in this attempted justification is the claim that whatever can be shown to be the outcome of a hypothetical contract is just. This is simply false. Imagine that, in exchange for a copy of this book you were to give me all your worldly possessions. This supposition is a hypothetical contract, as is any fictional contract that we could devise. But the result of it is hardly just, and in any case it obviously conflicts with the results of many other hypothetical contracts (for example the one in which you will not accept a copy of the book unless I also give you all *my* worldly possessions). Something obviously needs to be said to show why Rawls's hypothetical contract should be taken more seriously than either of these joke hypothetical contracts.

Rawls claims that his hypothetical contract has a privileged status because every element of the contracting situation—the original position—can be shown to be fair. The original position is, he says, 'a device of representation'. Every element represents something we accept, or could be brought to accept, on moral grounds. For example, making the parties in the original position ignorant of their sex reflects our belief that sexual discrimination is wrong. As we saw before, Rawls ensures impartiality by imposing ignorance.

That said, we can now see two quite different constraints on the make-up of the original position. One is that all its elements, all the assumptions about knowledge and ignorance, must properly reflect relatively uncontroversial moral beliefs shared by all, or almost all. The other is that agreement from the original position must be achievable. People must be characterized in the original position in such a way that they can come to some agreement or other; otherwise the method would have failed. It would be a very powerful argument against Rawls if it could be shown that, in order to reach agreement between the contracting parties, he has incorporated elements into the original position which are not fair.

One important criticism of this type questions Rawls's justification for requiring people to choose in terms of primary goods: liberties, opportunities, wealth, income, and the social bases of self-respect. We should recall that primary goods were introduced as a consequence of Rawls's decision to make people ignorant of their conception of the good. Consequently Rawls had to posit a 'thin theory of the good' so that people in the original position could make some choice or other, for otherwise, without a conception of the good, they would not know what they preferred. Rawls assumes that people want primary goods and that they prefer more of them to less. The philosophical justification of this move is to say that this is what rational people want, whatever else they want. That is, whatever you want from life these things will be a help. They are 'all-purpose means'. Hence they are neutral between conceptions of the good. But, in criticism, it has been said that these goods are not neutral. These goods are particularly suitable for life in modern capitalist economies, built on profit, wages, and exchange. Yet surely there could be non-commercial, more communal, forms of existence, and hence conceptions of the good in which wealth and income—even liberty and opportunity—have lesser roles to play. So, runs the criticism, Rawls's original position is biased in favour of a commercial, individualist, organization of society, ignoring the importance that non-commercial, communal goods could have in people's lives.

A different criticism focuses on the fact that Rawls wishes to make the contracting parties ignorant of their natural and social assets. Again, this may be necessary to achieve agreement between the parties, but how does it reflect a moral belief that we are all supposed to share? Rawls's answer is that one's possession of natural and social assets is 'arbitrary from a moral point of view'. No one deserves his or her strength, intelligence, or good looks, or to be born to wealthy and cultivated parents, and so no one deserves to benefit from these accidents of birth. This belief, then, is modelled by making people in the original position ignorant of these factors. We make natural assets 'common assets': things from which all members of society gain a benefit.

But is this right? Many people would resist the idea that we never deserve to benefit from using our talents. In particular, if someone has worked hard to develop a talent or skill which they then use to good effect then we often feel they deserve some reward for doing so. But Rawls says that even the ability to make an effort, or strive conscientiously towards a given goal, is so influenced by social and natural factors beyond one's control that one cannot even claim that developed talents deserve reward.

Perhaps Rawls is right about this, but he will not have convinced everyone by this argument. In that case some people will not accept that his description of the original position is correct, and they will also reject the claim that Rawls has justified his two principles of justice. For that attempted justification depends on the two principles being chosen from the original position, and on the original position being drawn up in such a way that whatever comes out of it will be fair. We have seen reasons for doubting both claims. But let us now turn to a different type of challenge to Rawls's views.

Nozick and patterns

Some have suggested that the main difficulty with Rawls's theory is not so much the method he uses, but the results he achieves with it. In particular, certain critics have argued that Rawls's two principles of justice are inconsistent. Specifically, they say that one cannot consistently adhere to both the Liberty Principle and the Difference Principle. This type of argument comes in two, diametrically opposed, forms. One argument contends that if we are concerned to equalize liberty then we must also equalize property—for it seems obvious that the rich can do more than the poor, and hence have more liberty. Thus the Difference Principle allows inequalities of liberty, in conflict with the Liberty Principle. However, the opposite complaint is made more often, and, if correct, is quite devastating to Rawls's project: to give people liberty means that *we cannot impose any restrictions on individual property holdings*. Limiting how much property people can acquire, and what they can do with it, is a way of reducing individual liberty. A proper respect for liberty rules out the Difference Principle, or, in fact, any other distributional principle. Robert Nozick has produced the most important version of this argument. It forms a central part of his libertarian defence of the free market, touched on in the first part of this chapter.

Nozick's argument against Rawls begins with some taxonomy. First he distinguishes what he calls 'historical' and 'end-state' theories of justice. An end-state theory of justice supposes that you can tell whether or not a situation is just simply by looking at its structure. So, for example, if you felt certain that the distribution depicted in the income parade described earlier in this chapter was unjust (or if you felt it was just) simply on the basis of the description given, then it might well be that you hold an end-state theory. But if you think that more information is needed about how people obtained their resources, or about the basis on which the resources were allocated, then you believe in a historical theory.

Nozick distinguishes two types of historical theory: patterned and unpatterned. Patterned theories say, obviously enough, that the distribution should be made according to some pattern: 'To each according to their . . .'. To each according to their need, to each according to their ability, to each according to their desert, or to each according to their status would all be examples of theories that appeal to a pattern. Unpatterned theories do not do this. Essentially they are 'procedural' theories. On an unpatterned theory the essence of just distribution is a matter of each person acquiring the goods they hold through legitimate procedures. Nozick's own theory is unpatterned. Almost all other theories, so he claims, are either patterned or end-state. And all can be defeated by a single example, which shows the consequences of giving liberty proper respect.

Nozick begins by asking us to imagine society regulated by our favourite pattern, whatever that may be. Suppose your view is that justice requires distribution according to need. The more one needs, the more one should have. Suppose, then, that property is distributed in society so that people are given money in proportion to their needs. Call this distribution of property $D1$. Nozick then asks us to imagine that a certain basketball player—Wilt Chamberlain—has made an arrangement with his team so that he gets 25 cents for every spectator who attends a home game. In addition to the standard gate money that they pay at the turnstile, they must each drop a quarter into a special box as they pass through the gate. At the end of the season a million people have dropped their quarter into the box. Accordingly Wilt Chamberlain is now $250,000 better off, and so a new distribution of property is the result. Call this new distribution $D2$. On the basis of this very simple example Nozick feels entitled to draw several important conclusions.

The first is that any pattern—whatever it is—is liable to disruption by people's free actions. In this case the pattern was 'each according to their needs', and it was disturbed, essentially, by people's consumption decisions. A million people decided to watch Wilt play, rather than, say, spending their money on chocolate. Whatever the pattern, it seems, certain free actions (exchanges, gifts, gambles, or whatever) are capable of disrupting it.

But what if people decided to stick to the pattern? This might be difficult to achieve in practice, but it might not be too difficult to stay within a certain range of variation. On the other hand, is it reasonable to expect everyone, or almost everyone, to be motivated in this way? If society is divided about the correct pattern, then, it appears, any pattern will be vulnerable.

Nozick's second claim is even more significant. If $D1$ is just, and people voluntarily moved from D_1 to D_2, then, he argues, surely D_2 is also just. But once we have conceded this then we have admitted that there can be just distributions which do not obey the original pattern. So all patterned conceptions of justice are refuted. It is vital, then, for defenders of patterns to resist this move. One strategy is to deny that the move from D_1 to D_2 was voluntary. Although it would seem foolish to argue that Wilt's supporters did not give him the money voluntarily, it does not follow that they realized that, in doing so, they would be bringing about D_2. This is a subtle point. Although D_2 has come about as a result of voluntary action, it does not follow that people have brought about D_2 voluntarily. How could they have if they did not even know that D_2 would be the result of their actions?

Another way of resisting the argument is to say that even if D_2 has come into existence in a purely voluntary way, it does not follow that it is just. Perhaps Wilt's riches will put him in a position to do other people harm, by exerting power through the market, hoarding goods, speculating, or whatever. After all, not everyone chose to pay to watch Wilt play, and these people—including the as-yet unborn—might have a legitimate complaint against Wilt's new wealth.

However, even if this reply can be sustained, Nozick's third argument is the most important of all. Patterns, he argues, can only be enforced at grave cost to liberty. Suppose we decided to maintain a pattern. Given that some people would wish to engage in Wilt-like exchanges, it seems likely that the pattern will soon be disrupted. So what should we do? Nozick argues that we have just two alternatives. Either we maintain the pattern by banning certain transactions (remember Vasili Grossman's would-be café-owner) or we constantly intervene in the market to redistribute property. Either way we need to make intrusions into people's lives: by stopping them from doing what they want to do, or by investigating their holdings of wealth and income, and removing some, from time to time. But whichever we choose we will be severely impeding people's liberty. Proper respect for liberty, then, rules out enforcing a pattern.

Nozick argues that these conclusions hold even for those who want to abolish private property altogether. In 'non-money communism' people will still have to be allocated goods, and some will want to make trades. Skilful traders may turn a profit. Furthermore, little industries could start up. Perhaps some will manage to make machines out of their legitimately acquired furniture or saucepans, and produce extra goods for exchange. This way, even without money, inequalities of possession will emerge.

What are the implications of the Wilt Chamberlain argument for Rawls? As far as Nozick is concerned, the Difference Principle represents a patterned conception of justice. Property is to be distributed so that it makes the worst off as well off as possible. But once people are given income and wealth according to the Difference Principle, some will spend it, while others will acquire more, and so sooner or later the Difference Principle will no longer be satisfied. Property will have to be redistributed. And, so Nozick has argued, this will greatly interfere with people's liberty to live their lives free from interference. Now recall that for Rawls the Liberty Principle takes priority over the Difference Principle. So if it really is true that maintaining the Difference Principle restricts liberty then, it seems, Rawls's own arguments compel him to give up the Difference Principle. A proper regard for liberty, so Nozick has argued, is incompatible with enforcing any patterned distribution of property.

Rawls, however, has several potential replies to this argument. The first is to point out that the Liberty Principle does not distribute liberty as such. Rather it is concerned with giving individuals an extensive scheme of what he calls 'basic liberties', such as freedom of speech, or the right to run for public office. It does not say that people should be absolutely free from interference. So there is no formal inconsistency between Rawls's two principles of justice.

Nevertheless, something more persuasive than this is needed to blunt the force of Nozick's attack. Even if there is no formal inconsistency in Rawls's views, should he not be troubled by

Nozick's observation that the Difference Principle, like all patterned conceptions of justice can only be maintained by constant
interference in people's lives? In response Rawls would argue
that Nozick has painted a strange picture of how a pattern would
be maintained. In the abstract it is true that to regulate society
by the Difference Principle it is necessary to ban some transactions, and enforce the redistribution of property. But this
could be done in a perfectly civilized, non-invasive, way, by the
sort of tax and welfare system we are so familiar with. Those on
large incomes will find themselves heavily taxed. Those on low
incomes will receive income supplements. Tax is both a way of
banning certain transactions and redistributing income—you
cannot pay someone a large income without it being the case
that they have to hand some of it over for the state to redistribute to others. And unpleasant though it is to pay tax, it hardly
seems to amount to a grave interference in one's life.

Still, Nozick has anticipated this reply. Taxation, he says, is on
a par with forced labour. And as we all object to forced labour,
then we should all object to taxation. Actually not everyone
does object to forced labour. Rousseau says that he thinks it less
opposed to liberty than taxation. But why should Nozick make
this claim, which, on the face of it, sounds absurd? The answer is
this. Suppose you work a forty-hour week, and 25 per cent of
your wages is taken in taxation for redistribution to the poor.
There is no way round this. If you are to do the work you do, at
the wages you do, you must pay this tax. Accordingly for ten
hours of the week (25 per cent of your time), you are, in effect,
forced to work for other people. For ten hours a week you are
little more than a slave. Taxation, then, is slavery—a theft of
your time. How can anyone who values liberty, suggests Nozick,
accept such a situation?

Again Rawls must reply that this is a massive exaggeration.
There does seem to be a grain of truth in the idea that taxation
forces one person to work for another, whether they wish to or
not. But calling it forced labour or slavery hardly seems appropriate. And, Rawls's defenders add, we must not overlook
something of perhaps even greater significance. Taxation for

redistribution also increases liberty, for by increasing the income of the poor, it gives them a range of choices that they would not otherwise have had. What type of system best advances liberty therefore remains a moot point. Nozick has not shown that Rawls's two principles of justice are inconsistent.

Conclusion

What, from all of this, should we conclude about distributive justice? Our initial question was whether valuing liberty was enough to determine how property should be distributed. I think we can conclude that it is not. All the theories considered (with the exception of utilitarianism) have been defended on grounds of liberty, among other values, but none of the arguments is uniquely convincing.

Does this mean that the question of distributive justice cannot be settled by argument, or at least not at this level of abstraction? We will look at some reasons for making this claim in the next chapter, but it would be too hasty to draw such a conclusion on the basis of what we have seen so far. Lack of success so far does not mean that success is impossible. If one accepts Rawls's general framework, as many philosophers are inclined to do, then we do have a way of reasoning about justice. This does not mean that Rawls's conclusions must be right, for it is possible that he has misused his own method. For example, it might be that rational people in the original position would choose utilitarian principles of distributive justice, or, more plausibly, utilitarianism subject to a 'social minimum'—a modified version of existing welfare states. But whether or not Rawls's principles of justice are correct, he has done political philosophy the great service of providing a means by which the debate can be continued. And Rawls is now such a dominant figure in political philosophy that those who reject his methodology need to explain why.

6

Individualism, Justice, Feminism

The entire history of social improvement has been a series
of transitions, by which one custom or institution after
another, from being a supposed primary necessity of social
existence, has passed into the rank of a universally stig-
matised injustice and tyranny. So it has been with the distinctions of slaves and freemen, nobles and serfs, patricians
and plebeians; and so it will be, and in part already is, with
the aristocracies of colour, race, and sex.

(John Stuart Mill, *Utilitarianism*, 320)

Individualism and anti-individualism

The earlier chapters of this book have addressed a number of
linked problems in political philosophy. We started with the
observation that the existence of political power—one person's
right to rule another—should not be taken for granted. So, in the
first chapter, we examined what life would be like without the
existence of political power, in a state of nature. Chapter 2,
following on, asked what justifies the state, while Chapter 3 was
concerned with the organization of the state, and, in particular,
whether it should have a democratic structure. The fourth chapter considered the question of the extent to which people should
have a sphere of individual liberty, immune from interference by
the state, and, finally, in Chapter 5 we looked at the issue of
justice in the distribution of property.

In each of these chapters several answers were presented and
discussed. However, some readers will object that a particular—
and controversial—assumption lies behind both the selection of
problems and the positions on them taken here. That assumption is variously called 'individualism', 'atomism', or 'liberal in-

dividualism'; often encapsulated by the rather obscure slogan that 'the individual is prior to society'. A good example of a liberal individualist position is Locke's assumption that human beings are naturally free, equal, and independent. And it is certainly true that each of the previous chapters has, one way or another, been preoccupied with the issue of how freedom and equality are to be secured. To this extent liberal individualism does seem to have been assumed here. But what, might one think, is wrong with that?

The most obvious challenge to the liberal individualist view that the individual is prior to society appeals to its own—diametrically opposed—slogan: 'society is prior to the individual'. We encountered one prominent version of such a view in Chapter 4: communitarianism. Human beings are naturally social, born into the customs and traditions of their own particular society. Much of what is significant about any individual is a consequence of their upbringing and social context. Thus human beings are in no sense naturally free and independent. And perhaps they are not even equal.

Should we try to debate the question of whether the individual really is prior to society? But can we make clear what we are arguing about? It is obvious that any individual now alive was born into some society or other. So in that sense clearly society is prior to the individual. But this does not seem to settle any philosophically interesting question. Is the issue whether there was ever a state of nature in which human beings lived outside of society? This is a very interesting question in itself, but the implications of any answer to it for political philosophy are not clear. A more philosophical debate concerns the nature of the moral bond between the individual and society. Yet even this so far remains vague and unfocused.

Thus individualism is a remarkably slippery concept, and to make any progress we will need a more articulated version of the view than we have seen so far. What I shall do, then, is to start by defining a view we could call 'extreme liberal individualism' (without worrying about whether this is a view anyone has ever actually held in its extreme form). At least if we do this we will see what there is to argue over. An extreme liberal individualist holds four views: a view about the nature of political philosophy; a view about political values; a view about the nature of the ideal political society; and a view about the foundation of rights and duties.

First, the extreme individualist assumes that the task of political philosophy is to devise principles of justice. These principles will be abstract and general, assigning rights, duties, and responsibilities to individuals. This does not mean that the individualist must believe in natural rights—some utilitarians are individualists in this sense. The point is, rather, that the individualist sees the task of political philosophy as the formulation of something akin to ideal legislation: rules allocating rights and duties.

Secondly, liberal individualists believe that the freedom and equality of individuals are of paramount importance. Hence they suppose that not only is the task of political philosophy to assign rights, but that the ultimate point of those rights is that they should protect the freedom and equality of individuals. This is a belief that utilitarians, for example, will not share. Even if they agree that political philosophers should try to devise systems of rights, those rights, on the utilitarian view, are designed ultimately to promote happiness, not freedom and equality. It is this second thesis that makes an individualist a *liberal* individualist: the utilitarians just mentioned are, strictly speaking, *non-liberal* individualists.

Thirdly, extreme individualists (liberal and non-liberal) believe in what we could call the priority or primacy of justice. Societies must be just, even if this has other sorts of costs. It might be hard to see the significance of this claim, but its importance will become clearer as this chapter develops. After Rawls, we will call it the view that justice is the 'first virtue' of social and political institutions.

Finally, the individualist picture supposes that any rights, duties, and responsibilities we have can be understood as somehow arising out of the actions—perhaps even voluntary actions—of individuals. This can be seen most clearly in the discussion of political obligation in Chapter 2. The contract approach assumes that we should think of our duties to obey the state as reducible to contracts or promises each of us has made. Thus we can model our moral relation to the state by imagining why and how we would have come to create it, if it did not already exist.

Extreme liberal individualism, then, is a complex view. It is certainly possible to endorse part of it without endorsing it all. For example, one could believe that political philosophy requires the formulation of abstract principles of justice to protect freedom and equality, but also think that justice is relatively unimportant: perhaps the first duty of any society is to create an environment in which great art and architecture can flourish, even if this leads to injustice. (Building the pyramids, for example, might have been impossible without slave labour.)

Furthermore, one could reject liberal individualism on many different grounds. Consider two quite different objections to the first claim. Communitarian critics of individualism often propose that the task of political philosophy is not to provide abstract principles of justice, but to generate a vision of the good society. Thus, rather than abstract principles of justice, political philosophy should provide rich and concrete accounts of what makes human society flourish. Certain conservatives, on the other hand, suppose that, strictly speaking, it is a mistake to think that political philosophy has any *tasks* at all. Edmund Burke (1729–97), in his work *Reflections on the Revolution in France* (1790)—an attack on the French Revolution and the political ideas that led to it—argued against the use of reason and theory in politics. Burke emphasized the importance of habits and traditions, which, although they may not be able to withstand criticism at the bar of reason, should not be expected to pass what he thought to be a quite inappropriate test. The theme has been resumed in this century by Michael Oakeshott (1901–90) who, in various writings, including *Rationalism in Politics* (1962), argues that our traditions and inherited institutions contain more wisdom than we do—the accumulated wisdom of generations—and that it is both wrong and damaging to reform and rebuild except in the most slow and careful manner. On this view liberal individualism is just one more form of pernicious rationalism, with a mistaken view about what reason in politics can achieve.

Just as there are various reasons for rejecting parts of the liberal individualist view, the rejection itself can come in many strengths. The fourth part is essentially the view that all rights and duties can be explained as arising out of the actions of individuals. An extreme form of opposition to this is often termed holism, and an example can be found in the writings of the British Hegelian philosopher F. H. Bradley (1846–1924). In a paper entitled 'My Station and its Duties' Bradley argues that a person's identity is so deeply penetrated by their social, cultural, and racial inheritance that it barely makes sense to think of someone as an individual at all: 'The mere individual is a delusion of theory; and the attempt to realise it in practice is the starvation and mutilation of human nature, with total sterility or the production of monstrosities' (*Ethical Studies*, 111). In place of liberal individualism Bradley recommends the theory of 'my station and its duties': one is born into a station in life, and has the duties applicable to that station. This idea goes hand in hand with a particular view of the state. 'The state is not put together, but it lives; it is not a heap nor a machine; it is no mere extravagance when a poet talks of the nation's soul' (*Ethical Studies*, 120).

The state, on this view, is an organism—a living whole—and the individual an organ: 'always at work for the whole' (*Ethical Studies*, 113). The metaphor of the 'body politic' is taken very seriously. Your station and duties are as fixed as those of your own organs. Giving your heart, say, the liberty to do what it wanted—if that were conceivable—would be disastrous. Similarly your own duties are defined by your relation to society or the state as a whole. They are given to us, not created by our own actions.

It would be a mistake to think that if we are not individualists then we must be holists. Extreme liberal individualism asserts that all rights and duties can be explained as arising out of individual actions, while holism asserts that none of them can. But there is a middle possibility—in fact a range of possibilities. Perhaps some social rights and duties can be explained as arising out of individual actions, but others cannot. Indeed real-life individualists and holists both accept the middle ground. Holists like Bradley accept that we can create obligations through voluntary actions such as making promises or contracting, while individualists like Locke accept that we have some moral duties, such as the duty not to harm others, whether or not we have created these duties ourselves. The real debate is over *how many* of our political and moral obligations can be explained as arising out of individual action.

It seems, then, that by debating the question of the truth of liberal individualism we open up a dizzying array of issues. Little insight is to be gained by trying to puzzle out whether or not the individual is prior to society: detailed attention needs to be given to a multitude of claims and objections. But how best to approach this highly complex issue? I said earlier that something akin to liberal individualism has been assumed in the selection of topics and the positions taken on them in this book. I would deny that extreme liberal individualism has been taken for granted here, but certainly the assumptions in the background are closer to individualism than to anti-individualism. Now it is clear from what I have said so far that there are many alternatives to liberal individualism. What may not be so clear is why anyone should want to adopt any of them. What, precisely, is meant to be wrong with liberal individualism? All the main objections really come down to the same thing: *liberal individualism offers a false picture of human nature and social relations, and with it a misleading and damaging vision of what it is possible for human beings to achieve politically.* The details of this objection vary from opponent to opponent—conservatives will say that liberal individualism offers much more than is feasible; radicals that it offers much less than is desirable. But there could hardly be a more important objection to a political philosophy than that it offers a misleading and damaging vision. So it is vital to consider whether the objection is well founded. And this can only be done in detail.

In contemporary political philosophy the debate about the limits to liberal individualism is being played out on many fronts: conservatives, communitarians, socialists, and environmentalists all pick out elements from what I have called extreme liberal individualism as objects of their attack. But the most lively and considered debate is currently taking place within feminist political philosophy. We shall turn our attention to this debate now, both for the intrinsic interest and importance of the topic, and as a case study in 'the limits to liberal individualism'. I will start by looking at feminist arguments that operate within a liberal individualist framework, and then consider whether that framework is adequate, or whether, as feminist critics of liberalism suggest, it requires to be revolutionized, both in theory and practice. This will lead us back to the question of the adequacy (or otherwise) of liberal individualism.

Rights for women

Perhaps the earliest feminist demand was for equal rights for women—a liberal individualist programme if ever there was one! And the demand is not surprising when we recognize how unequally women have been treated. As the French feminist and philosopher Simone de Beauvoir (1908–86) put it in 1949:

in no domain has woman ever really had her chance. That is why a great many women today demand a new status; and . . . their demand is not that they be exalted in their femininity . . . they wish to be accorded at last the abstract rights and concrete possibilities without the concurrence of which liberty is only a mockery. (*The Second Sex*, 149)

The historical subordination of women is truly remarkable. We have seen that British women were denied the vote until the early part of this century. Until the various Married Women's Property Acts of the late nineteenth century, a woman's property on marriage became her husband's. Before the Equal Pay Act of 1970 it was standard practice in Great Britain to offer jobs with two rates of pay: one (higher) rate for men, and another for women. This is now illegal, but it is quite astonishing how recently the change was made.

Women have certainly made great strides towards equal rights. Open and explicit discrimination in employment is now much rarer than it was even a decade ago, and there are reasons to believe that the situation will continue to improve. So if women have, or shortly will have, equal rights, what more could a feminist want?

It does not take much to see that a policy of equal rights, while highly desirable in itself, is not enough to satisfy demands for equality. Even if women rarely now suffer open and explicit discrimination in employment this does not rule out more subtle forms of discrimination. It is illegal to have different pay scales for men and women, but women still tend to cluster near the bottom of the scale. According to a recent report, in Great Britain in 1970, before the first Equal Pay Act, women on average earned 63 per cent of men's hourly pay. By 1993 the rate had risen significantly, but still only to 79 per cent. Furthermore, while it is illegal to discriminate in employment practices, the state hardly has the resources to supervise every employment panel. In other words, as we noted in an earlier chapter, laws can be free of a defect without society being free of that defect. Making discrimination illegal is not a way of ensuring that it never happens, nor even that it never happens in a systematic fashion.

Yet even if we can eliminate deliberate discrimination, a policy of equal rights may still be problematic. Again, as Marx argued, a right to equality in one respect may lead to inequality in another. Equal incomes will not ensure equal living standards if one person has elderly dependants and another has not, or if one is handicapped and another not. So if men's and women's needs differ in significant ways then a policy of equal rights will not be a way of achieving equality. Is there, in fact, a relevant difference? Here feminists have sometimes felt themselves to be in a dilemma. Admitting that women's needs are different from those of men, and, furthermore, arguing that such needs give rise to specific claims, is sometimes taken by men as special pleading or an admission of weakness: a tacit admission of inferiority. So some feminists have been tempted to deny that women need their own distinctive rights.

Yet there is no reason why an acceptance that differences

exist between men and women should imply that women are weaker: this is simply how we often construe the position. Men have special needs too: for example, a man generally needs a higher daily intake of calories than a woman. But this has never been thought of as a sign of men's inferiority to women. So accepting that a group has special needs is not, in itself, to say that they are weaker. And a refusal to admit that women have special needs—particularly those connected with their biological nature—may be a way of ensuring them an inferior standing. So, for example, we can hardly ignore the fact that women, not men, give birth to children. This fact gives rise to special needs, and with it the need for special rights.

However, this type of argument needs to be handled very carefully. How much of what is considered distinctive about women is really due to their biological nature? One way that feminists highlight this problem is by drawing a distinction between 'sex' and 'gender'. Sex is identified as a purely biological category; gender a social or 'socially constructed' category. Thus it is often observed that gender roles differ quite arbitrarily from society to society. To take one apparently trivial example, in some societies only men tend goats, in others only women. Clearly there is no biological reason why this should be: the difference is obviously a matter of custom—a social construction. And what has been socially constructed can be reconstructed some other way. Gender roles seem open to evaluation and change, in principle at least.

So the recognition that there are biological differences between the sexes does not mean that we must endorse all traditional differences in gender roles. Yet our imaginations are often very limited. In almost all societies it has been treated as a virtually inescapable fact that women are the primary carers for young children, at least in the first few months of a child's life. As a response to this difference, which generates differences in need, modern societies have in recent decades devised various systems of maternity leave as a way of trying to treat women and men as equals. Yet maternity leave alone is not sufficient to guarantee women equality in the workplace. However generous her leave, a mother's career is almost certain to be affected by the birth of a child in a way in which a father's rarely is. Generous maternity leave may even stand in the way of a woman's career development, particularly when we remember that a woman's childbearing age coincides with the stage of her life when she is likely to be building a career, if she is to have a good chance of achieving at a high level. As the contemporary feminist political philosopher Susan Moller Okin has put the point, at the root of the problem

are two commonly made but inconsistent presumptions: that women are primarily responsible for the rearing of children; and that serious and committed members of the workforce . . . do not have primary responsibility, or even shared responsibility, for the rearing of children. The old assumption of the workplace, still implicit, is that workers have wives at home. (*Justice, Gender, and the Family*, 5)

So some feminists have sought to challenge the assumptions upon which the policy of maternal leave is based. Why is it assumed that a mother will be the person to look after her child in the first few months? There is no longer any biological necessity. Why should the father not take on this responsibility, if that is more appropriate in the circumstances? So it has been proposed that maternity leave should be replaced by 'parental leave' which could be taken by either parent (or both for a shorter time). This seems a liberating proposal. It will become a matter of choice whether the mother or father takes on the role traditionally assumed by the mother. Not everyone, of course, will be happy with this suggestion. Some women will feel that the apparent 'choice' offered is simply another avenue of oppression: to be forced back to work when they would rather spend time with their newborn baby. Nevertheless, the general point remains. Social policy can be used to permit gender roles to be reconstructed when these are seen as unfair.

This example also helps to illustrate the connections between two domains of particular concern to feminists: the workplace and the family. For much of history marriage, for a woman, was seen as a refuge from unsatisfying and low-grade work. Often, though, it was not much of an improvement, and, even at best, perpetuated women's subservient social role. However, the attempt—through choice or through economic necessity—to combine a career and a family has led many women into an exhausting 'double day' of work and housework, which in turn has often hampered their career prospects. Few men have been prepared to share domestic burdens with their working wives. It has been claimed that: 'husbands of wives with full-time jobs averaged about two minutes more housework per day than did husbands in housewife-maintaining families, hardly enough additional time to prepare a soft-boiled egg' (Barbara R. Bergmann, cited in *Justice, Gender, and the Family*, 153). Whether in paid employment or not, a wife rarely has the power, status, and economic autonomy enjoyed by her husband, and this, in part, explains why even a working wife normally has primary responsibility for domestic chores. These inequalities need to be addressed both in themselves and as a means of allowing women equal opportunity in the workplace. A policy like parental leave is a small step towards this goal.

But what else is to be done? One additional suggestion is that women should be the beneficiaries of programmes of 'affirmative action'—active policies to favour the careers of a disadvantaged group, in this case women.

Affirmative action

Affirmative action takes many forms. It could simply be a matter of encouraging people from certain backgrounds to apply for jobs or for promotion through a policy of active recruitment. More often, though, affirmative action involves 'preferential' hiring or admissions policies. Again there are different ways this can be done. Imagine the case of a university that wishes to enrol more female students. It might have a strict quota of places which must be awarded to female candidates. Or it might have no quota, but view applications from women more favourably. Or it might simply use sex as a tie-breaker between equally able candidates. No doubt other policies are possible too. Broadly, though, policies of affirmative action appear consistent with liberal individualism. They are ways of assigning rights and duties with the ultimate goal of achieving a form of freedom of occupational choice and equality.

However, many people, including some who call themselves 'liberals', react very strongly against affirmative action programmes. It is frequently objected that the policy is self-contradictory. After all, affirmative action programmes are supposed to be a remedy for discrimination, but all they seem to do is discriminate on different grounds. Common though it is, this is a very superficial objection as it stands. Any policy must discriminate on some grounds. The university admissions office ought to discriminate between the clever and the not-so-clever, for example. We cannot possibly say that all discrimination is unjust. The real question is whether the discrimination involved in affirmative action programmes is acceptable or not.

Why might it not be? Objectionable discrimination might be defined as 'choosing on non-relevant grounds'. And, it is said, sex and race are never relevant grounds for choice. Perhaps it is wrong to treat people as members of groups, rather than as individuals. The fact that someone is black or white, male or female, should be irrelevant to the treatment they receive, particularly when the allocation of scarce resources is at issue. The argument against racial or sexual discrimination can be turned into an argument against affirmative action. Everyone should be treated on their individual merits. To do otherwise is unjust. Furthermore, it can even make things worse. What is the justice, for example, of helping middle-class women into medical school if they do not have the qualifications of certain men, perhaps from less fortunate backgrounds, who will lose out?

A further objection to affirmative action is that it can be counter-productive. Those who owe their place to a policy of affirmative action may be stigmatized by this fact. Even worse, those members of disadvantaged groups who would have gained a job or a place anyway will be treated as if they are beneficiaries of the programme, and so stigmatized too. These people cannot win. Affirmative action, on this view, is patronizing and degrading, and, in the long term, may do more harm than good.

These are forceful criticisms. Can affirmative action be rescued? Various defences are possible, not all of equal power. One argument is that affirmative action is little more than an extension of the idea of equality of opportunity. In any meritocratic system positions should go to the most able, but relying on formal qualifications will systematically discriminate in favour of those who went to better schools, or had more comfortable family backgrounds, or more support and encouragement at home. Affirmative action is a way of compensating for the exaggerated qualifications of the advantaged.

If the advantaged simply looked better on their application forms than they were in real life, then this argument would be persuasive. But often those who have achieved qualifications have a training as well as a certificate, and so are in a better position to use an opportunity offered, or to perform well in a job. It may well be that justice requires equality of opportunity in the acquisition of skill; this is Rawls's view. But that would seem to demand intervention at the level of remedial education, not affirmative action later on.

A second argument defends affirmative action on the grounds of social utility. It is claimed that people feel more comfortable dealing with professionals of their own race and sex. More importantly, poor black neighbourhoods are particularly badly served for doctors, dentists, lawyers, and other professionals. Black doctors and lawyers are needed by society, and law and medical schools have a social duty to train people from all backgrounds to fill these roles. Again this is an argument that needs handling with great care. Apart from the fact that the argument is very limited in scope, is it really true that people have preferences for professionals of their own race and sex? And should we simply accept these preferences without further question if people do have them? Furthermore, why should we assume that black doctors and lawyers will choose to work in the neighbourhoods where they are needed if they can earn more elsewhere?

A third argument is based on the idea of reparation or compensation for past injustices. This is particularly clear in the case of black Americans whose current disadvantages are, in part at least, a legacy of the slave trade. Affirmative action is one policy in a package which tries to compensate for these past injustices. Against this, it is argued that whites living today do not have slaves, and so have not acted unjustly to blacks. But this misses the point. Whites are the beneficiaries of past injustices, even if they are not the cause of them. And men are the beneficiaries of a culture in which men are more favourably treated than women. Hence there is reason to make reparation.

Each of these arguments has some force, but we are not finished yet. A fourth argument points to the symbolic power of a policy of affirmative action. It is a way of symbolizing the idea that black people and women are welcome in the universities and professions, and that their earlier exclusion is a matter for regret. For the time being at least, their way must be eased if they are to make a contribution. This goes hand in hand with a fifth argument: that it is essential to break the mould by which certain opportunities have seemed closed to women and minorities. Affirmative action provides role models, opening the eyes of a new generation to what is possible for them.

The great advantage of these two arguments is that they allow us to make the concession that a world which includes affirmative action is not an ideal one. As a long-term policy, affirmative action is undesirable, and in certain respects unjust. People should be treated on their individual merits, as critics of affirmative action claim. But without a temporary policy of affirmative action it will be much harder to create a world in which affirmative action is unnecessary: in which people *are* treated on their individual merits. So we should see affirmative action as a transitional policy in a step towards a more just world.

Transcending liberal individualism?

If affirmative action, together with a social policy to reconstruct gender roles, will bring us closer to a just world, should feminist political philosophers perhaps restrict their efforts to designing the best affirmative action programmes and social policies?

Many feminists have serious objections to this proposal, and the reason why is well expressed by Seyla Benhabib:

to understand and to combat women's oppression it is no longer sufficient to demand woman's political and economic emancipation alone;
it is also necessary to question those pychosexual relations in the domestic and private spheres within which women's lives unfold, and
through which gender identity is reproduced. ('The Generalized and
the Concrete Other', 95)

The general point can be illustrated by observing that affirmative action and social reform take place within existing society,
and so concentrating one's efforts on such policies in the name
of justice signals a general acceptance both of society in the
broadly liberal, capitalist form in which it now exists, and of
political philosophy in its traditional form. Set against this we
find two particularly striking feminist positions: that feminists
should reject capitalism; and that they should stop using the
language of justice. This second claim takes us directly to the
critique of liberal individualism. But let us first see why some
feminists believe that capitalism should be rejected.

There is, of course, one obvious reason: some feminists are
socialists, and socialists reject capitalism. But this does not give
us a distinctive feminist reason for its rejection. The next step is
to claim that there is an intrinsic link between capitalism and
'patriarchy', or male dominance. This claim comes in two (or
three) versions.

One argument is that capitalist economic structures necessarily give rise to a system of male dominance—for example,
capitalist work relations constantly reproduce oppressive relations within the family. So capitalism must be overturned before
male dominance can be ended. Reform within a capitalist system is incapable of ending systematic male domination.

A second version argues that the causation goes in the other
direction: male dominance creates capitalism. Equalizing gender
roles will therefore create a new form of society. For example, in
1972 Sheila Rowbotham wrote:

It is only when women start to organize in large numbers we become a political force, and begin to move towards the possibility of a truly democratic society in which every human being can be brave, responsible, thinking and diligent in the struggle to live at once freely and unselfishly. Such a democracy would be communism, and is beyond our present imagining. (*Women, Resistance and Revolution*, 12–13)

Finally, combining the two views, a third claim is that capitalism and patriarchy are in a reciprocal relation. One cannot be removed without the other, and thus the system must be revolutionized in its entirety.

It would be very surprising to find *no* link between the nature of a society's economic system and its other social institutions and relations. For example, it is often observed that power within a household tends to be held by whoever earns the highest income: be it the husband/father, the wife/mother or, exceptionally, the teenage son or daughter. So if a local economy, for example, creates large-scale unemployment for adult men, but produces opportunities for young women, it is bound to have enormous social effects as young women find themselves relatively affluent and powerful. (In fact, some observers suggest that in such cases daughters begin to take on the aggressive and rowdy behavioural traits previously associated with their fathers!) In the other direction, we are also seeing that changes in ideas about responsibility within the household are leading to changes in the types of employment people are prepared to take on: perhaps fathers of young children are now less prepared to take on work requiring extensive absence from home. But such scattered observations are hardly enough to show that there are entrenched and systematic links between capitalist economic structures and patterns of male domination. It remains to be seen how much of the latter can be changed by piecemeal reform, rather than outright revolution. Thus policies like parental leave and affirmative action might go a long way to equalize the positions of the sexes. Then again, they might not. As yet, we do not know whether capitalist economic structures are compatible with sexual equality.

So let us turn our attention back to the 'extreme liberal individualism' we defined earlier in this chapter. This combined four views: that political philosophy is a matter of fashioning abstract principles of right and justice; that such rights should protect individual freedom and equality; that justice is the first virtue of social and political institutions; and that social rights and duties can be seen as arising out of the actions of individuals. Feminist critics have challenged all four of these views, and we can see why by examining the claim that feminists should stop using the language of justice.

The general reason for this claim is easy to state: justice, it is said, is a 'gendered' concept. To imagine that political philosophy requires us to devise principles of justice is already to accept a male perspective. On the face of it this is an astonishing charge: justice, after all, was supposed to be about treating everyone equally. Why should we give the claim any attention? One kind of argument that would give it force is to be found in the work of Nancy Chodorow. In *The Reproduction of Mothering* (1978), Chodorow argues that women seek 'connectedness' with others, while men value 'separation', often finding it very hard to form deep personal relations with others, even with members of their own families. Women have far greater success in this area, yet at a cost to their own development. In attending to, and serving, the needs of others, women typically neglect themselves. These observations certainly ring true, but what can explain this difference?

On Chodorow's view, we must look to 'mother-only child-rearing' as the cause of these patterns of behaviour. In brief, it is claimed that the first few years of life are the most important from the point of view of the formation and development of individual personality. Typically, during this time a child is raised solely by its mother (or, if not, then by some other woman or women) while the father is a distant, largely absent figure. In identifying himself as male, a boy must separate himself from the mother, while for the girl identification and connectedness with the mother is crucial. In this process separation and maleness come to merge, as do connectedness and femaleness.

These characteristics are then reproduced through subsequent generations.

This argument provides the first premiss in the feminist 'anti-justice' argument: men, much more than women, value abstraction and separation. A vital second premiss is that justice is an ethic of abstraction and separation, from which it seems to follow that men value justice much more than women. Hence, in this sense at least, justice is a gender-biased concept. The claim is not so much that so-called just outcomes favour men—and so are unjust—but that to be supremely concerned with justice is to adopt a male perspective.

The empirical studies in Carol Gilligan's *In A Different Voice* (1982) seem to confirm this conclusion. Following others, Gilligan supposes that there are essentially two types of approach to moral questions: the approach of 'justice' and the approach of 'care'. The justice approach is a matter of seeking abstract rules or principles which can be used to resolve specific moral difficulties. The care perspective, by contrast, requires one to consider the particularities of the situation—who will be hurt, who will benefit—and so make a decision on a much more concrete, case-by-case basis. Many theorists argue that, to a very great extent, men tend to adopt the perspective of justice and rights, women the perspective of care. However, it is often assumed that the male perspective of justice and rights is a 'higher' or 'more mature' form of moral reasoning. Female care morality is seen as a deviation, a sign of deficient moral development.

Gilligan's immediate project is to show that the care perspective is not immature, or undeveloped, but just as valid a way of approaching moral issues as the rights perspective (in fact, some have taken it as evidence that female moral reasoning is superior). She illustrates her case with reports of interviews with Jake and Amy, two intelligent and articulate 11-year-olds. They are each told a story in which Heinz considers whether to steal a drug he cannot afford to buy, in order to save his wife's life. Should Heinz steal the drug? Jake says he should, and defends himself in these terms:

For one thing, a human life is worth more than money, and if the druggist only makes $1,000, he is still going to live, but if Heinz doesn't steal the drug, his wife is going to die. (Why is life worth more than money?) Because the druggist can get a thousand dollars later from rich people with cancer, but Heinz can't get his wife again. (Why not?) Because people are all different and so you couldn't get Heinz's wife again. (*In A Different Voice*, 26)

Amy, on the other hand, resists giving a straight answer to the question of whether Heinz should steal the drug:

Well, I don't think so. I think there might be other ways besides stealing it, like if he could borrow the money or make a loan or something, but he really shouldn't steal the drug—but his wife shouldn't die either.

If he stole the drug, he might save his wife then, but if he did he might go to jail, and then his wife might get sicker again, and he couldn't get more of the drug, and it might not be good. So, they should really just talk it out and find some other way to make the money. (*In A Different Voice*, 28)

Gilligan comments that while Amy sees a 'narrative of relationships that extends over time' Jake sees the issue as a 'math problem with humans' (*In A Different Voice*, 28). This is starkly confirmed in response to a later question: when responsibility to oneself and responsibility to others conflict, how should one choose? Amy agonizes over the way situations can vary, while Jake responds: 'You go about one-fourth to the others and three-fourths to yourself.'

If one accepts that Jake and Amy represent characteristically male and female perspectives (and, of course, little follows from just one example) then there is empirical reason to think that men value abstract and general notions of justice more than women. Chodorow's work provides a possible explanation of why this is so. But the argument falls far short of proof. Chodorow's work is largely speculative. Many women value justice, and many male theorists reject the idea that the point of political philosophy is to devise abstract principles of justice. It would be a form of crude reductionism to think that all beliefs of this nature can be explained on the basis of how each individual was brought up—at least without extensive biographical research. Yet Chodorow's argument should give the liberal pause for thought. Why are the Lockean assumptions about natural freedom, equality, and independence so perennially attractive? Many political philosophers find them hard to dispute. Is this because the assumptions are self-evidently true? Or could the attraction simply be a consequence of the early upbringing of the theorists?

This argument—if we accept it—seems to undermine several elements of the extreme liberal individualist view. Only men will accept that the task of political philosophy is to design abstract principles of justice. Only men will suppose that political philosophers should concern themselves, above all, with the values of freedom and equality. And only men will claim that justice is the first virtue of political and social institutions.

But what is the alternative to an ethic of justice? There are, in fact, many circumstances in which appeals to justice and rights seem out of place. Thus the contemporary political philosopher Jeremy Waldron notes:

Claims of right should have little part to play in the context of a normal loving marriage. If we hear one partner complaining to the other about a denial or withdrawal of conjugal *rights*, we know that something has already gone wrong with the interplay of desire and affection between the partners. (*Liberal Rights*, 372)

Waldron's contrast is between justice or rights, on the one hand, and affection—mutual concern and respect—on the other. This example is very useful for thinking about the limitations of all aspects of extreme liberal individualism, and particularly the fourth strand: that social rights and responsibilities are to be understood as arising out of individual actions. For individualism seems particularly inept at explaining the moral relations that arise within a family. Hobbes, for example, was interested in the question of the nature and source of a mother's rights over her child in the state of nature. And these are the startling, pseudo-contractual, terms in which he settles the issue: 'In the condition of meer Nature . . . the right of Dominion over the Child . . . is . . . hers. . . . Seeing the infant is first in the power of the Mother, so as she may either nourish, or expose it, if she nourish it, it oweth its life to the Mother; and is therefore obliged to obey her' (*Leviathan*, 254).

Kant, writing in the late eighteenth century, notoriously viewed marriage as a contract for 'life-long reciprocal possession of the sexual faculties'. Yet the idea that marriage, or any element of family life, is, at bottom, a commercial relation in which there is a mutually beneficial reassignment of rights and duties surely mischaracterizes at least how we want to think about marriage. It is, of course, true that one normally has a choice whether or not to marry. But the nature of the relationship—at least in its broad outlines—is not simply a matter of choice, but also a matter of the customs, laws, and traditions of one's own society. (This is true in part too even for those couples who choose to remain unmarried.) And, in the case of other family members, as the old saying goes, you can choose your friends, but you can't choose your relations. One is simply born into many of one's family relationships. An individualist might reply that it is open to any individual to repudiate their family obligations, so an important element of choice remains. Yet it is interesting that we think the worse of anyone who has exercised this 'option', at least if they do so without excellent reasons. Hence it does seem that we are prepared to accept the existence of positive obligations which exist independently of the will or actions of individuals.

A better liberal individualist response is to accept the non-voluntariness of many family relations, but to point out that, nevertheless, we are often prepared to rethink our ideas about what counts as acceptable relations within a family in deference to liberal values. Family law is constantly under review. A wife is no longer considered her husband's property. Rape within marriage has finally been acknowledged as a conceptual possibility and a grave crime. The existence of child abuse is increasingly recognized and punished. Thus the family is being reformed in the direction of liberal individualism. Family members are being assigned rights to protect their autonomy. And no doubt there is much further to go.

Still, the model of the family provides an interesting contrast to the extreme liberal individualist picture. Love, or at least affection, not justice, is the first virtue of the family. Should mutual affection also be the first virtue of social and political institutions? This seems unlikely. However easy it might be to *call* everyone brother or sister, only a saint could act as if the entire human race (or even the residents of one's street) made up a big, happy family, with the special ties of affection and concern that family members ideally have for each other.

Nevertheless these thoughts do point in a more promising direction. Even if you cannot be brother or sister to everyone, you can be a good citizen. The good citizen is prepared, for example, to help another even when that other person has no right to expect help. Thus one alternative to thinking that political philosophy should derive a system of rules and principles of justice is to suppose that it should try to set out the conditions under which people of a certain character could flourish. That is, on this view, the task of political philosophy is to work out how to encourage people to become good citizens; to try to create a world populated by people who care about one another, and do not press their own claims in the face of the greater claims of others.

Indeed this is a view we have encountered at various places in this book. Rousseau, as we saw in Chapter 3, was concerned to design a society which encouraged the development of moral and political virtues. Mill, we also saw, measures the quality of our social institutions partly in terms of the quality of the people they will tend to produce. Recall, too, Marx's criticisms of liberalism from Chapter 4: liberal rights of security, equality, property, and liberty encourage us to view others as limitations on our own freedom. They encourage feelings of separation and isolation. For Marx, we have to transcend this narrow, bourgeois perspective. For feminist critics of liberal individualism we should add: this narrow, bourgeois, *male* perspective. Here, though, many strands of anti-individualist thought—Marxism, feminism, communitarianism, conservatism—coincide in making the broad claim we saw that they all share: justice, or, at least, too rigid and exclusive a concern with it, undermines genuinely valuable human relations. (Think of the person who always calculates his *exact* share of the bill in a restaurant!)

Perhaps this idea of the virtue of citizenship should supplant the liberal individualist concern for justice, both as the primary concern of political philosophy and the first virtue of society? It is hard, however, to see how we could, or why we should, attempt to remove justice entirely from consideration. If political philosophy in practice concerns the design and assessment of a society's laws and institutions, then abstract rules and principles seem intrinsic to the subject. Care, affection, and other virtues may inform how we run our individual lives, and so may govern our relationships with others, but the public world of political decision-making seems fated to remain dominated by 'math problems with humans'. We have no understanding of how we could conduct public regulation of property, liberty, or power without appealing to abstract ideas of justice.

Yet it does not follow that we must exclude considerations based on the idea of care. For, as we have seen, it is one thing to say that we need principles of justice, and another to say what those principles should be. And as soon as we start to think about distributive justice we see that people's particular needs *are* of concern to the liberal political philosopher. The welfare state is a system for institutionalizing care, mediated by social workers, nurses, and volunteers. Hence the liberal's concern for justice already incorporates the values of care, albeit through a division of labour.

Furthermore we might suggest that such expanded ideas of justice should co-exist with attachment to the virtues of active citizenship, as they do in Mill's political philosophy. On this approach political philosophers should work out abstract principles of justice, while at the same time trying to set out the conditions under which the virtues can flourish. This surely seems to be the correct compromise to adopt.

But is it a compromise that will work? If justice is to be the first virtue of social and political institutions, what room is there for anything else? Consider again the analogy with a marriage: if husband and wife insist on their rights, this would seem to undermine the possibility of their treating each other with normal love and affection. A marriage in which a couple insist on their rights is a marriage gone wrong. But it does not follow from this that we should abandon the concept of marital rights: after all, marriages do—rather often—go wrong. Waldron claims that the need for such rights is 'not to constitute the affective bond, but to provide each person with secure knowledge of what he can count on in the unhappy event that there turns out to be no other basis for his dealings with his erstwhile partner in the relationship' (*Liberal Rights*, 374).

There is a sense, then, in which it is quite wrong to say that justice is the first virtue of social and political institutions. It might be better to say that it is the *last* virtue, or, at least, the last resort. Rights, or considerations of justice, are like an insurance policy: something offering security to fall back on. Rights do not (or need not) undermine ties of affection. And the point, of course, is not restricted to marriage, but generalizes to the whole of social life. Justice need not undermine an ethic of virtue and care, but provides a safety-net when virtue wears thin.

We can illustrate this point another way. Much human social life depends on trust. We make promises to each other, we rely on each other's word or understanding, and we expect others to behave in certain ways. A world without trust would be awful, perhaps even inconceivable. But some would say that granting individuals enforceable rights presupposes that we cannot trust each other. If we could, what would be the need for rights? And in any case, once we have rights we no longer have a need for trust, and so rights subvert or undermine trust.

It is not clear, though, that trust and rights need be in conflict. For example, one commentator has argued that, for Locke, the 'state of nature . . . is a condition in which the need or demand for rational trust hopelessly exceeds the available supply' (John Dunn, *Interpreting Political Responsibility*, 24). The remedy for this is to design institutions that 'economize on trust': essentially laws of justice. Trust is important, valuable, and a permanent feature of our social and political world. Yet we simply cannot rely on it all the time. This is why we need abstract enforceable rules of justice, granting individuals rights: not because we think it is a good thing for people to invoke their rights and demand justice, but because we know that sometimes this is all they have left.

But justice is a very broad concept. It is wrong to think that seeking justice is simply a matter of constructing abstract and completely general principles, as the argument against justice supposes. A concern for justice should not exclude attention to detail. Many factors need to be taken into account, and not only to see how principles are to be applied in particular cases. The assumption of this book is that the main demand for justice is the demand to remedy illegitimate inequalities. Feminist criticism requires, not that we replace the ethic of justice with the ethic of care at the heart of political philosophy but that we apply the idea of justice with an enriched sensitivity to the ways in which our institutions can embody and reproduce injustice. Feminists cannot, and should not, give up the struggle for genuine freedom and equality for women.

Thus feminist theory does not require the overthrow of our most fundamental ideas of justice, but their consistent application. It also points us back to a very ancient thought: we should not be indifferent to the question of the type of people our political institutions are liable to produce. A society that has a tendency to create ruthless, egotistical exploiters is worse than one with a tendency to produce charitable, altruistic co-operators, even if, in formal terms, both societies can be described as just. Perhaps this thought will help us see how far extreme liberal individualism needs to be modified. But we will not attempt a definitive statement here.

Final word

I hope in this book to have conveyed some of the reasons why political philosophy has been an object of study and fascination for 2,500 years. But I also hope to have made clear that it is far from complete. Not only are there unsolved problems and unexplored byways at every turn, but some claim that we have to start all over again. Does this mean we can never make any progress? That, I think, is more pessimistic a view than is warranted. Mill claimed that in political philosophy 'considerations may be presented capable of determining the intellect either to give or withhold its assent to the doctrine', which is surely correct. He went on to add, though, that 'this is equivalent to proof' (*Utilitarianism*, 255). Yet it is unclear how. Mill himself would agree that, however powerful any considerations seem at any one time, perhaps yet more powerful considerations will later be presented in favour of an opposing view. Thus while there can be more and less plausible positions and arguments, there can be no final word in political philosophy. Still, for the time being, this is where we shall end.

Guide to Further Reading

A list of the principal works discussed appears at the end of this guide.

Preface

As indicated in the Preface, this book is not meant to be a systematic account of the present state of play in political philosophy, nor a scholarly history of the subject. But there are excellent books which do these things. Of the many introductions to contemporary political philosophy I would particularly recommend: Will Kymlicka, *Contemporary Political Philosophy: An Introduction* (Oxford: Oxford University Press, 1990) and Raymond Plant, *Modern Political Thought* (Oxford: Blackwell, 1991). *A Companion to Contemporary Political Philosophy*, ed. Robert E. Goodin and Philip Pettit (Oxford: Blackwell, 1993), contains many useful introductory articles. The best recent introduction to the history of political theory is Iain Hampsher-Monk, *A History of Modern Political Thought* (Oxford: Blackwell, 1992). This includes reliable and readable accounts of the views of many of the philosophers discussed here, including Hobbes, Locke, Rousseau, Marx, and Mill.

Introduction

The citation from Thucydides' *The Peloponnesian War* is from the 1972 Penguin edition. The quotation from Engels is from his *Socialism: Utopian and Scientific*, available in many editions of Marx and Engels' selected works.

Chapter 1

The citation from William Golding's *Lord of the Flies* is taken from the 1954 Penguin edition.

Many editions of Hobbes's *Leviathan* are available. References in the text are to the edition by C. B. MacPherson (Harmondsworth: Penguin, 1968). For an introduction to Hobbes see Richard Tuck, *Hobbes* (Oxford: Oxford University Press, 1989). More advanced, but highly recommended, is Jean Hampton, *Hobbes and the Social Contract Tradition* (Cambridge: Cambridge University Press, 1986).

References to Locke are to *Two Treatises of Government*, ed. Peter Laslett (Cambridge: Cambridge University Press, student edn., 1988).

References in the present book give section, as well as page, numbers, for users of other editions. David Lloyd Thomas, *Locke on Government* (London: Routledge, 1995) is an excellent introduction to Locke's political thought.

The most useful edition of the various works of Rousseau referred to here is *The Social Contract and Discourses*, ed. G. D. H. Cole, J. H. Brumfitt, and John C. Hall (London: Everyman, 1973), and the page numbers given are taken from this edition (in the case of *The Social Contract*, book and chapter numbers are also given). This edition contains all of Rousseau's major philosophical works, with the exception of *Émile*, which is also available in an Everyman edition, published in 1974.

An account of societies without the state is contained in Harold Barclay, *People Without Government* (London: Kahn & Averill, 1990). Many discussions of the prisoners' dilemma are available. A good introduction to this and related issues is Jon Elster, *Nuts and Bolts for the Social Sciences* (Cambridge: Cambridge University Press, 1989) (the Sartre example is taken from Elster). George Woodcock (ed.), *The Anarchist Reader* (Glasgow: Fontana, 1977) contains an interesting selection of anarchist writings, including portions of William Godwin's *Enquiry Concerning Political Justice*, and Peter Kropotkin's *Mutual Aid*. Full-length reprints of these two works are: Godwin, *Enquiry Concerning Political Justice*, ed. Isaac Kramnick (Harmondsworth: Penguin, 1976); Kropotkin, *Mutual Aid*, ed. Paul Avrich (London: Allen Lane, 1972). A useful survey of positions is contained in David Miller, *Anarchism* (London: Dent, 1984).

Chapter 2

The page references to John Stuart Mill's *On Liberty* are to the very convenient edition of *Utilitarianism and Other Writings*, ed. Mary Warnock (Glasgow: Collins, 1962). The references to Locke are again to the Laslett edition of the *Two Treatises*. Bentham's utilitarianism is set out in his *Introduction to the Principles of Morals and Legislation*, ed. J. H. Burns and H. L. A. Hart (London: Methuen, 1982). The first five chapters of this are printed in the Mary Warnock edition of Mill.

Max Weber's definition of the state is presented in his article 'Politics as a Vocation', in *Essays from Max Weber*, trans. H. Gerth and C. W. Mills (London: Routledge & Kegan Paul, 1948).

Two excellent general treatments of the problem of political obligation are A. John Simmons, *Moral Principles and Political Obligations*

(Princeton, NJ: Princeton University Press, 1979) and John Horton, *Political Obligation* (London: Macmillan, 1992). Simmons defends 'philosophical anarchism', as does R. P. Wolff in *In Defense of Anarchism* (New York: Harper, 1973). A recent defence of consent theory is Harry Beran, *The Consent Theory of Political Obligation* (London: Croom Helm, 1987).

The theory of participatory democracy is defended by Carole Pateman in two works: *Participation and Democratic Theory* (Cambridge: Cambridge University Press, 1970) and *The Problem of Political Obligation* (Oxford: Polity Press, 1985).

The quotation concerning tacit consent is from Hume's 'Of the Original Contract', in his *Essays Moral, Political, and Literary*, ed. E. F. Miller (Indianapolis, Ind.: Liberty Press, 1985), 465–87, and the citation from Rousseau is from *The Social Contract and Discourses*, ed. Cole *et al.*

H. L. A. Hart presented the theory of fairness in his article 'Are There Any Natural Rights?', reprinted in J. Waldron (ed.), *Theories of Rights* (Oxford: Oxford University Press, 1984). It has received a book-length defence in George Klosko, *The Principle of Fairness and Political Obligation* (Lanham, Md.: Rowman & Littlefield, 1992). Nozick's objections are set out in his *Anarchy, State, and Utopia* (Oxford: Blackwell, 1974), and are discussed by Simmons and Horton.

Bentham's theory appears in his *A Fragment on Government*, ed. Ross Harrison (Cambridge: Cambridge University Press, 1988). A good discussion of utilitarianism is J. J. C. Smart and Bernard Williams, *Utilitarianism: For and Against* (Cambridge: Cambridge University Press, 1973). The case of the Birmingham six is discussed in detail in Chris Mullin, *Error of Judgement* (Dublin: Poolbeg Press, revised edn., 1990).

In addition to the essay 'Of the Original Contract', referred to above, Hume discusses justice and political obligation in book III of his *A Treatise of Human Nature*, ed. L. A. Selby-Bigge (Oxford: Oxford University Press, 2nd edn., 1978). See also his *An Enquiry Concerning the Principle of Morals*, in his *Enquiries*, ed. L. A. Selby-Bigge (Oxford: Oxford University Press, 3rd edn., 1975).

Chapter 3

The most helpful philosophical treatment of democracy is Ross Harrison, *Democracy* (London: Routledge, 1993). Also useful is David Held, *Models of Democracy* (Cambridge: Polity, 1987) and Keith

Graham, *The Battle of Democracy* (Brighton: Wheatsheaf, 1986). A more detailed development of some of the themes of this chapter is contained in Jeremy Waldron, 'Rights and Majorities: Rousseau Revisited', in his *Liberal Rights* (Cambridge: Cambridge University Press, 1993).

Many editions of Plato's *Republic* are available. The citations here are from H. P. D. Lee's edition (Harmondsworth: Penguin, 1955). A famous extended attack on Plato's view is Karl Popper, *The Open Society and its Enemies*, i (London: Routledge, 1945). An excellent introduction to *The Republic* as a whole is Nickolas Pappas, *Plato: The Republic* (London: Routledge, 1995). Condorcet's argument is summarized in Brian Barry, 'The Public Interest', in A. Quinton (ed.), *Political Philosophy* (Oxford: Oxford University Press, 1967), and set out in detail in Duncan Black, *The Theory of Committees and Elections* (Cambridge: Cambridge University Press, 1958). The trade union examples illustrating the idea of the general will are adapted from Barry's article.

References to Rousseau's *Social Contract* and *A Discourse on Political Economy* are to the Everyman edition by Cole *et al.* Mary Wollstonecraft's *Vindication of the Rights of Women* is available in Miriam Brody's 1992 Penguin edition. The distinction between positive and negative freedom is famously discussed by Isaiah Berlin in 'Two Concepts of Liberty', in his *Four Essays on Liberty* (Oxford: Oxford University Press, 1969). It is reprinted, with other relevant papers, in *Liberty*, ed. David Miller (Oxford: Oxford University Press, 1991). Berlin's essay makes several of the criticisms of Rousseau pointed out here. The works of Carole Pateman on participatory democracy (cited above) are also particularly relevant. Mill's position is set out in *Considerations on Representative Government*, in *Utilitarianism, On Liberty, and Considerations on Representative Government*, ed. H. B. Acton (London: Dent, 1972).

Chapter 4

References to Mill's *On Liberty* and *Utilitarianism* are again to the Mary Warnock edition of *Utilitarianism*. An excellent discussion of Mill's position is contained in the essays in *J. S. Mill, On Liberty In Focus*, ed. John Gray and G. W. Smith (London: Routledge, 1991). For a treatment of Mill's political ideas in the broader context of his thought, see John Skorupski, *John Stuart Mill* (London: Routledge, 1989). The reference to Rousseau is again to the Everyman edition of *The Social Contract and Discourses*, ed. Cole *et al.* Mill's defence of freedom of thought is critically discussed in detail by R. P. Wolff, *The Poverty of Liberalism* (Boston, Mass.: Beacon Press, 1968). The 'rich aunt' example is taken from David Lloyd Thomas, 'Rights, Consequences, and Mill on Liberty', in A. Phillips Griffiths (ed.), *Of Liberty* (Cambridge: Cambridge University Press, 1983). Bentham's attack on natural rights is set out in his *Anarchical Fallacies*, reprinted in *Nonsense Upon Stilts*, ed. Jeremy Waldron (London: Methuen, 1987). As well as a good general discussion of the concept of a right, this volume also contains a version of Marx's 'On the Jewish Question', which is widely available in anthologies of Marx's writings. Particularly recommended is *Karl Marx: Selected Writings*, ed. D. McLellan (Oxford: Oxford University Press, 1977), from which citations of 'On the Jewish Question' in the present book are taken.

Henry Sidgwick's position is set out in his *The Methods of Ethics* (London: Macmillan, 1907). The term 'government house utilitarianism' comes from the introduction to Amartya Sen and Bernard Williams (eds.), *Utilitarianism and Beyond* (Cambridge: Cambridge University Press, 1982). James Fitzjames Stephen, *Liberty, Equality, Fraternity*, is available in a reprint (Chicago: Chicago University Press, 1991). Patrick Devlin's 'Morals and the Criminal Law', first published in 1958, is reprinted in his *The Enforcement of Morals* (Oxford: Oxford University Press, 1965) and has been critically discussed by H. L. A. Hart in *Law, Liberty and Morality* (London: Oxford University Press, 1963). For the communitarian critiques of liberalism see the essays in *Communitarianism and Individualism*, ed. Shlomo Avineri and Avner de-Shalit (Oxford: Oxford University Press, 1992), especially those of Michael Sandel, Charles Taylor, Alasdair MacIntyre, and Michael Walzer, the philosophical founders of modern communitarianism. Michael Sandel, *Liberalism and the Limits of Justice* (Cambridge: Cambridge University Press, 1982) is an influential full-length presentation of a communitarian position, concentrating on criticism of John Rawls, *A Theory of Justice* (Oxford: Oxford University Press, 1971).

Chapter 5

The quotation from Hume's *Second Enquiry* is from the Selby-Bigge edition. Mill's *Chapters on Socialism* is available in *On Liberty and Other Writings*, ed. Stefan Collini (Cambridge: Cambridge University Press, 1989). Nozick's *Anarchy, State, and Utopia* is discussed at length in my own *Robert Nozick: Property, Justice and the Minimal State* (Cambridge: Polity, 1991). See also G. A. Cohen, *Self-Ownership, Freedom, and Equality* (Cambridge: Cambridge University Press, 1995), and the essays in Jeffrey Paul (ed.), *Reading Nozick* (Oxford: Blackwell, 1982). An excellent collection of essays on John Rawls's *A Theory of Justice* is Norman Daniels (ed.), *Reading Rawls* (Oxford: Blackwell, 1975). Rawls has modified his views over the last two decades, and his latest views are presented in his *Political Liberalism* (New York: Columbia University Press, 1993). Some of these changes are documented in C. Kukathas and P. Pettit, *Rawls* (Cambridge: Polity Press, 1990), which also contains other useful material.

Jan Pen, *Income Distribution*, is published by Penguin (1971). A recent report on income and wealth in Britain, using Pen's idea of the income parade, is John Hills, *Joseph Rowntree Foundation Inquiry into Income and Wealth*, vol. ii (York, 1995). The quotation from Rousseau is again taken from the Everyman edition of *The Social Contract and Discourses*. Locke's discussion of property is contained in chapter 5 of his *Second Treatise* (citations from the Laslett edition). Useful treatments of the topic of property rights are Lawrence C. Becker, *Property Rights* (Boston, Mass.: Routledge & Kegan Paul, 1977) and Alan Carter, *The Philosophical Foundations of Property Rights* (Hassocks: Harvester, 1988).

A good general philosophical discussion of the market is Allen Buchanan, *Ethics, Efficiency and the Market* (Totowa, NJ: Rowman & Allanheld, 1985). It contains a useful brief summary of F. A. von Hayek's position, which is set out by Hayek at great length in various writings, but especially in *The Constitution of Liberty* (London: Routledge & Kegan Paul, 1960). The writings of Milton Friedman are more accessible: see particularly his *Capitalism and Freedom* (Chicago: Chicago University Press, 1962) and (jointly written with Rose Friedman), *Free to Choose* (Harmondsworth: Penguin, 1980). A discussion of Marx's reasons for advocating the planned economy is contained in my article 'Playthings of Alien Forces', *Cogito*, 6/1 (1992). Engels's *Speeches in Elberfeld* are reprinted in K. Marx, F. Engels, and V. I. Lenin, *On Communist Society* (Moscow: Progress Press, 1974). The edition of Marx cited is *Early Writings*, ed. Lucio Colletti (Harmondsworth: Penguin, 1975).

The quotation from Adam Smith is from *The Wealth of Nations*, first published in 1776 (Harmondsworth: Penguin, 1970). The quotation from Alec Nove's *The Economics of Feasible Socialism* is from the first edition (London: George Allen & Unwin, 1983). It is now published in a second edition entitled *The Economics of Feasible Socialism Revisited* (London: Harper Collins, 1991).

The main source for Marx's writings on alienation is his *Economic and Philosophical Manuscripts* (1844), especially 'Alienated Labour'. This is available in many editions: for example *Karl Marx: Selected Writings*, ed. D. McLellan and *Early Writings*, ed. Colletti. On the phenomenon of 'de-skilling' under capitalism see Henry Braverman, *Labour and Monopoly Capitalism* (New York: Monthly Review Press, 1974). The reference to Engels's *The Condition of the Working Class in England*, first published in 1845, is taken from *Marx and Engels on Britain* (Moscow: Marx–Engels–Lenin–Stalin Institute, 1953). Other editions are also available.

Many of the objections to Rawls are raised in the collection edited by Norman Daniels, *Reading Rawls*, referred to above. See in particular the papers by Ronald Dworkin, Thomas Nagel, and Thomas Scanlon. The idea of the 'social minimum' is usefully discussed in Jeremy Waldron's 'John Rawls and the Social Minimum', in his collection *Liberal Rights*. For a version of 'Left-wing libertarianism' see Hillel Steiner, *An Essay on Rights* (Oxford: Blackwell, 1994).

Chapter 6

A good introduction to the diversity of feminist political thought is contained in Jane J. Mansbridge and Susan Moller Okin, 'Feminism' in Robert E. Goodin and Philip Pettit (eds.), *A Companion to Contemporary Political Philosophy* (Oxford: Blackwell, 1993). This also contains a substantial bibliography. Will Kymlicka's *Contemporary Political Philosophy* includes a (partly) sympathetic response to feminist thought from a liberal perspective. The Simone de Beauvoir quotation is from *The Second Sex* (New York: Vintage, 1952). Susan Moller Okin, *Justice, Gender and the Family* (New York: Basic Books, 1989) is a much-discussed liberal feminist position. One of the best discussions of affirmative action is Thomas E. Hill, Jr., 'The Message of Affirmative Action', in his *Autonomy and Self-Respect* (Cambridge: Cambridge University Press, 1991).

Useful anthologies of feminist writings are Janet A. Kourany, James P. Sterba, and Rosemarie Tong (eds.), *Feminist Philosophies* (Hemel Hempstead: Harvester Wheatsheaf, 1993) and Nancy Tuana and Rosemarie Tong (eds.), *Feminism and Philosophy* (Boulder, Colo.: Westview Press, 1995). New anthologies of feminist philosophical writings appear almost by the month.

The quotations from F. H. Bradley's *Ethical Studies* are taken from a reprint of the second edition (Indianapolis, Ind.: Bobbs-Merrill, 1951).

Burke's *Reflections on the Revolution in France* is available in a 1968 Penguin edition. Michael Oakeshott's *Rationalism in Politics* is published by Methuen (London, 1962). See also Roger Scruton, *The Meaning of Conservatism* (London: Macmillan, 2nd edn., 1984).

A collection of essays on the relationship between capitalism and patriarchy is *Women and Revolution*, ed. Lydia Sargeant (Boston, Mass.: South End Press, 1981). This includes Heidi Hartmann's famous paper 'The Unhappy Marriage of Marxism and Feminism' (also reprinted in Kourany, Sterba, and Tong, *Feminist Philosophies*), which begins with the words: 'The "marriage" of marxism and feminism has been like the marriage of husband and wife as depicted in English common law: marxism and feminism are one, and that one is marxism.' The quote from Sheila Rowbotham is from *Women, Resistance and Revolution* (London: Penguin, 1972) and Seyla Benhabib's article 'The Generalized and Concrete Other' is printed in Seyla Benhabib and Drucilla Cornell (eds.), *Feminism as Critique* (Cambridge: Polity Press, 1987).

The main feminist writings discussed in the text are Nancy Chodorow, *The Reproduction of Mothering: Psychoanalysis and the Sociology of Gender* (Berkeley, Ca.: University of California Press, 1978) and Carol Gilligan, *In A Different Voice* (Cambridge, Mass.: Harvard University Press, 1982). Other particularly influential writings are Catherine MacKinnon, *Feminism Unmodified* (Cambridge, Mass.: Harvard University Press, 1987), Alison M. Jaggar, *Feminist Politics and Human Nature* (Hemel Hempstead: Harvester, 1983), and Carole Pateman, *The Sexual Contract* (Stanford: Stanford University Press, 1988). Susan Moller Okin, *Women in Western Political Thought* (Princeton, NJ: Princeton University Press, 1979) is a very interesting account of the place of women in the thought of Plato, Aristotle, Rousseau, and Mill.

The article referred to by Jeremy Waldron is 'When Justice Replaces Affection: The Need For Rights', reprinted in his *Liberal Rights*. John Dunn's article 'What is Living and What is Dead in the Political Theory of John Locke?' appears in his *Interpreting Political Responsibility* (Cambridge: Polity, 1990). Michael Ignatieff, *The Needs of Strangers* (London: Hogarth, 1984) can be seen as a study of how care can be institutionalized.

Principal works discussed in the text

BENTHAM, JEREMY, *Anarchical Fallacies*, in *Nonsense on Stilts*, ed. Jeremy Waldron (London: Methuen, 1987).

—— *A Fragment on Government*, ed. Ross Harrison (Cambridge: Cambridge University Press, 1988).

—— *An Introduction to the Principles of Morals and Legislation*, ed. J. H. Burns and H. L. A. Hart (London: Methuen, 1982).

GODWIN, WILLIAM, *Enquiry Concerning Political Justice*, ed. Isaac Kramnick (Harmondsworth: Penguin, 1976).

HART, H. L. A., 'Are There Any Natural Rights?', repr. in J. Waldron (ed.), *Theories of Rights* (Oxford: Oxford University Press, 1984).

HOBBES, THOMAS, *Leviathan*, ed. C. B. MacPherson (Harmondsworth: Penguin, 1968).

HUME, DAVID, *An Enquiry Concerning the Principle of Morals*, in *Enquiries*, ed. L. A. Selby-Bigge (Oxford: Oxford University Press, 3rd edn., 1975).

—— 'Of the Original Contract', in *Essays Moral, Political and Literary*, ed. E. F. Miller (Indianapolis, Ind.: Liberty Press, 1985).

—— *A Treatise of Human Nature*, ed. L. A. Selby-Bigge (Oxford: Oxford University Press, 2nd edn., 1978).

KROPOTKIN, PETER, *Mutual Aid*, ed. Paul Avrich (London: Allen Lane, 1972).

LOCKE, JOHN, *Two Treatises of Government*, ed. Peter Laslett (Cambridge: Cambridge University Press, student edn., 1988).

MARX, KARL, *Early Writings*, ed. Lucio Colletti (Harmondsworth: Penguin, 1975).

—— 'On the Jewish Question', in *Karl Marx: Selected Writings*, ed. D. McLellan (Oxford: Oxford University Press, 1977).

MILL, JOHN STUART, *Chapters on Socialism*, in *On Liberty and Other Writings*, ed. Stefan Collini (Cambridge: Cambridge University Press, 1989).

—— *Considerations on Representative Government*, in *Utilitarianism*, ed. H. B. Acton (London: Dent, 1972).

—— *On Liberty*, in *Utilitarianism and Other Writings*, ed. Mary Warnock (Glasgow: Collins, 1962).

NOZICK, ROBERT, *Anarchy, State, and Utopia* (Oxford: Blackwell, 1974).

PLATO, *The Republic*, ed. H. P. D. Lee (Harmondsworth: Penguin, 1955).

RAWLS, JOHN, *A Theory of Justice* (Oxford: Oxford University Press, 1971).

—— *Political Liberalism* (New York: Columbia University Press, 1993).

ROUSSEAU, JEAN-JACQUES, *Émile* (London: Everyman, 1974).

—— *The Social Contract and Discourses*, ed. G. D. H. Cole, J. H. Brumfitt, and John C. Hall (London: Everyman, 1973).

STEPHEN, JAMES FITZJAMES, *Liberty, Equality, Fraternity* (Chicago: Chicago University Press, 1991).

VON HAYEK, F. A., *The Constitution of Liberty* (London: Routledge & Kegan Paul, 1960).

WOLLSTONECRAFT, MARY, *Vindication of the Rights of Women*, ed. Miriam Brody (Harmondsworth: Penguin, 1992).

Index

OXFORD

MORE OXFORD PAPERBACKS

This book is just one of nearly 1000 Oxford Paper-backs currently in print. If you would like details of other Oxford Paperbacks, including titles in the World's Classics, Oxford Reference, Oxford Books, OPUS, Past Masters, Oxford Authors, and Oxford Shakespeare series, please write to:

UK and Europe: Oxford Paperbacks Publicity Manager, Arts and Reference Publicity Department, Oxford University Press, Walton Street, Oxford OX2 6DP.

Customers in UK and Europe will find Oxford Paperbacks available in all good bookshops. But in case of difficulty please send orders to the Cash-with-Order Department, Oxford University Press Distribution Services, Saxon Way West, Corby, Northants NN18 9ES. Tel: 01536 741519; Fax: 01536 746337. Please send a cheque for the total cost of the books, plus £1.75 postage and packing for orders under £20; £2.75 for orders over £20. Customers outside the UK should add 10% of the cost of the books for postage and packing.

USA: Oxford Paperbacks Marketing Manager, Oxford University Press, Inc., 200 Madison Avenue, New York, N.Y. 10016.

Canada: Trade Department, Oxford University Press, 70 Wynford Drive, Don Mills, Ontario M3C 1J9.

Australia: Trade Marketing Manager, Oxford University Press, G.P.O. Box 2784Y, Melbourne 3001, Victoria.

South Africa: Oxford University Press, P.O. Box 1141, Cape Town 8000.

WORLD'S ✿ CLASSICS

PRINCIPLES OF HUMAN KNOWLEDGE AND THREE DIALOGUES

GEORGE BERKELEY

Edited by Howard Robinson

Berkeley's idealism started a revolution in philosophy. As one of the great empiricist thinkers he not only influenced British philosophers from Hume to Russell and the logical positivists in the twentieth century, he also set the scene for the continental idealism of Hegel and even the philosophy of Marx.

There has never been such a radical critique of common sense and perception as that given in Berkeley's *Principles of Human Knowledge* (1710). His views were met with disfavour, and his response to his critics was the *Three Dialogues* between Hylas and Philonous.

This edition of Berkeley's two key works has an introduction which examines and in part defends his arguments for idealism, as well as offering a detailed analytical contents list, extensive philosophical notes and an index.

OPUS

TWENTIETH-CENTURY FRENCH PHILOSOPHY

Eric Matthews

This book gives a chronological survey of the works of the major French philosophers of the twentieth century.

Eric Matthews offers various explanations for the enduring importance of philosophy in French intellectual life and traces the developments which French philosophy has taken in the twentieth century from its roots in the thought of Descartes, with examinations of key figures such as Bergson, Sartre, Marcel, Merleau-Ponty, Foucault, and Derrida, and the recent French Feminists.

'*Twentieth-Century French Philosophy* is a clear, yet critical introduction to contemporary French Philosophy. . . . The undergraduate or other reader who comes to the area for the first time will gain a definite sense of an intellectual movement with its own questions and answers and its own rigour . . . not least of the book's virtues is its clarity.'
Garrett Barden
Author of *After Principles*

OXFORD

FOUR ESSAYS ON LIBERTY

Isaiah Berlin

'those who value liberty for its own sake believe that
to be free to choose, and not to be chosen for, is an
inalienable ingredient in what makes human beings
human'
Introduction to *Four Essays On Liberty*

*Political Ideas in the Twentieth Century
Historical Inevitability
Two Concepts of Liberty
John Stuart Mill and the Ends of Life*

These four essays deal with the various aspects of
individual liberty, including the distinction between
positive and negative liberty and the necessity of
rejecting determinism if we wish to keep hold of the
notions of human responsibility and freedom.

'practically every paragraph introduces us to half a
dozen new ideas and as many thinkers—the land-
scape flashes past, peopled with familiar and un-
familiar people, all arguing incessantly'
New Society

OXFORD

RETHINKING LIFE AND DEATH

THE COLLAPSE OF OUR TRADITIONAL ETHICS

Peter Singer

A victim of the Hillsborough Disaster in 1989, Anthony Bland lay in hospital in a coma being fed liquid food by a pump, via a tube passing through his nose and into his stomach. On 4 February 1993 Britain's highest court ruled that doctors attending him could lawfully act to end his life.

Our traditional ways of thinking about life and death are collapsing. In a world of respirators and embryos stored for years in liquid nitrogen, we can no longer take the sanctity of human life as the cornerstone of our ethical outlook.

In this controversial book Peter Singer argues that we cannot deal with the crucial issues of death, abortion, euthanasia and the rights of nonhuman animals unless we sweep away the old ethic and build something new in its place.

Singer outlines a new set of commandments, based on compassion and commonsense, for the decisions everyone must make about life and death.

WORLD'S ✿ CLASSICS
OXFORD

PHYSICS
ARISTOTLE

Translated by Robin Waterfield
Edited with an introduction by David Bostock

This book begins with an analysis of change, which introduces us to Aristotle's central concepts of matter and form, before moving on to an account of explanation in the sciences and a defence of teleological explanation.

Aristotle then turns to detailed, important, and often ingenious discussions of notions such as infinity, place, void, time, and continuity. He ends with an argument designed to show that the changes we experience in the world demand as their cause a single unchanging cause of all change, namely God.

This is the first complete translation of Physics into English since 1930. It presents Aristotle's thought accurately, while at the same time simplifying and expanding the often crabbed and elliptical style of the original, so that it is very much easier to read. A lucid introduction and extensive notes explain the general structure of each section of the book and shed light on particular problems.

OPUS

A HISTORICAL INTRODUCTION TO THE PHILOSOPHY OF SCIENCE

John Losee

This challenging introduction, designed for readers without an extensive knowledge of formal logic or of the history of science, looks at the long-argued questions raised by philosophers and scientists about the proper evaluation of scientific interpretations. It offers an historical exposition of differing views on issues such as the merits of competing theories; the interdependence of observation and theory; and the nature of scientific progress. The author looks at explanations given by Plato, Aristotle, and Pythagoras, and through to Bacon and Descartes, to Nagel, Kuhn, and Laudan.

This edition incorporates an extended discussion of contemporary developments and changes within the history of science, and examines recent controversies and the search for a non-prescriptive philosophy of science.

'a challenging interdisciplinary work'
New Scientist

Oxford
Paperback
Reference

THE OXFORD DICTIONARY OF PHILOSOPHY

Edited by Simon Blackburn

* **2,500 entries covering the entire span of the subject including the most recent terms and concepts**

* **Biographical entries for nearly 500 philosophers**

* **Chronology of philosophical events**

From Aristotle to Zen, this is the most comprehensive, authoritative, and up to date dictionary of philosophy available. Ideal for students or a general readership, it provides lively and accessible coverage of not only the Western philosophical tradition but also important themes from Chinese, Indian, Islamic, and Jewish philosophy. The paperback includes a new Chronology.

'an excellent source book and can be strongly recommended . . . there are generous and informative entries on the great philosophers . . . Overall the entries are written in an informed and judicious manner.'
Times Higher Education Supplement